THE COMPLETE
WHITEWATER
RAFTER

THE COMPLETE
WHITEWATER
RAFTER

JEFF BENNETT

Ragged Mountain Press
Camden, Maine

International Marine/
Ragged Mountain Press

A Division of The McGraw·Hill Companies

Published by Ragged Mountain Press

10 9 8 7 6 5 4 3

Copyright © 1996 by Jeff Bennett

Library of Congress Cataloging-in-Publication Data
Bennett, Jeff, 1961–
    The complete whitewater rafter / Jeff Bennett.
        p.   cm.
    Includes index.
    ISBN 0-07-005505-X (alk. paper)
    1. Rafting (Sports)—Handbook, manuals, etc. I. Title.
GV780.B447 1996
797.122—dc20   95-49247
                             CIP

Questions regarding the content of this book
should be addressed to:
Ragged Mountain Press
P.O. Box 220
Camden, ME 04843

Questions regarding the ordering of this book
should be addressed to:
The McGraw-Hill Companies
Customer Service Department
P.O. Box 547
Blacklick, OH 43004
Retail customers: 1-800-822-8158
Bookstores: 1-800-722-4726
www.raggedmountainpress.com

A portion of the profits from the sale of each Ragged Mountain
Press book is donated to an environmental cause.

♻ *The Complete Whitewater Rafter* is printed on 60-pound Renew
Opaque Vellum, an acid-free paper which contains 50 percent
recycled waste paper (preconsumer) and 10 percent postconsumer
waste paper.

Printed by Quebecor Printing, Fairfield, PA
Design and Production by Dan Kirchoff
Edited by Jonathan Eaton, Jacqueline Boyle, Tonya Bennett

All photos by Jeff and Tonya Bennett unless otherwise noted.
Illustrated by Jeff Bennett
Additional technical review by: Les Bechdel, Jim Cassady, Bill
Cross, Casey Garland, Doc Loomis, Vera Loomis, Jack Nelson,
Dave Prange, Julie Prange, and Gary Stott.

"The face of the river, in time, became a wonderful book . . . which told its mind to me without reserve, delivering its most cherished secrets as clearly as if it uttered them with a voice. And it was not a book to be read once and thrown aside, for it had a new story to tell every day."

—from *Life On The Mississippi*, by Mark Twain

This book was previously published as *Rafting!* by Swiftwater Press, 1993.

CONTENTS

6. Propulsion Basics: 65
Different Strokes for
Different Boats

7. Paddle Captaining: 77
The Art of Whitewater
Choreograhy

8. Whitewater: 82
Running the Rapids

9. Safety and Rescue: 99
Keeping Your Head
and Gear Above Water

10. Advanced Rafting: 122
Rafting on the
Cutting Edge

Glossary   193

Index   195

INTRODUCTION

The First Splash

My skin prickled with electricity as our raft slipped onto the long, slick tongue leading into the heart of the rapid. All around me, cool canyon air reverberated with the thunderous applause of crashing waves. From my perch in the front of the raft I could hear our guide musing, "Well, isn't it Jeff's turn to get doused?" Suddenly, the immensity of the experience snatched away his final words. With my ears echoing the pounding of my heart, my remaining senses reeled in excitement. Our guide leaned on the oars one last time, turning our raft into the first standing wave.

Splash! Our raft surged skyward, twisting along the path of a huge, liquid roller coaster. As we reached the crest of the first wave, a wall of water reared to meet us, then crashed down all around me. The river's icy fingers reached through the air and descended into the small openings in my paddle jacket. I shivered, not so much from the chilling water, but from the rush of adrenaline through my limbs.

I imagined myself an explorer, a voyageur, a daredevil . . . flirting with death itself, but never feeling so alive!

Little did I realize the impact that first raft trip would have on my life. Today I reflect upon that adventure with remarkable clarity and fondness. And no matter how many times I board a raft, I find myself captivated by the river, enraptured by whitewater, and consumed by the thrill of running rapids.

Since then I've been fortunate enough to raft scores of rivers in many countries, and to share countless river experiences with commercial passengers, friends, and fellow racing competitors. On my journey as a rafter,

I've found myself floating from the peaceful rivers of my backyard to the outer limits of whitewater.

Using the finest equipment and techniques available, I pursued my penchant for Class V river explorations and first descents. Yet I never lost my simple fascination with the basic dynamics of running water. With each passing bend I let the river share its secrets, and I've carried them with me from put-in to put-in.

It is my hope that this handbook captures and reveals those things rivers have taught me. It is not my intent to *teach* you how to raft, for only the river is the true teacher, of which we are each forever a student. Instead, it is my intent to share with you my knowledge of whitewater in hope that it will enhance your own river-running experience.

Whether you are about to embark on your first whitewater trip or your seasonal pilgrimage to a favorite river, I wish you the best in your whitewater endeavors!

About the Author

I began my river-running career in the early 1970s humbly paddling an old canoe down the gentler rivers of America's mid-Atlantic states. Always looking with curiosity and desire toward burlier rivers, I finally got my first taste of whitewater in 1978 while rafting Wyoming's Snake River. From the moment our crowded boat emerged from the Snake's renowned Lunch Counter Rapid, I was forever changed.

Over the course of the last couple of decades, I have had the good fortune to explore hundreds of North and Central American rivers as a professional river guide, a whitewater instructor, and an international racer. Along the way, hundreds of friends and acquain-

Your rafting adventure is just about to begin!

tances have taught me more about rivers and rafting than I ever knew existed.

Now a freelance writer and columnist for *Paddler, Canoe & Kayak, Snow Country, Adventure West,* and other magazines, and an author or coauthor of a half-dozen books (*A Guide to the Whitewater Rivers of Washington, Class Five Chronicles, The Complete Inflatable Kayaker, The Complete Snowboarder, Soggy Sneakers Guide to Oregon Rivers,* and *No Shit, There I Was . . .*), I rarely drift far from the river. It is there that I am at home. It is there that I feel complete.

The Complete Whitewater Rafter is the culmination of my river experiences and the progeny of my immensely popular book, *Rafting!* Soon after *Rafting!* hit the bookshelves, it became the worldwide manual of choice for professional and amateur rafters alike. *The Complete Whitewater Rafter* includes everything found in *Rafting!*, plus new sections on whitewater photography, rafting for the physically challenged, alternative whitewater craft, and more.

Writing these books has provided an excellent way to share my ideas with fellow river runners. Bear in mind, however, that *The Complete Whitewater Rafter* is not the sole creation of the author. Instead, it is the culmination of a river-running evolution that has been ongoing for the last half-century. This book borrows tips and techniques from contemporary instructors and classic technique handbooks alike. Its roots spread wide throughout river-running circles and find their strength in the wealth of information that is available to river runners. However, this book remains unique in that it tailors river-running techniques and equipment to you, the whitewater rafter.

A Little Help from My Friends

Over the course of countless river journeys, I have met many friendly faces and helpful compatriots. Each has added significantly to my rafting endeavors. Without their support and contributions, this book would have been little more than a dream.

I would like to give special thanks to those who have spent endless hours with me, sharing river trips and tall tales, and those who have listened patiently while I babbled incoherently about river books and whitewater dreams. My helmet goes off to Al Ainsworth, Dan Baxter, Brian Beffort, Bill Bowey, Eugene Buchanan, Dan Buckley, Eric Burge, Bruce Bergstrom, David Bolling, Eric Burge, Fryar Calhoun, Bob Carlson, Bryan Cavaness, Jim Cassady, Jim Clements, John Connelly, Rick Croft, Bill Cross, Connie Davis, Jerry Davis, Dick DeChant, Dianne Dinkins, Bonnie Doyle, Mike Doyle, Brooke Drury, Dick Edgely, Jerry Eline, Bernie Fandrich, Rick Freimuth, Debbie Foust, Jim Foust, Debbie Frieze, Dale Fuller, Casey Garland, Rorie Gotham, Todd Grannis, John Hall, Alan Hamilton, Carol Hammond, Dave Hammond, Dave Harrison, Lars Holbek, John Holland, Phyllis Horowitz, Ole Hougan, Megan Kalstad, Robert Koch, Larry Laba, Mark Leder-Adams, Ronnie Leder-Adams, Glenn Lewman, Mark Lisk, Mike McCleod, Steve Miesen, Tom Moore, Marianne Moore-DeChant, Dave Mullins, Jack Nelson, Richard Penny, Rocky Perko, Matt Polstein, David Prange, Julie Prange, Scott Quinn, Greg Ramp, Slim Ray, Ron Reynier, Craig Richter, Kathleen Ring, Beth Rundquist, Dennis Schell, Val Shaull, Dave "Harpo" Sher, Jim Stohlquist, Gary Stott, Mike Strickland, Dennis Stuhaug, Dave Thomas, Doug Tims, Tom Wagner, Kris Walker, Todd Walker, Doug Zeal, and everybody else credited throughout this book.

I would also like to thank the following manufacturers, retailers, outfitters, publications, and organizations for their support: AAA Rafting, *Adventure West,* AIRE, Alpine Rafting Company, The American Whitewater Affiliation, B & A Distributing, Beyond Limits Adventures, *Canoe & Kayak,* Canyons Incorporated, Carlisle Paddles, Carlson Designs, Cascade Outfitters, Colorado Kayak, Columbia Sportswear, Custom Inflatables, The Dig Dogs, Down River Equipment Company, Downstream Products, Eastern River Expeditions, Extrasport, FlashBack Photographics, Guy Cables Enterprises, High Country River Rafters, Michael Hodgson, Hyside, Hy-Tek Helmets, Kokatat, Maravia Mountain and Surf Pro Shop, National Organization for River Sports, New England Whitewater Center, North American Paddlesports Association, North American River Runners, The North West Rafters Association,

Northwest River Supply, OS Systems, Pacific River Supply, *Paddle Sports, Paddler,* Patagonia, Perception, Polzel Manufacturing, Power Bar, Predator, Preferred Modes, Project RAFT, Rapid Shooters, REI, Rescue 3 Northwest, Riken, Rios Tropicales, Rivers and Mountains, Rogue Equipment, Sawyer Paddles and Oars, Sierra Designs, Sierra South, *Snow Country,* SOAR Inflatables, Sunshine River Adventures, Team SOTAR, Tributary Whitewater Tours, Western River Expeditions, Whitewater Manufacturing, Whitewater Photography, and Yakima.

Finally, I must thank my family—Paul, Bobbi, Tonya and Michelle Bennett—for having shared a singular vision of the world, one that knows no limitations, and bases quality of life on experience and adventure.

What Are You Getting Yourself Into?

Whitewater rafting bestows upon each of us endless opportunities for waterborne adventure. For some boaters, rafting adventures entail peaceful camping trips amid majestic arid canyons or pine-covered slopes. For others, first descents mark the apex of whitewater adventures. For still others, rafting ties friends and family together during lively river outings. Whichever category you fall into, whitewater rafting is an exhilarating way to travel across water.

Rafting is an endless process of learning, where experience is piled atop experience, and continuously evolving skills soon correct the misplaced strokes and ill-chosen routes of past trips. If you have any friends who have gone whitewater rafting, you've surely heard how fun this sport can be. Rafts are stable and forgiving when used properly, and are designed to support first-time river runners safely even in moderate whitewater. If you give it your best, you can acquire enough skill in your first day or two to carry you comfortably from easy Class II rapids to more powerful Class III rapids. As your confidence and ability grow, those same basic skills will guide you down more challenging rivers with only slight modification.

Ultimately, whitewater rafting will become whatever you make of it. Your raft can be a tool to bring you back in touch with the natural splendor of river canyons, or provide an opportunity to push river running to its limits. With the enormous flexibility of whitewater rafting, you will always have a fantastic array of rafting choices, from the equipment you use to the types of river you paddle.

How to Use This Book

The Complete Whitewater Rafter—as its name implies—is a complete course in river running. Arranged in a simple, user-friendly format, the book is designed to take you from the showroom of your local paddle shop to the put-in of your favorite river. Each chapter builds upon the ideas learned in the previous chapter, and provides a solid foundation for more progressive rafting adventures.

After a discussion of raft history and hints on undertaking your first trip, you will embark upon a journey through the jungle of available rafting equipment and accessories. Next you will explore rivers themselves, probing underwater currents, surface hydraulics, and the many forces that make up whitewater rapids. Finally, you will study actual river running, from basic maneuvers to the advanced techniques used on Class V rivers. You'll also learn about safety and rescue, how to pack gear for overnight trips, how to plan rafting expeditions, and much, much more.

By the time you finish this book you should have a broad-based understanding of the concepts that underlie whitewater rafting. Hopefully, all the safety information will follow you from river to river, and you will glean enough information from these pages to plan a safe outing. Still, no book—especially one on whitewater sports—can replace the teachings of professional instructors and on-the-river application of these concepts. Start easy. Take a trip with a commercial outfitter or some highly skilled friends. Sign up for a guide school in your area or join a club that emphasizes safety and enjoyment of whitewater rivers. Then, let your own desires dictate how far you will follow this sport.

With the sound judgment and finely tuned skills you'll develop, whitewater rafting will provide an endless source of recreational pleasure.

1

THE EVOLUTION OF RAFTING:

FROM POWELL TO PADDLE CATS

"There warn't no home like a raft," exclaimed Huck Finn in Mark Twain's timeless novel, *The Adventures of Huckleberry Finn*. Though written in 1885, Huck's words live on, emblazoned upon the pages of guidebooks, magazines, and outfitters' brochures. At a glance, it may seem as if rafting didn't begin until Huck shoved off onto the great Mississippi. But the evolution of rafting reaches much further into the past than Mark Twain's lifetime.

Rivers and streams have been liquid highways for millennia, transporting Indians in buffalo-skin boats, French voyageurs in massive canoes, and early American explorers on log rafts. Though these craft bear little resemblance to today's high-tech rafts, the techniques used to maneuver and propel river boats have changed little over the years. Rivers themselves—though subject to the forces of gravity, erosion, and geological change—have remained essentially the same.

The Fremont Expeditions

Modern rafting dates back as far as 1842, when Lieutenant John Fremont of the U.S. Army first chronicled his explorations of the Platte River. The raft he used was most likely designed by Horace H. Day, the ultimate holder of a patent to a remarkable, albeit rudimentary, design. Constructed from four independent india rubber cloth tubes and a wrap-around floor, Day's first rafts were easily distinguished from other inflatable craft by their suspended floors. Day's *Air Army Boats,* as they came to be known by Fremont, were square or rectangular in shape and designed to seat passengers and gear atop an interior floor. Other craft of that era—distant ancestors of the multiple-pontooned Huck Finn and the modern cataraft—usually consisted of independent tubes connected and topped by a stable platform.

Fremont used Air Army Boats with varying degrees of success, running rapids that would have destroyed wooden craft, and flipping in rapids a bit too severe for first-time rafters. Ultimately, Fremont and his men abandoned their rubber rafts and never wrote of them again.

John Wesley Powell

In 1869, 27 years after Fremont's first rafting trip, John Wesley Powell led a team of explorers through the Grand Canyon of the Colorado River in decked wooden oarboats. Powell and his companions were brave souls, using the only techniques known at that time to test uncharted rivers and rapids. Approaching each new rapid, Powell's men heaved on their oars, backs facing downstream, hoping that a clean run would deliver their rigid craft to the safety of calmer pools below. Unable to maneuver in this fashion, Powell's boats were crushed, capsized, and lost in rapids whose names live on in the genre of modern river tales. Yet in the midst of Powell's tribulations, the first glimpse of modern whitewater sport emerged. Powell wrote:

With difficulty we manage our boats. They spin about from side to side, and we know not where we are going, and find it impossible to keep them headed down the stream. At first, this causes us great alarm, but we soon find there is but little danger; and it is the merry mood of the river to dance through this deep, dark gorge; and right gaily do we join the sport.

For almost three decades after Powell's historic Colorado River journey, boaters continued using the same equipment that had caused Powell so much consternation: heavy wooden craft that had to be sturdy enough to withstand being dragged around rapids and pounded by rocks and hydraulics. The immense weight of these early boats meant that they were not only difficult to portage but also quite unwieldy in whitewater. Early explorers also persisted in running rivers backward as Powell had done, sitting with their backs to the rapid, unable to view the dangers lurking downstream.

Nathaniel Galloway

In 1896, Nathaniel Galloway, a hunter and trapper from Utah, revolutionized whitewater travel by turning his seat around and looking downstream. With this simple change came the ability to *face the danger.* Equipped with Galloway's light, flat-bottomed craft, river travelers used their newfound rowing techniques

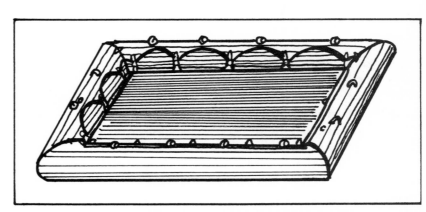

Horace H. Day's Air Army Boats were used by Lieutenant John Fremont to explore rivers in the mid-1800s.

to slow down, position their craft, and maneuver around obstacles. By 1909 Julius Stone's Grand Canyon expedition—considered by some historians to be America's first commercial whitewater trip—uniformly used Galloway's techniques, tackling rapids with an effortless style that had eluded Powell many years earlier. A new era of whitewater travel had begun.

The U.S. military resurrected rubber rafts between World Wars I and II for use as life rafts. Amos Burg used a custom-designed rubber raft to run Idaho's Middle Fork of the Salmon in 1938, and Bus Hatch soon followed Burg's lead on many other rivers. But the big explosion in whitewater rafting came after World War II.

The Post-World War II Era

After World War II, surplus neoprene rafts—similar in shape, size, and design to modern rafts—found their way into the hands of private adventurers all around North America. Though impossibly heavy, shapeless, and quite unseemly by modern standards, these boats were durable and affordable, and they provided reliable flotation. It was probably with little surprise that the first real rafter discovered that early military assault rafts and ocean life rafts were well suited to Galloway's techniques. All a rafter had to do was fit the raft with a strong wooden rowing frame and the boat was all set to go.

As rafting entered the 1950s, a growing fraternity of river runners took their equipment to new locations, accumulating many first descents and attracting the interest of river lovers everywhere. It didn't take long before entrepreneurial rafters began taking paying customers along for the ride. In 1952, Bus Hatch, who had been running rivers like the Green and Yampa near Dinosaur National Monument, Utah, was granted the first commercial river-running concession, and a new industry was begun. Meanwhile, river pioneers—like Georgie White, Smuss Allen, Shorty Burton, Mac Ellingson, Don Harris, and Amos Burg—were plying their favorite rivers and gaining legendary reputations as news of their adventures spread. Out of those adventures arose the realization that these early neoprene craft were quite suitable for whitewater travel.

Georgie White, firmly devoted to building a safer and more responsive whitewater vehicle, approached Rubber Fabricators of West Virginia to build the *Green River,* an extraordinary whitewater raft that revolutionized raft design. The Green River, along with its smaller cousins, the Yampa and the Selway, actually looked like modern rafts. Their turned-up bows rose over cresting waves while the remainder of the raft comfortably carried rafters and their gear. Elsewhere, Bryce Whitmore worked together with R. C. Flemmings of RF Incorporated to manufacture some of the first rafts ever built for river running. Patterned after the Navy's 15-man *basket boats*—peculiar life rafts with arching overhead hoops designed to support sun-shielding tarps—the new raft deleted the hoops and incorporated a new rip-stop nylon and neoprene material.

Not happy with the big-water performance of the Green River, Georgie White designed the *G-rig,* an enormous three-part craft specially designed to safely float the Colorado River passing through the Grand Canyon. Applying the same concepts that culminated in Georgie White's G-rig, Jack Smith constructed a new multiple-pontoon raft known as the *Smith rig.* These massive craft were constructed of hot dog–shaped pontoons lashed side by side to form an immense barge that could withstand even the worst hydraulics of rivers like the Colorado, the Fraser, and the Ottawa. Interestingly, a miniaturized, yet similar, concept was applied in 1965 by Bryce Whitmore, who lashed rowing frames onto a handful of small surplus pontoons to form incredible self-bailing rafts. One of Whitmore's creations was a two-tubed craft called a Spiderboat. However, it was Whitmore's four-tube design that would have pleased Mark Twain, for this raft was respectfully dubbed the Huck Finn.

As rafting's popularity grew, the call for improved designs and materials rang throughout the canyons. Soon, people like B. A. Hanten, Lou Elliot, Eddie Sowden, and Vladimir Kovalik began working with manufacturers like Rubber Fabricators, Avon, and Rubber Manufacturers to design even better river rafts. By 1969, timeless craft like Avon's Adventurer and Professional appeared on rivers. Elsewhere, the practical designs of Gordon Holcombe and Vladimar Kovalik—the Havasu, the Miwok, the Shoshoni, and the Hopi—sprang to life. Manufactured first through Campways and later through Riken, these rafts joined the burgeoning showcase of legendary craft on new rivers throughout the world.

Following the onslaught of new raft designs in the late 1960s, rafting's evolutionary period all but ended by 1972.

The Self-Bailing Generation

After a long period of hibernation, raft designers clambered into rafting's renaissance age in the early 1980s. Gordon Holcombe—working first under the name of Holcombe Industries and then with Maravia—had spent the 1970s working on military assault rafts. His rafts featured I-beam floors and self-bailing designs, but did not catch the popular attention of whitewater

rafters. While Holcombe's military assault rafts quietly crept into the 1980s, other primitive self-bailing rafts began to evolve under the direction of Vladimir Kovalik, Rafael Gallo, the Metzler Company of Germany, and others. Still elsewhere, two visionary American rafters were busy collaborating on a self-bailing raft that would finally take the river-running community by storm.

Building upon the floating mattress concept, Jim Cassady, Randy Shelman, and Glenn Lewman engineered a raft with a laced-in inflatable floor. Reclaiming and updating the design and aesthetics of the old surplus rafts, these new rafts had an inflated floor whose surface floated 4 to 6 inches above the river. That floor was then laced to the raft's side tubes through a series of matching grommets. When water fell over the raft's tubes and onto the floor, it flowed sideways and back into the river through the lacing

A Russian ploht competing at the 1989 Chuya Rally. (Photo by Doc Loomis)

holes. These first-generation self-bailing rafts were dubbed *SOTARs*, an appropriate acronym for *State-of-the-Art Raft*.

By the mid-1980s, many other manufacturers were offering self-bailing rafts, and countless new rivers fell to the daring first descents of intrepid rafters. The long, heavily obstructed rapids that once were the nemesis of standard-floor boats were now being run without the fear of swamping or losing control. For almost a decade self-bailing rafts were not only considered state-of-the-art equipment but were the sole means of transportation on many Class V rivers.

The Russian Influence

In the late 1980s, rafting found itself entangled in a series of historical events of worldwide importance. Russia began dismantling its Iron Curtain, and as the barriers between East and West fell, human commonality and curiosity created links between the people of distant lands. In a moment of shared visions, a handful of rafters from the United States teamed up with Russian boaters to explore some of Asia's great rivers. Led by Jib Ellison, Project RAFT soon created a pipeline for American-Russian rafting exchanges.

In 1989, Russia opened the door to its most popular rafting competition, the Chuya Rally. Rafters from around the world came to compete on Siberia's Chuya River where they found two- and four-person teams paddling curious-looking catarafts, and adept rafters maneuvering giant oar-powered plohts through seemingly impossible river mazes. Though oar-powered catarafts had already plied North American rivers in small numbers for many years, these unique craft leapt to the forefront of river gear after the Chuya Rally, and impressed the rafting community with their sensible designs. Soon, North American rafters began to see catarafts showing up on popular streams, with Russian-style paddle cats becoming a common sight. Today, catarafts are on the way to becoming nearly as popular as the more traditional rafts.

Looking Toward Tomorrow

Rafting is in a perpetual state of evolution. While you pore over this book, someone is undoubtedly tinkering with new materials, different shapes, and cutting-edge designs. Thanks to the passion, creativity, and imagination of folks like these, rafters have myriad craft from which to choose. From traditional standard-floor rafts to high-tech paddle cats, there are boats and accessories for any rafter and any river. Plus, today's river runners can draw upon techniques perfected over more than a hundred years of whitewater rafting in order to set upon the safest adventures ever undertaken.

Whether you are a first-time rafter or a seasoned veteran of whitewater rivers, it is truly an exciting time to be a river runner and a witness to the power and splendor of the river's mighty rapids.

2
G E T   W E T
YOUR FIRST RAFTING ADVENTURE

With rafting showing up everywhere these days—on television, on magazine covers, in colorful brochures—the tenderfoot may still scratch his or her head and wonder what it takes to get on the river. For the beginner, the first step into whitewater rafting can be intimidating and confusing. Unless you have some experienced friends, you're bound to ask yourself, "Where do I find whitewater? What do I need to know? Don't I need experience? Isn't rafting crazy?" Fortunately, rafting has grown into an enormous commercial industry. Hundreds of outfitters, clubs, and whitewater organizations cater to novices seeking to get *wet* for the first time.

Outfitters

One of the easiest ways to get your first taste of whitewater is through a reputable commercial outfitter. In North America, rafting companies abound in just about any state and province that has hills and streams. You can find these outfitters in the yellow pages under *River Trips, Rafts and Rafting,* or *Guides.* America Outdoors and other outfitters organizations listed in the Appendix maintain lists of active, reputable members and will be happy to share information with you. If you're still striking out, check out your local outdoor store. They'll often have some brochures from local outfitters. Even government agencies such as the Bureau of Land Management, the National Forest Service, and local tourism departments maintain lists of qualified outfitters. If none of these prospects turns up a good outfitter, check out the advertisements in one of the popular outdoor magazines at your local bookstore.

Once you find an outfitter, inquire about the types of trips it offers. If you or members of your group don't care to paddle, ask the outfitter if they will carry you down the river in an oar boat, in which the guide does most of the work. More adventurous first-timers will probably enjoy the thrill of being part of a paddle crew on a Class III river. Although many outfitters now offer rivers with Class IV and V rapids, ask the outfitter what you're getting into. Daring and physically fit novices can often run rivers with one or two user friendly Class V rapids, but only those with prior paddling experience should consider rivers with dozens of difficult rapids.

One easy way to figure out what types of rivers the outfitter offers is to read between the lines in its brochure. *Scenic float trips* are usually peaceful journeys along easy waterways with a few riffles to spice things up. *Fun for the whole family* often means the river has

One way to get your first taste of whitewater rafting is to go with a reputable outfitter.
(Photo courtesy of Whitewater Photography, Fayetteville, WV)

some whitewater but that the rapids are forgiving of uncoordinated paddlers and swimmers. Once the word *adventure* pops up—especially when combined with an adjective like *ultimate*—you may be getting into more difficult whitewater. Unless you have paddled whitewater before, or have the utmost confidence in your aquatic abilities, you may want to reorient your thinking and slide back to *family class* trips for your first rafting voyage.

Remember, don't overestimate your abilities! It is better to leave the river hungry for more challenging adventures than to scare yourself out of the sport on your first trip.

Other Ways to Get Wet

CLUBS AND ORGANIZATIONS

Local outdoor clubs, whitewater organizations, and college outdoor programs offer appealing alternatives to the "pay to play" option offered by outfitters. Clubs and organizations can usually save you a lot of money by asking you to contribute your own food, transportation, and personal gear, yet they frequently offer the identical rivers that outfitters advertise in their brochures.

RAFT RENTALS

On some of North America's more popular rivers it is possible to rent rafts, lifejackets, and all the gear you'll need to undertake your own whitewater adventure. Since this alternative gives intrepid greenhorns direct access to whitewater, it is best to have an experienced river runner along for guidance.

3

E Q U I P M E N T
FROM OARS TO FLOORS, HELMETS TO HI-FLOATS

The concept of floating on air-filled bladders isn't anything new. In fact, people were drifting on inflated animal skins thousands of years before the first World War II–surplus rafts found their way onto whitewater streams. And, conceptually at least, today's rafts vary little from their ancient predecessors.

Rafts, in the most basic sense, are little more than misshapen balloons, high-tech bladders bent and distorted to conform to some waterlogged inventor's notion of the perfect river craft. Yet, despite the apparent simplicity of floating on air, today's high-quality rafts are masterpieces of contemporary engineering.

More than mere balloons, modern rafts are specifically designed for whitewater use. They are durable, maneuverable, and equipped with a dazzling array of specialized accessories and options.

Basic Raft Anatomy

If you flip through the pages of your favorite whitewater catalog or walk the showroom of your local rafting shop, it soon becomes obvious that rafts vary as widely as their manufacturers' imaginations.

On the other hand, the more closely you examine raft designs, the more similarities begin to appear. In the end, most rafts fit into one of three categories: standard-floor rafts, self-bailing rafts, and catarafts. Other designs—such as J-rigs, G-rigs, triple rigs, and plohts—appear on North American rivers less often, so they'll receive only a passing mention.

Any fully assembled raft consists of many independent components, each of which is important to the raft's performance. The list of components includes *tubes, baffles, seams, panels, thwarts, valves, floors, pressure-release valves, D-rings, rubbing strakes, chafe pads,* and *carry handles.* In the accompanying diagram you'll see that most of these parts show up in a typical self-bailing raft. Standard-floor rafts differ from self-bailing rafts only slightly, while catarafts, though unique in shape, display most of the features common to other rafts.

TUBES

All high-quality self-bailing whitewater rafts have one continuous outside tube that gives the raft its distinctive oval shape. The tubes, in turn, are divided by *baffles* or *bulkheads* into multiple *chambers.* The independent air chambers keep the raft afloat even if one chamber is punctured, and add rigidity by holding the internal air in place. In a typical 12- to 18-foot raft there may be as many as four separate tube chambers. One interesting twist on the multichamber design is the bladder system, which is similar to a car tire and inner tube. Rather than filling the outer tube with air, a bladder is inserted into the outer tube and filled with air. If the inner bladder is damaged it can be removed and patched faster and more easily than could a more conventional, single-layer tube. (Some river runners have gone so far as to carry a spare bladder on extended trips just in case one blows out!) The bladder system also lets manufacturers cut production costs significantly.

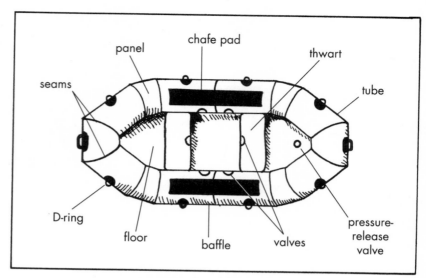

Anatomy of a self-bailing raft.

PANELS AND SEAMS

Tubes are constructed from many separate pieces of material, or *panels,* welded or glued together. Their overlapping joints are sometimes concealed and strengthened with welded or glued strips of material known as *seams.* When discussing the shape and configuration of panels at the bow and stern, rafters sometimes refer to the individual panels as *miters.*

Many PVC and urethane rafts are now being constructed with a *thermo-welding* process, which actually fuses the panels and seams together without the use of toxic glues or solvents. Welded rafts tend to be more bombproof than glued rafts since there is no possibility of a seam delaminating on a hot day. Nonetheless, glued joints and seams rarely separate and can be repaired.

VALVES

Each chamber has its own valve. Most rafts feature one of three types of valve: *military style, Halkey-Roberts,* and *AD-1.* Military-style valves open and close by twisting the outer assembly; when it is open, air flows freely in either direction. Halkey-Roberts and AD-1 valves have spring-loaded center posts that let you pump air one way into the raft. To release the air you just depress the post.

Valves should be durable, maintenance free, and eas-

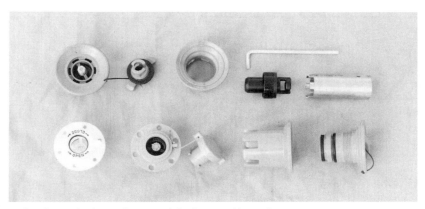

Raft valves (clockwise from top left): low-profile Halkey-Roberts valve parts and tools; full-size Halkey-Roberts valve parts; AD-1 valve; plastic military-style valve.

ily accessible. Some manufacturers place valves in the passenger compartment to provide quick and easy access in an empty raft; frames and other equipment can cover the valves once the raft is fully loaded. Valves mounted on the outside of the main tubes give easy access at any time but run the risk of damage in the event of a direct collision.

THWARTS

Thwarts are the inflated cross-tubes that run at right angles to the main tubes. Whether glued, welded, clipped, or strapped in place, thwarts help the raft maintain its shape by holding the main tubes an equal distance apart.

Besides adding torsional rigidity to a raft, thwarts give paddlers more surface area to brace themselves against. If you are going to be using a rowing frame, removable thwarts can be detached to add valuable storage space without compromising the raft's structural integrity. Keep in mind, however, that removable thwarts should have a bomb-proof binding system to keep them in place when they are needed (for example, when paddlers need to brace their legs against the thwarts).

FLOORS

Rafting floors are generally described as either *standard* or *self-bailing*. In a standard-floor raft, the floor is glued to the main tubes, in effect creating a giant bathtub. Some standard-floor rafts are built with *wrapped*

floors, which merely means that the floor continues upward around the outside of the main tubes. Wrapped floors generally extend up to a *rubbing strake—* an additional piece of thick, durable material bonded to the perimeter of the tubes to act as a protective bumper.

Self-bailing rafts have buoyant floors designed to float the floor's upper surface higher than the surrounding river level. When water enters the raft it lands on the floor's top, then pours off the floor and out of the raft through a series of holes or slots.

Most self-bailing floors have either an *I-beam* or a *drop-stitch* construction. In I-beam construction, indented pleats run the length of the floor, giving the floor the appearance of a common air mattress. In drop-stitch construction, thousands of tiny threads hold the floor's surfaces an equal distance apart. A drop-stitch floor has a smooth top and bottom unlike the deeply channeled surfaces found on I-beam floors. Either type of floor can be attached to the raft by welding or gluing, or by lacing the floor to the main tubes with guy lines that run through matching slots or grommets.

The advantages of the removable laced-in floor are that it can be replaced if damaged, can be separated from the raft for long portages, and can be cut loose to free pinned rafts. Only rarely do the ropes or straps holding the floor in place snap. Glued-in floors, on the other hand, are simpler, have no ropes that could fail, and can be built with a lower, faster profile. However, they sometimes bail more slowly and are difficult to replace.

The last floor component—the *pressure-release valve*—saves self-bailing floors from being damaged by overinflation or hot, expanding air. The pressure-release valve opens when internal air hits a preset pressure level and lets the excess air out before it can do any damage.

ACCESSORIES

The most common raft accessories are *D-rings, rubbing strakes* (discussed in the previous section), and *chafe pads.* D-rings are heavy-duty steel rings mounted on

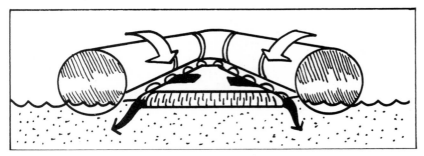

A self-bailing floor is buoyant and its upper surface floats higher than the surrounding river. When water spills into the passenger compartment it flows toward the sides and back into the river through holes along the edge of the floor.

short straps that are sewn and glued under a patch made of the same material as the raft. D-rings provide a fixed point for strapping down frames and gear, tying your raft to a trailer, or retaining a hand line. Rubbing strakes and chafe pads are extra layers of heavy-duty fabric that are bonded to the outer tubes to protect the raft from collisions and abrasion.

Another popular accessory found on many rafts is the carrying handle. Somewhat akin to those found on large suitcases, these handles make lifting and carrying a raft much easier. They can even double as handholds when mounted inside the passenger compartment.

FOOTCUPS

Footcups are sturdy, foot-size cones built to work a lot like the back foot of a slalom waterski. Once footcups are welded or glued to the floor, passengers can wedge their feet in deep and lean far out of the raft with total confidence—even in heavy whitewater. This is really important in Class V rapids, where a few extra strokes are more important than a passenger's ability to lean inboard and hug the thwarts! If things get *too* rough, the cup shape prevents the paddlers' feet from jamming and allows paddlers to release their feet quickly.

Properly mounted footcups should fit any paddler. Take your raft out for a test ride before mounting the cups and carefully observe where people's feet touch the floor. This will tell you the best location for the footcups. To keep your crew smiling—and inside the raft—glue in at least one cup for the inside foot of each paddler. (To accommodate a broad range of preferences, mount the footcups at a 60- to 90-degree angle to the raft's long axis.)

Materials

Rafts are constructed from a variety of materials that vary in durability, life expectancy, stiffness, and overall feel. In order to give rafters some idea of how materials compare, I'll describe many of the common fabrics and coatings used when this book was written. Keep in mind, however, that raft technology is ever changing. By the time the ink dries on these pages there will be

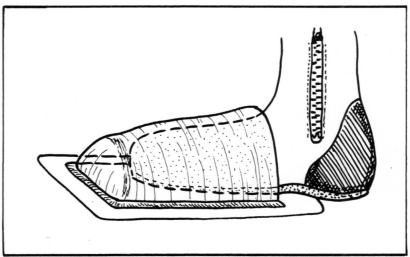

Footcups are to rafts what seat belts are to cars: They keep you in your seat when the going gets rough.

something new on the market, and the only way to keep up with the new technology will be to read whitewater magazine reviews, obtain literature from raft manufacturers, and talk to local retailers. Once you've heard the hype you can use the comparisons in this book to decipher their claims.

Raft materials have two parts: the *base fabric* and the *coating*. The base fabric provides tear and puncture protection, and the coating provides abrasion resistance, air retention, and protection from ultraviolet (UV) rays.

BASE FABRICS

Base fabrics consist of cloth sheets made from woven or knitted polyester or nylon threads. Single polyester threads are less stretchy, but tend to be weaker than nylon threads. Single nylon threads, in turn, are stretchier but stronger. I've used the term *single threads* because the cloth's *weave* can also affect how much each thread stretches. In fact, it is possible to weave a nylon thread into cloth that is less stretchy than polyester cloth.

One of the most common terms you'll hear regarding material is *denier,* which is but one of many ways to measure material strength. Denier measures the weight of one 9,000-meter-long thread, in grams: The heavier that thread, the higher its denier will be. High-quality whitewater rafts are usually constructed of materials with a minimum of 420 denier, the more durable rafts featuring deniers of 1,000 or more. If you see two numbers describing the denier (i.e., 420/840), the fabric is woven from yarns of two different deniers. Since polyester tends to be a little weaker than nylon, polyester-based materials generally use a higher-denier thread to achieve the same characteristics as a lower-denier nylon cloth.

The quality of the base cloth can also be measured by *thread count* and *fabric weight*. Thread count simply measures the number of threads per inch and fabric weight measures the weight of one square yard of cloth. As with denier, higher numbers tend to indicate better materials.

COATINGS

Most fabric coatings fall into two general categories: *rubber coatings* and *plastomers*. The most popular rubber coatings are Hypalon (polyethylene chlorosulfone) and neoprene (polychloroprene). Popular plastomer coatings, on the other hand, include PVC (polyvinyl chloride) and urethane (ether-based polyurethane).

It would be pretty easy to keep coatings straight if there really were only four types. However, each coating just mentioned can have many variations—for example, there are more than 20 neoprene compounds. Still, even the newest coatings will probably fall within the rubber and plastomer categories, and will undoubtedly compare themselves to the coatings in use today.

Common to all coatings are fillers such as stabilizers, UV inhibitors, antioxidants, and pigments.

Hypalon. Hypalon is a lightweight rubber coating developed by the DuPont Company. It stands up well to abrasion and UV rays, is fully cured when applied, and bonds securely to the base fabric. In top-quality rafts, Hypalon makes up almost 80 percent of the coating; cheaper rafts might be as little as 25 to 50 percent Hypalon.

Many rafters like Hypalon for its durability, long shelf life, ease of repair, and ability to be deflated and stored in a tight bundle. On the other hand, Hypalon rafts can be more flexible than PVC or urethane rafts, and tend to stick to obstacles more often. Hypalon's sticky or rubbery feel is partly due to the nylon that usually makes up its base fabric. However, some manufacturers use stiffer base fabrics and higher-quality Hypalon coatings to give their rafts a more solid, slick feel.

Neoprene. Neoprene—one of the most popular coatings on early model rafts—is showing up on fewer whitewater rafts these days. Still an effective coating for general whitewater use, neoprene is similar to Hypalon but heavier and less abrasion resistant. Its best feature is its ability to hold air. Top-quality carbon-black neoprene holds air extraordinarily well and is highly resistant to UV degradation. Finally, neoprene rafts are a breeze to build or repair with simple gluing techniques.

PVC. While comparable in abrasion and UV resistance to Hypalon, PVC (a plastomer) is a much lighter and stiffer coating—especially when used with polyester base fabrics. PVC's light weight and increased rigidity lets rafts glance off rocks and hold their shape in powerful hydraulics a little better than the softer Hypalon rafts. The tradeoff for this increased rigidity shows up the moment you try to roll up your raft at the end of the day: PVC rafts don't wrap up as tight and can crack if rolled up in very cold temperatures. Also, PVC isn't fully cured when applied to the base fabric; its plasticizers leach out slowly, leaving the coating brittle and weak after many years of use. One advantage of PVC rafts is their ability to be welded rather than glued, thereby creating an inseparable bond between panels.

Urethane. Polyurethane—another plastomer—is particularly durable and appears on many state-of-the-art rafts. It is extremely rugged and long-lasting (perhaps more so than Hypalon and PVC), it recaptures some of the *hand* of Hypalon, and it can be welded like PVC. Urethane can be used alone (without any other coatings) or sprayed over other coatings as a protective outer layer.

Adhesion. The bonding of the coating to the base fabric has a remarkable effect on raft materials. Since the coating adheres to the base fabric, the material works as a single unit. If the coating adheres too tightly to the base fabric, the threads will be locked in place and the material's tear resistance will be lowered. Too little adhesion, on the other hand, leads to delamination and lowered abrasion resistance. The way coatings are layered can also be important. Some manufacturers use one coating on top of another to combine the best performance characteristics of each.

Design Characteristics

Many factors affect a raft's performance, from the type of material used in its construction to the size and shape of its floor, tubes, and thwarts. The most apparent differences among traditional rafts are their length, width, tube size, thwart size and attachment, number of thwarts, number of chambers, type of floor, and bow and stern shape. Each of these factors can enhance or hinder a raft's whitewater performance depending on the type of river it is being used on.

LENGTH AND WIDTH

Most modern raft designers construct rafts with a width equal to about half its overall length. Using that as a starting point, the more square feet of raft floor you have on the water, the more stable the raft will usually be. That's why rafters choose long, wide rafts for big-volume rivers like the Thompson, the Snake, the Colorado, or the Zambezi and short, narrow rafts for small streams.

Moving beyond these simple ideas, you'll find that smaller rafts can be more exciting and livelier than their bigger, more cumbersome cousins, but can also flip more easily in powerful hydraulics. When it comes to turning, a longer raft takes more time to pivot than a shorter raft, making it more difficult to maneuver through a technical, rock-strewn rapid.

TUBE SIZE

Tube size should be proportional to the raft size since the tubes give the raft buoyancy, deflect water, and provide seats for paddlers. If the tubes are too small (less than 15 or 16 inches in diameter) waves will readily roll into the passenger compartment and paddlers will find themselves seated too low to paddle effectively.

SYMMETRY

Many traditional 14- to 18-foot rafts have five to seven panels in the bow or stern sections (two to three panels on each side, plus one at the end). Once assembled, they create a semirounded shape that deflects waves and holes that would otherwise knock the raft off course. Some manufacturers incorporate pointier bows and squared-off sterns into their rafts, creating *asymmetrical* boats. Rafts with smaller stern compartments have less gear space but may make it easier for paddle captains to lock themselves into position. *Symmetrical* rafts often have more storage space than asymmetrical rafts of equal size and they handle equally well when moved forward or backward.

RISE

Rise—also known as *kick*—helps lift the bow over waves and holes, prevents diving in steep drops, and provides a drier ride through rapids. Stern rise also makes back ferrying (discussed later) easier by letting the stern slide over the water instead of trying to push it aside.

Building the right amount of kick into the raft is tricky. For example, too much bow rise creates a bulldozer effect and allows the raft to bend too much, both of which can cause the raft to run more slowly and stall in strong hydraulics. Manufacturers incorporate these ideas into their designs and offer rafts with a good compromise that works best in a variety of rapids.

In place of kick, some manufacturers use diminished tubes, which taper down to smaller diameters toward the bow and stern. Although less rigid than uniform-diameter tubes, diminished tubes increase space in the passenger compartment and can, in theory, also help the bow pierce or ride over holes and steep waves. The piercing action of diminished tubes also makes for a wet ride.

WATERLINE

Waterline is the amount of raft that is actually in the water. The waterline of an empty raft is governed by the raft's length, bow rise, and stern rise. But once the raft is loaded, the added weight will cause it to sink deeper into the river's surface, extending the waterline toward the bow and stern. If the raft has a shorter waterline, it will spin faster but will be difficult to track straight in a chosen direction. The inverse is also true: A longer waterline helps the raft to track straight but hampers its ability to turn.

FLOORS

Floor design can have a profound effect on a raft's handling characteristics. Standard-floor rafts capture water in the passenger compartment like a giant bathtub, rendering the raft heavy and unwieldy once it gets waterlogged. To keep the standard-floor raft light and maneuverable, the water must be bailed out manually. If there isn't a pool or eddy close by to pull into and bail, the extra water could be a real hazard. However, on rivers with short, steep drops and long pools the standard-floor raft works just fine. In fact, on forgiving pool-drop rivers, standard-floor rafts can be more exciting for passengers, and the extra weight of surplus water has been credited with helping more than a few rafts survive boat-flipping hydraulics.

The best standard floors are very taut when the raft is inflated; floppy, loose floors sag and hold more water, making bailing more difficult.

Self-bailing rafts, with their remarkable water-shedding capabilities, perform well in almost any type of whitewater. On small, technical streams the self-bailing raft remains light and nimble. On large-volume rivers the self-bailer's quick reactions let rafters turn quickly into oncoming waves and deftly ferry around big holes and pourovers.

Self-bailing rafts, like standard-floor rafts, handle very differently from one another. For example, self-bailing rafts with smooth, flat-bottomed drop-stitched floors are highly maneuverable and easy to turn, but may not track as well as deeply furrowed I-beam floors. (This can be a nuisance if the raft isn't built correctly. To keep the raft from continually sliding off course the floor must be correctly attached to the tubes at just the right height—an engineering feat accomplished by most reputable manufacturers.) I-beam

A raft's kick (A), tube size (B), and waterline (C and D) affect the way it feels and performs. The waterline of an unloaded raft (C) is elongated when you add passengers and gear (D).

floors, on the other hand, track quite well but tend to take a little extra effort to turn.

Catarafts

Made up of just a couple of pontoons and a frame, the cataraft displays some distinct differences from other types of rafts—such as its lack of a floor. Because catarafts have no floor, there is no passenger compartment to bail. This cuts down on drag on shallow rivers and lets the tubes pierce all but the most stubborn hydraulics. If the cataraft ever *does* find itself wrestling a sticky hole, the river will pour through the open tubes, making it harder to flip the boat. The decreased drag also makes *cats* faster to row and paddle than regular rafts.

The flip side of all this added mobility and stability is a big loss in buoyancy. Without a floor to provide added lift, all the weight of the frame, passengers, and gear rests on two to six tubes. This makes it a tougher craft to outfit and use as a paddle boat, and means that

SELF-BAILING RAFTS

By the early 1980s I had become a fanatical river runner, progressing from canoes to kayaks to the leading edge of whitewater rafting. At the same time, I was doing first descents on some pretty difficult rivers. The standard-floor rafts being used at the time were pretty good, but could hardly stand up to the demands we placed on them. As the rivers got harder, the old *bathtub boats* started to become a weighty burden. I hadn't yet heard of the early self-bailing designs of Gordon Holcombe and others, and I was in desperate need of a new, water-shedding craft.

In the spring of 1982 Randy Shelman of Whitewater Manufacturing journeyed down to California to demo some prototype raft designs. As the operations manager for a local rafting company, I got to join a group of professional river runners on the North Fork of the American to try out the new boats.

One boat was a modified Huck Finn, with upturned ends on smaller inside pontoons rather than outside pontoons. The design stirred up a lot of interest, but I was more intrigued by a second raft, which combined the outer tubes of a conventional raft with a suspended, carpeted wooden floor. Strangely akin to a floating dance floor, it was the brunt of many jokes from my fellow rafters. Still, its self-bailing design had piqued my imagination.

After a few more conversations with Randy Shelman and his partner, Glenn Lewman, we decided that a laced-in, I-beam inflatable floor should replace the heavy wooden boards. I felt so confident about this design that I sent Whitewater Manufacturing a deposit to make the boat, and even featured it in Pacific River Supply's new flyers before the first raft ever arrived!

When the first self-bailing rafts came off the assembly line in May of 1983, we were amazed. The new design worked like a charm. The raft was light and nimble, could be paddled or rowed, and was incredibly buoyant. Top California rafters like Jib Ellison, Bill McGinnis, Mark Helmus, Mike Doyle, Bill Carlson, and Jack Morrison were so stoked about the boat after their first trips that they all put in orders too!

One customer said the new craft was a *state-of-the-art raft*, and we just reduced it to its acronym . . . *SOTAR*. Soon, self-bailing rafts started showing up on showroom floors everywhere, with manufacturers like AIRE, Avon, Hyside, Maravia, Northwest River Supply, and Riken incorporating self-bailing designs into their top-quality rafts.

Today, just about every leading manufacturer builds—and believes in—self-bailers. The rest, as they say, is history.
—Jim Cassady, co-author, *Western Whitewater* and *California Whitewater*

Catarafts are becoming more popular every year.

rafters on multiday trips must pick a cat big enough to haul all their gear.

TYPES OF CATARAFTS

From short, sleek, highly rockered cats to big multi-tube cats, catarafts are as varied as their more traditional cousins. However, catarafts frequently incorporate many of the same features found on traditional rafts: D-rings, valves, multichambered tubes, baffles, and even rubbing strakes and wrapped floors. Accordingly, I don't think you'll be disappointed if I don't repeat everything I just said about raft components. (If you are severely disappointed, just flip back a couple of pages, start reading again, and substitute the word *cataraft* wherever you see *raft!*)

CATARAFT DESIGN CHARACTERISTICS

As with traditional rafts, tube length, width, and shape all affect the cataraft's performance characteristics. If you compare two catarafts with straight tubes of equal diam-

eter, the cat with longer tubes or additional tubes will provide a more buoyant ride. This can be a real plus for running large-volume rivers or carrying additional gear or people. The tradeoff for this increased stability is a slight decrease in the cataraft's ability to spin quickly. Shorter tubes, though not as buoyant, tend to turn faster without losing much of their ability to track well.

The addition of *rocker,* or tube curvature, drastically changes the way catarafts handle whitewater. Small cats with a lot of rocker have a very short waterline, offer little surface area for the river to grab and flip them, and they turn on a dime. Because they conform to the shape of some waves, highly rockered cats surf well and make great playboats. Even larger catarafts gain a lot of turning ability when manufacturers build in a moderate amount of rocker to longer tubes. As always, there's a tradeoff when rocker is increased. The decreased waterline brings with it less buoyancy—reducing the number of people or amount of gear that can be carried—and makes it more difficult to keep the

OAR CATS AND PADDLE CATS

Almost any cataraft can be rowed or paddled with the right gear. Oar frames take great advantage of the cataraft's light weight by placing the weight of the rower and gear over the middle of the raft. This provides a low center of gravity and a central pivot point.

To paddle a cat you've got to outfit it with saddles, quick-release straps, or paddle frames. These accessories allow rafters to straddle the tubes while being firmly braced against straps or bars. Plus, the saddles and paddle frames help keep paddlers' knees and feet off the water and away from rocks.

Some catarafts are better for paddling than others. Four or six paddlers can line up two or three to a tube and power through big holes when riding big cats, but they'll find turning to be a challenge. Outfitters have upped the ante, however, by adding an oar rig to the back of the big paddle cats. This paddle-assist configuration is both powerful and maneuverable in the right hands.

Two-person teams can paddle small cats in just about anything, and often find it easier to spin and dart about the river's surface than with larger cats.

No matter which way you go, catarafting is a ton of fun!

A paddle cat in action.

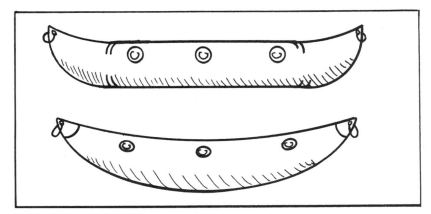

Rocker: This diagram shows one tube with no rocker (top), and another with a lot of rocker (bottom).

boat on track when trying to ferry or maintain a straight line in currents.

ROTOCATS AND PLASTIC CATS

Rotocats and plastic cats are the newest addition to the rafting market, their first significant acceptance coming in the early 1990s. Rotocats differ from ordinary catarafts in that they are molded out of solid plastic rather than welded together out of sheets of flexible fabrics. This lets rotocat manufacturers borrow both technology and designs from plastic kayak makers. In fact, the rotomolding process used to construct these catarafts lets manufacturers build in features like climbing and tracking edges, asymmetric hulls, and storage wells. This provides a unique ride—one that is stiffer and slicker than on an ordinary cataraft—whether the cat is rowed or paddled. Of course, this added stiffness is permanent. Rotocats aren't meant to fold up and store compactly, and the tubes retain their shape until someone runs over them with your cousin's giant pickup truck!

Other Types of Rafts

NORTH AMERICAN RAFTS

On some rivers—especially giants like the Colorado, the Fraser, the Thompson, and the Katun—the raft of choice may be a J-rig, G-rig, triple rig, Smith rig, or ploht.

The *G-rig* was first designed by legendary Grand

Plastic cats (rotocats) blend kayak manufacturing technology with traditional raft designs.

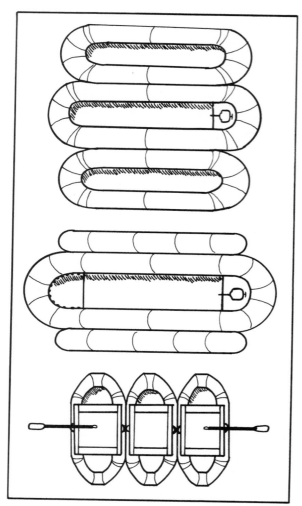

Three types of big-water rafts used on North American rivers (from top to bottom): a G-rig, a Smith rig, and a triple-rig.

ily laden with passengers and gear. With frames mounted on the two outside rafts, maneuvering a triple rig becomes a fantastic demonstration of teamwork: Two guides are needed to operate the oars at either end of the rig. If all three rafts are fitted with rowing frames, triple rigs can be separated for smaller rapids, then reattached for the big rapids.

J-rigs, Jack Currey's innovative variation on the G-rig, consists of two to five sausage-shaped tubes lashed side by side. The entire barge can also be fitted with a frame and is usually powered by an outboard motor.

The final type of giant motor-driven raft found on North American rivers is the *Smith rig.* Named for Ron Smith, the Smith rig combines a single doughnut-shaped pontoon—like the ones used on the G-rig—but adds two of the sausage-shaped pontoons to the sides.

PLOHTS

Not to be upstaged by American ingenuity, Russian rafters have come up with myriad inventive raft designs. Plohts, a generic name for many of Russia's favorite raft designs, are multitube rafts joined together by steel or wooden frames.

Although plohts, like big catarafts, can be rowed or paddled, most are rowed with oars over the bow and stern, more akin to North American *sweep boats* than to catarafts. Sweep boats, in turn, are nothing more than traditional rafts with special frames and long oars that reach out over the bow and stern rather than over the sides. This lets one or two rowers maneuver the raft diagonally and horizontally with downstream ferries rather than using upstream ferries. Plohts, though frequently constructed from independent pontoons, are usually configured and rowed like sweep boats.

Purchasing a Raft

TRADITIONAL RAFTS

Buying a new raft can be a big investment, especially if you're going to purchase a top-of-the-line cataraft or self-bailer. Fortunately, supply and demand economics affects raft manufacturers the same as it does any other

Canyon guide Georgie White and consists of three giant oval-shaped pontoons. The pontoons are lashed side by side with a motor mounted on the middle pontoon. These behemoths may measure more than 30 feet in length, providing incredible stability even in the largest rapids.

The *triple rig* is quite similar to the G-rig except that it uses smaller, more conventional oar-powered rafts. When joined together as a single unit, the individual rafts create a remarkably stable boat, capable of tackling treacherous stretches of whitewater even when heav-

A massive J-rig in action in the Grand Canyon.
(Photo courtesy of Western River Expeditions, Salt Lake City, UT)

industry, and there are now rafts for almost any budget.

Budget should be only one of your concerns when buying a raft, and not necessarily the biggest. You should also consider what type of rivers you'll be running, the amount of abuse you expect to inflict upon your raft, and the amount of gear or passengers you'll be carrying. Since you may buy and use only one raft, your ideal raft will be a compromise of as many desired features as possible.

Don't be afraid to pepper retailers and manufacturers with questions. Most raft dealers are proud of their products and very informative. Since they want you to be happy, they'll often go out of their way to help you select the raft that is right for you. Some are so honest, they'll send you to another company if they can't sell you the right boat!

Before purchasing your next raft, consider each of these factors:

1. Do you wish to row, paddle, or both?

2. Will you be running Class III rapids? Class V rapids?

3. Will you be running day trips? Overnight trips?

4. How many people and how much gear do you intend to carry?

5. How many days will you use the raft this year?

6. Will you be rafting small, steep rivers, or large, high-volume rivers?

7. What is your budget?

8. What warranties will you get with the raft?

9. What is the dealer's/manufacturer's reputation?

10. Do you intend to use the raft commercially or on boat-damaging rivers?

A Russian ploht at the 1991 Chuya Rally.
(Photo by Doc Loomis)

11. Where can you go for major repairs?
12. Will you use the raft for racing?
13. Will you be carrying the raft over long distances?

Next, take a look at the adjoining raft size selection table. The last two columns indicate the approximate number of people that can comfortably fit in an oar boat or paddle raft without much added gear. To find a raft that might fit your needs for day trips, figure out how many people you intend to carry, then select the raft that matches that number from the left column. If you plan to do many overnight trips, your extra gear will have the same affect on the table as extra people. Get a larger raft so you can fit all your equipment inside comfortably.

CATARAFTS

Buying a cataraft is much the same as buying a traditional raft. First, ask yourself the questions listed on the previous page, then discuss your answers with manufacturers and retailers. If you think that most of your outings will be one-day trips, or that you'll be rowing without passengers, the giant multitube cats may be overkill. Pick a smaller cat that is still buoyant and stable enough to survive the rapids of your favorite rivers. If you plan to carry extra gear and passengers, start looking at catarafts with larger or additional tubes.

USED RAFTS

Used rafts can be a great way to break into the private whitewater game. Since properly maintained equipment lasts for many years, you're likely to find high-quality rafting gear available at reasonable prices.

When looking for a used raft, spend enough time to adequately *kick the tires*. Ask a lot of questions like, "How old is this raft?" "What rivers have you used it on?" and "Does it hold air?" Next, inflate the raft and listen for air leaks. Inspect the material for any fading or discoloration that might indicate too much exposure to damaging ultraviolet rays. Check the seams to see if they're intact, and see how carefully any patches have been applied. You should also make sure that the valves open and close smoothly. To check the integrity of the baffles, inflate one chamber at a time. Finally, the true measure of the raft's prior use and care is its floor. Examine the floor in good lighting to see if the material's outer coating is worn away from the base cloth. Expect to find some wear, but if large patches of cloth are showing through, chances are the raft has seen some heavy use.

Keep in mind that used equipment is bound to have some damage—patched tubes, broken D-rings, marred floors—but with some time and effort many rafts can be inexpensively reconditioned and used for many more years.

Raft Length (in feet)	Raft Width (in feet)	Tube Size (in inches)	Rowing/ People	Paddle/ People
10	5	16	1–2	2–3
12	6	18	2–3	3–4
13	6	18	3–4	3–6
14	6.5–7	20	3–5	4–8
15	7	21	4–5	6–8
16	7.5	22	4–6	6–10
18	8	24	5–6	8–10

Raft size selection table for standard-floor and self-bailing rafts: The chart above provides a useful starting point for selecting the proper raft by its capacity rating. Keep in mind that rafts aren't all the same shape and size, as described earlier. Also, factors such as the amount of gear you plan to carry and the type of rivers you will be rafting will affect your choice of raft.

Raft frames provide a fulcrum for the oars, seats for rowers and passengers, and lash points for cargo.

Frames

Rowing frames—constructed from aluminum, steel, or other metals—secure gear, stiffen the raft, support a rower's weight, and provide a fulcrum for the oars. Wooden frames can work just as well as their metallic counterparts, but they're slowly disappearing into rafting's nostalgic history. In the future, new materials will inevitably fall into the hands of innovative frame builders, giving rafters broader choices in frame construction and design.

TRADITIONAL RAFT FRAMES

Basic rowing frames consist of side rails that rest atop the tubes; cross bars to keep the frame square; oarlock stands to hold oarlocks or pins; and a seat for the rower. As builders add new pieces and bars to the basic frame, raft frames become more varied and personalized. For example, some rafters prefer slanted seats—long boards that slant downward toward the rower's feet—over more conventional seats, while others prefer the comfort of a large padded seat. A dropped foot brace, mounted across from the rower's seat, is often added to frames to give the rower a solid platform from which to start pulling the oars. Other additions—such as ammo can wells, cooler retainers, movable oarstands, and breakdown frames—add some luxurious amenities for the rafter willing to invest a little more in indulgences.

Frames can be built to fit in the center of the passenger compartment or in the stern. If there is only one guide, and no one else around to assist with paddling, the center frame works best since it puts the pivot point near the middle of the raft. Stern frames, on the other hand, are often used in conjunction with paddle teams to provide some extra power when the guide really needs it.

SELECTING A FRAME

What type of rafting do you plan to do when rowing? One-day trips or overnighters? Steep, technical streams or broad, lazy rivers? Will you be in a traditional raft or a cataraft? There are so many frames available today that it is easy to select and tailor one to your needs.

If you plan to spend most of your time doing short trips on very difficult rivers, all you'll probably need is a sturdy bare-bones frame. A simple add-on for cataraft frames is a set of footplates, which provide a solid platform when you're standing up, shifting weight, or pushing through huge waves and holes. Frames that have a built-in cooler retainer are nice for almost any river, expanding your raft's versatility by turning it into a food carrier. If you plan on doing long trips with a lot of gear, larger, more complicated frames may make river life easier by supplying multiple tie-down points and wells for kitchen boxes or ammo cans.

Frames also come with a variety of seat options, including tractor-style seats, flat boards, cooler seats, and slant boards. Cooler seats and flat boards provide the least seating stability for rowers but make it easy to move about the passenger compartment. Tractor seats and slant boards, on the other hand, hold rowers more firmly in place, allowing them to concentrate on rowing rather than staying seated.

Before you buy any frame, your first step will be to determine your raft's dimensions. Take these measurements and give them to your retailer, who will then be able to recommend the right frame for your raft.

1. Center compartment width: the distance between the main tubes in the center compartment.
2. Center compartment length: the distance between the thwarts in the center compartment.
3. Tube size: the tube diameters (the raft manufacturer will be able to tell you this if you don't know).

4. The size (in quarts) and make of the cooler you plan to use.
5. For self-bailing rafts, the distance from the top of the main tubes to the top of the floor.

OTHER CONSIDERATIONS

Any frame should be free of burrs or sharp corners that could snag and puncture tubes or injure paddlers. If the frame breaks down into separate sections, make sure that the pop buttons or cotter pins don't rub against the raft's material. Finally, it's always a good idea to cover the bottom and corners of the frame with padding to help save the skin of both your raft and crew.

CATARAFT FRAMES

Frames are an essential component of any cataraft system and much more critical to the performance of a cataraft than to that of a traditional raft. Cataraft frames tend to be stronger and better supported than traditional raft frames since they must hold the pontoons firmly in place while the river's hydraulics try to twist the whole rig into a pretzel.

Some cataraft frames include safety nets. This helps the rower stay aboard if bounced from his seat, but makes it impossible to climb back through the center if the raft flips.

Because cataraft frames don't have floors, some rafters install durable safety nets across the bottom opening. The reasons for this are obvious: On my first cataraft ride, I stared at the Class III rapids gurgling below the open bottom of the cataraft and felt like I was on a trapeze without a net. Many rafters prefer to leave the interior open so they can put their feet down and walk the boat across shallows. The open floor design also lets the rower climb through the center when the cataraft is upside down.

A recent addition to the cataraft frame market is the *paddle saddle*. Paddle saddles allow paddlers to ride the tubes like a horse while maintaining a firm grip on the raft. Whether constructed from the same curved metal tubing used to build raft frames, or merely from quick-release strap harnesses, paddle saddles cradle rafters' legs while they kneel on top of the tubes, and support and protect the lower legs by keeping them up off the river's surface.

COOLER FRAMES

A cooler frame is a narrow rectangular frame designed to hold a cooler firmly inside the raft's passenger compartment. It's great for single-day trips or for light overnighters and can even be used to keep dry bags and other gear off the floor.

Oars

From the timeless aesthetics of wooden oars to the rugged reliability of aluminum and composite oars, whitewater oars are built to be durable enough to withstand powerful hydraulics and menacing boulders, yet light enough to respond all day long to a rower's efforts.

OAR CONSTRUCTION

Most contemporary oars fall into one of three categories: *wooden, aluminum,* and *composite.* Wooden oars have been in use since rafting first started. Whether crafted from solid ash or laminated strips of Douglas fir, wooden oars flex and straighten during the course of a single stroke. To many rafters, the feel of a wooden oar is incomparable.

Aluminum oars now equal wooden oars in popularity due to their sturdy construction, ease of maintenance, and ability to accept different blades or oar extenders. Starting with a hollow aluminum shaft, aluminum oars are coated with a colorful protective plastic or vinyl sleeve, then fitted with a solid handle at one end of the shaft and a cavity specially designed to accept removable blades at the other end. Usually sold separately, the blade has a pole-like end that slips into the shaft's cavity and locks into place. This allows easy replacement of damaged blades and more compact storage with the blade removed, and it lets rafters change from one blade size to another.

Composite oars are constructed from a multitude of exotic materials, including fiberglass, carbon, and graphite shafts, and polypropylene or compressed foam handles. When properly laminated, these materials can mimic the feel of a wooden oar while providing much of the durability of aluminum oars. Some manufacturers even go so far as to weight the handles of composite oars to counterbalance the blades and make the entire oar feel as light as balsa wood.

SELECTING OARS

Oars come in so many different materials—all of which have good and bad characteristics—that your choice of material is a personal one. Ask your retailer and friends plenty of questions. Do you want a one-piece oar or interchangeable parts? Are you willing to maintain a wooden oar or do you want a maintenance-free synthetic oar? Do you prefer the lightness of a graphite shaft or the weight of wooden and aluminum oars?

When purchasing wooden oars, it is important to

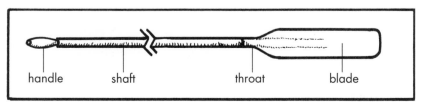

handle   shaft   throat   blade

Parts of an oar.

buy the best wood you can afford—one that combines great bending strength and medium flexibility with high impact resistance. For medium- to heavy-duty river use, fir, ash, oak, and spruce make excellent oars. Laminated softwoods such as fir and spruce also hold up well to the rigors of river running if properly constructed. Ash oars are often cut from a solid piece of wood and are considered by some to be the toughest oars available. However, ash's quality does not come without a price: These oars tend to be heavier and more expensive than others. Other types of wood, such as basswood and cottonwood, don't last as long in tough river conditions, but work well for light-duty use.

Before buying a wooden oar, examine it closely. The strongest oars will have grains running parallel to the shaft and will be free from strength-sapping knots. If the oar is prepainted, the manufacturer may be trying to conceal flaws. The throat of the oar—the point where the shaft and blade meet—should be thick and strong. Test the oar's flexibility by holding it out to your side at a 45-degree angle with the blade touching the floor. Holding the handle with one hand, exert pressure halfway down the oar with the opposite foot. A good oar will have some flex, but not too much.

OAR LENGTH

It is important to pick out the right oar length for your raft. Generally, a properly sized oar leaves one-third of its overall length between the oarlock and your hand. First-time buyers can generally select a proper oar length by measuring the distance between oarlocks or pins, then adding 50 percent to that distance to get the proper oar length. Another way to estimate proper oar length is to measure two-thirds the length of the raft.

Keep in mind that many factors govern oar length. Longer oars may be needed on wider rafts, on rafts with large tubes, and on frames with high or widely spaced oarlock

stands. Shorter oars might be better on technical streams and in stern rowing frames; larger-bladed oars may perform best on a large-volume river or when the raft is heavily laden. Even a rower's strength and arm length will affect oar length selection: Strong, long-armed rowers often like a slightly longer oar.

SETTING UP OARS

No matter which oar you buy, you may need to do some finishing work before it is river-ready. If you have purchased a set of unfinished wooden oars, they will require special treatment before you can take them out on the river. Here's what you'll need to do:

1. Paint the entire oar with a light coat of quality wood sealer such as linseed oil. To get the best results, try to do this when the air temperature is at least 70 degrees Fahrenheit. Let the sealer dry completely.
2. Paint the entire oar with a high-oil-content marine spar varnish that has been thinned slightly with good varnish thinner. Brush the varnish on in the same direction as the wood's grain. Again, let this coat dry completely. (In place of varnish, many rafters use marine-grade paint.)

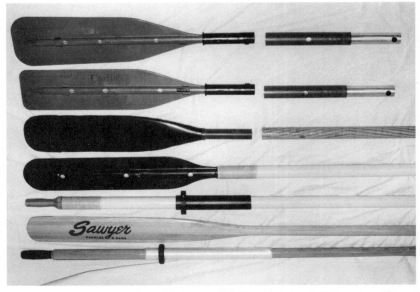

Oars blades and shafts come in a wide variety of materials and lengths.

Raft Length (in feet)	Raft Width (in feet)	Oar Length (in feet)
11–12	5–6	7–8
12–13	5.5–6	7.5–9
13–14	6–7	8–10
14–16	6.5–8	9–11
16–18	7	21
16	7–8	10–12

Oar length selection table: This provides a rough estimate for proper oar length based on the size of your raft.

3. Apply another coat of varnish or paint in the same manner as the first coat. Let it dry completely and your oars will be finished.

If you are using oarlocks, the next thing any oar will need is an *oarstop*. These tight-fitting rubber or plastic doughnuts slide or bolt onto the shaft where it rests against the oarlock to prevent the oar from sliding out of the oarlock and into the river. Oarstops should be positioned about one-third of the way down the oar from the handle. To install your oarstops, start by marking the point on the shaft where the oarstop will go. Next, slide or bolt them into place on the oar shaft. Finally, put the oars in the oarlocks to make sure that the handles are positioned comfortably for you.

Oarstops are usually used with *stopper sleeves* that slide over the shaft and protect it at the point that the oarlocks rub the shaft. (Without the sleeve, the oarlocks can quickly cut deep grooves in any oar material.) As an alternative to sleeves, many rafters form a protective shield by wrapping 60 to 70 feet of solid-braided ¼- to ³⁄₁₆-inch multifilament polypropylene rope or parachute cord tightly around the shaft and gluing it into place. (This can also be done with about 6 feet of seat belt strapping or 1½-inch webbing.)

PINS AND CLIPS

Pins and clips make up one of the two most common tools for supporting an oar midway on a rowing frame. (The second tool—oarlocks—will be discussed in a moment.)

In a pin and clip system, a vertical steel rod called a

thole pin is placed into the oarlock stand and bolted into place. A plastic or nylon *stirrup* is mounted in a U shape on the pin to hold the oar in place if the oar pops loose from the pin. Finally, the oars are fitted with beefy steel clips, which are bolted securely to the shaft with two or more radiator hose clamps. Once everything is in place, the oar can be jammed onto the pin, where it is free to pivot around the pin's axis.

Note that when using pins and clips, the oar should be kept in front of the pin (toward the bow) so that it doesn't create too much stress. The added benefit of this oar position is that it lets a rower execute a few extra strokes after an oar pops loose if a stirrup was used to hold the loose oar in place. Also, to prevent accidental injury, the pin is kept as short as practicable and capped with a large plastic or rubber ball.

Pins and clips have long been a favorite of beginner rafters with little or no rowing experience because they keep the oar length and blade angle perfectly set at all times. Experts also like this feature because it cuts down on the number of missed strokes in difficult rapids. The drawback of pins and clips is that the oar can only be *shipped* parallel to the raft, not drawn into the raft. Also, since the blades can't be *feathered*, or twisted, they occasionally catch strong submarine currents in heavy hydraulics.

OARLOCKS

Oarlocks—steel U-shaped oar retainers—allow more oar movement than pins and clips, but they take some getting used to. With oarlocks, the rower can feather the oars (which makes it easier to row against the wind or through big hydraulics), draw the oars into the raft, or pull the oars out of hydraulics. The tradeoff for this added flexibility is that the blade may twist in the wrong direction just when you need to make a critical stroke. One cure for this problem is the use of an *Oar Right*—an oar stopper with a guide that keeps the oar aligned vertically in the oarlock. Oar Rights recapture the blade angle benefits of pins and clips while letting the rower ship and feather the oar freely.

FINE TUNING

Unless you've already got a good feel for how you like to position your oars, you should mount the oarstops

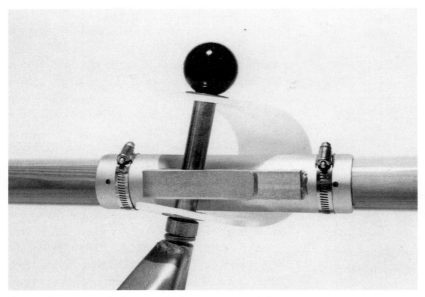

A complete pin and clip set up, showing a properly mounted oar and stirrup.
(Photo courtesy of Cascade Outfitters, Springfield, OR)

still be used if they pop free.

If you are using oarlocks, adjust the oarlock opening with a rubber mallet so that it is slightly narrower than the oar shaft. This will hold the oar in place while you row but will let it pop free under intense pressure. Once properly adjusted, the only way to insert an oar is to slide it in blade first. Also, to avoid losing the oarlock, thread a sturdy cotter pin through the oarlock's base.

When you mount oars on either pins or oarlocks, you may also wish to add a short *safety line* to retain the oar should it pop free. The safety line should be just long enough to reach from the clip or oarstop to the oarlock stand, but not so short that it prevents you from shipping the oars inward. Keep in mind that the safety line is a matter of personal choice. Some rafters prefer not to use safety lines because they can entangle passengers in the event of a flip or wrap.

and clips on the shaft so that the oar handles are never less than a fist's width apart. This will prevent your hands from getting caught between the handles and will maximize your leverage on the blades.

If you are using pins and clips, bolt the thole pins into the oarlock stand with just enough pin showing to accommodate the oar, stirrup, and cap ball. (Most thole pins come preset, making customization unnecessary.) Next, adjust the opening on the clip with a rubber mallet so that it snaps securely onto the pin but will pop free if it hits a rock or gets caught in a powerful hydraulic. (If you make the clip opening too small, the oar will violently pop free of the pin when it releases.) Finally, mount the oars inside the stirrup on the bow side of the pin. That way the oars can

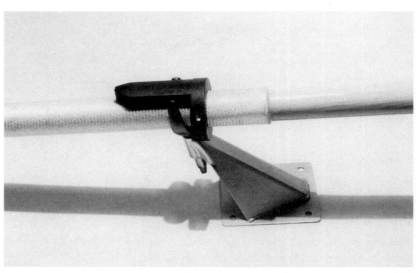

This oar is in an oarlock mounted on the oarstand. The oarstop shown here is an Oar Right.
(Photo courtesy of Cascade Outfitters, Springfield, OR)

Paddles

Paddle rafting may be exhilarating for your crew members, but it tests the limits of your paddles. Rafting paddles must be able to withstand the same rigors as oars: rock collisions, powerful hydraulics, and the torque that results when paddlers pit their strength against the river's current.

The main considerations in choosing rafting paddles are length and materials. Most rafters use paddles ranging from 54 to 60 inches in length, with the 60-inch paddle being the most popular length for commercial customers. Paddle captains, on the other hand, often prefer slightly longer paddles—66 to 72 inches long. The extra length gives the captain added leverage to execute ruddering strokes. (I like the extra length because I can reach forward and poke inattentive passengers when they're not paddling correctly!)

Paddles, like oars, come in a variety of materials. Outfitters usually use paddles constructed with aluminum shafts and some type of plastic handle and blade because they are durable and reasonably priced. However, many experienced paddlers are discovering that wooden paddles—constructed from ash, fir, and other woods—and composite paddles sacrifice a minimal amount of durability while their light weight makes paddling easier. In fact, many top rafting competitors choose wood and fiberglas paddles for their light weight, incredible feel, and stellar performance characteristics.

The last criteria to consider when selecting paddles is blade size. Paddle blades are generally 7 or 8 inches wide by 20 inches high. Guides often like beefier blades—up to 8 inches wide by 26 inches high—which give them extra leverage to crank the stern around. However, the rest of the crew will find that larger blades slow down their stroke rate and require some extra muscle to move.

Essential Riverwear

Novice rafters are often astonished when they first discover how cold most rivers are. Whether fueled by snowmelt, rainfall, or dam releases, many popular rivers are cold enough to require some form of outerwear even on the warmest days. Plus, rivers are rocky. You may only have to worry about the rocks near the surface, but they're there, just waiting to take a shot at you if you swim by.

The first layer of protection between you and the river environment is your personal gear: clothing, lifejackets, and helmets. Carefully designed and selected riverwear not only improves the quality of your river experience but makes whitewater rafting much safer. Wetsuits, drysuits, lifejackets, and helmets protect rafters from the debilitating effects of hypothermia, provide them with flotation in powerful currents, and protect them from injury amid rock-strewn channels.

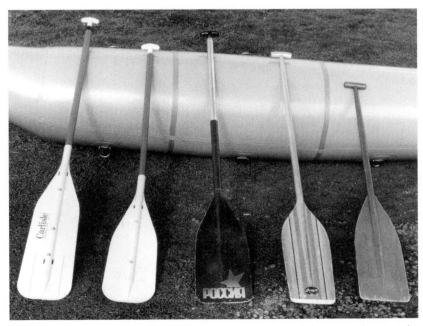

Raft paddles come in a variety of shapes and materials.

CLOTHING

When choosing riverwear, select garments that provide (1) comfort, (2) flexibility, and (3) sufficient insulation to ward off hypothermia. You may be able to get away with shorts or bathing suits when the river is forgiving and the air is warm, but such conditions are the exception to the rule. Experienced rafters consider river and air temperatures, the type of river they'll be rafting, and their expected level of activity to determine their clothing requirements. Novices, on the other hand, can follow the *120-degree rule:* If the combined air and water temperatures equal less than 120 degrees Fahrenheit, don wetsuits, drysuits, paddle jackets, and booties to stay warm. You can always peel off layers during the trip if you get *too* warm!

Wetsuits. Wetsuits made of body-hugging neoprene have been a favored form of insulation for many years. A *farmer john*–style wetsuit—which leaves the arms and shoulders uncovered—provides the first layer of insulation, with pile sweaters and paddle jackets or dry tops making up the outer layers.

The wetsuit works by shielding unprotected skin from direct splashes and trapping a thin film of water between the suit and your skin during swims. Once water fills the suit it is warmed by your skin and insulated from the river by the suit itself. Wetsuits also provide some extra flotation and padding—nice to have if you're swimming a boulder-strewn river.

When you select a wetsuit, try not to get the same type of suit worn by scuba divers; a rafter's higher activity level and increased range of motion demand a thinner wetsuit. A thickness of ⅛ inch (2 to 3 millimeters) provides both warmth and flexibility. Also check for proper fit: A farmer john wetsuit should follow the contours of your body without being too tight.

Paddling Jackets and Dry Tops. Paddling jackets and dry tops are high-tech rain jackets similar in design to the upper half of a drysuit (described below). The main difference between paddling jackets and dry tops is in their ability to shed water. The more affordable paddling jacket combines loose layers of waterproof cloth with water-resistant neoprene or Lycra closures at the neck and wrist. The dry top, on the other hand, incorporates waterproof latex closures at the neck and wrist.

Both paddling jackets and dry tops are effective when you're sitting up in the raft, but they let water in through the waist opening when you're swimming. They're usually used as an outer waterproofing layer with wetsuits, to help prevent chilling blasts of cold water from finding their way down the front of your suit. However, on warmer days paddle jackets and dry tops can be enough to keep hearty rafters warm with nothing more than a synthetic sweater underneath.

Drysuits. Drysuits differ dramatically from wetsuits in both appearance and function. Instead of trapping water near the skin, the drysuit keeps water off your body by enclosing it in a loose-fitting layer of waterproof fabric. The suit has a large waterproof zipper or flap closure that allows easy entry and exit, and is made totally waterproof with tight-fitting latex gaskets at the neck, wrist, and ankle openings.

Though drysuits lack the insulating qualities of wetsuits, they are baggy enough to fit over inner layers of clothing. As with other outdoor sports, the best way to choose clothing that will keep you warm is to follow the *layering* concept. The innermost clothing layer should wick sweat away from your skin, and the next layers should be warm and absorbent. Since the drysuit will seal in body moisture, it is important to choose inner layers made of synthetic materials like nylon or polypropylene fleece.

Other Clothing Accessories. Booties, gloves, and insulating caps vastly improve the quality of your rafting experience on cold rivers. Thick neoprene booties with semirigid soles keep feet warm and provide decent traction during slippery portages. In warmer climates, specially designed river sandals (with extra straps to hold them securely on your feet) work great. Waterproof caps help the body retain an enormous amount of body heat by providing another layer of insulation over your head. Hands can be kept comfortably warm with neoprene gloves.

LIFEJACKETS

Lifejackets—also called *personal flotation devices* or *PFDs*—must be worn by rafters on any river. They not only increase your buoyancy in the event of a swim, but their foam-filled shells provide some extra insula-

River clothing, from left to right: wetsuit, paddling jacket, and drysuit.

in mind that you'll be adding bulky layers of riverwear under the jacket when you're out rafting, so make sure there's enough space left to accommodate your clothing.

The second factor in selecting a proper lifejacket is flotation or *buoyancy*. Lifejackets work on some fairly basic principles. An average person is surprisingly buoyant, weighing only 10 to 12 pounds when immersed in water (less if you're thin, more if you're heavy), so anything that attaches to the body and provides more upward lift than its sinking weight will increase the buoyancy.

The main purpose of a lifejacket is to keep your mouth and chin above water long enough to let you breathe. Before you can decide how much flotation *you'll* need on your next river trip, you'll need to evaluate your own abilities and the river's difficulty. Ask yourself what type of water you will be paddling; how much you weigh and your body type; the clothing you intend to wear under the lifejacket (a wetsuit can add 6 to 8 pounds of buoyancy, and an air-filled drysuit can

tion on cold days and even some welcome body armor in the event of a swim.

When choosing or purchasing lifejackets you must consider two important factors: *fit* and *flotation*. A properly fitted lifejacket is comfortable enough to wear all day and doesn't interfere with rowing, paddling, or swimming. It will cinch snugly around your torso and won't ride up over your face or head in rapids. Many lifejackets achieve a customized fit through the use of different sizes (from extra-small child sizes to extra-large adult sizes), flexible contoured foam panels, and buckled cinch straps.

To make sure you're getting the best fit possible, try a few on. First select a lifejacket that has ties or straps that tighten at the waist, and after you put it on and cinch the ties, have a friend yank on the shoulders. If the lifejacket fits properly, it will budge only slightly while remaining comfortable. Keep

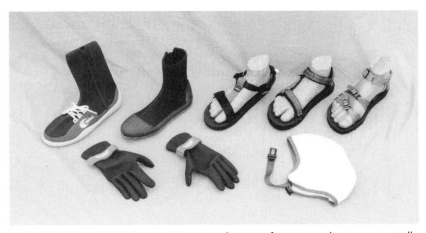

Accessories: a selection of neoprene booties, specially designed river sandals, gloves, and a helmet liner.
(Courtesy of Cascade Outfitters, Springfield, OR)

RESCUE LIFE JACKETS

U.S. Coast Guard regulations discouraged lifejacket innovations in this country during much of the 1980s. At the same time, teams of imaginative European river runners filled in the creative gaps, coming up with practical, safety-minded personal flotation devices. Their designs finally caught the eyes of North American rafters in the early 1990s, and now provide some great alternatives for all sorts of whitewater use.

The main difference between rescue lifejackets and ordinary personal flotation devices is accessories. A stripped-down rescue lifejacket might look like a common PFD, but it has all sorts of attachments for rescue tools, and adjustment straps for tighter fits. Items such as integral harnesses (for vertical resuces), quick-release belts (for strong-swimmer rescues), gear bags (for carabiners), and throwbag pouches are common to most rescue lifejackets.

If you're a professional guide, a Class V rafter, or just want to have the best in safety gear, consider wearing a resuce lifejacket on any river trip.

HELMETS

Helmets have become de rigueur for rafters on many whitewater rivers, and are mandatory on any Class IV and V outing. Helmets consist of a sturdy outer shell, a shock-absorbing liner, and a chin harness

(continued on page 33)

add more); whether you are likely to swim this river; and whether you're a strong swimmer.

If you're a weak swimmer or about to embark on a very difficult run, a lifejacket with maximum flotation may increase your safety during a swim. However, the more foam added to the lifejacket (to increase its buoyancy), the more it will interfere with your ability to swim, row, or paddle. Also, high-flotation lifejackets might make it tougher to escape holes or reversals. Strong swimmers on gentle rivers may be able to get away with slim, low-flotation lifejackets.

Since there are so many factors involved in choosing a lifejacket, ask your dealer to help you select one, or get a couple of lifejackets so you'll be ready for anything.

Lifejackets range from beefy, high-flotation jackets (left) down to slim low-float jackets (right).
(Courtesy of Cascade Outfitters, Springfield, OR)

to keep the helmet on your head. Outer shells can be made of plastic, fiberglass, Kevlar, or other strong, rigid materials. However, since reputable whitewater stores are unlikely to carry helmets with shells made of inferior materials, the shape and fit of the outer shell becomes more important than its durability.

A properly shaped and fitted helmet covers the entire head—including the top of the head, temples, and ears—but remains unobtrusive to the wearer. Some helmets even have face guards to protect against injuries caused by rocks, flailing paddles, or collisions with other paddlers.

When selecting a helmet, check out its liner. You may prefer foam padding to a suspension type of shock-absorbing system, but either works well. Finally, make sure that the helmet fits your head comfortably: The chin strap should hold the helmet securely in place so the helmet won't ride up and expose your forehead or slide down and block your vision.

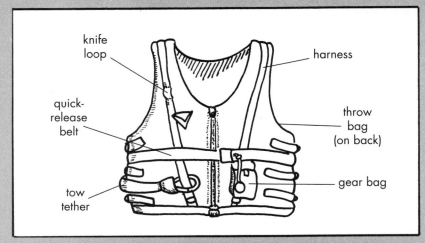

Rescue lifejackets provide a great alternative for experienced, safety-conscious rafters and Class V enthusiasts. Items like integral quick-release harnesses and belts, lash points for carabiners, and throwbag pouches are common features of these remarkable devices.

Well-designed helmets cover all the important parts of the head, including the forehead, temples, and ears.
(Courtesy of Alder Creek Kayak Supply, Portland, OR)

4

S A D D L E   U P

ASSEMBLING YOUR GEAR AND CREW

A fully outfitted raft is like a fine car: It looks great just sitting there, but it doesn't work worth a darn until there's somebody behind the wheel.

In this chapter you'll learn much more than how to sit behind the wheel. You'll take your new-found knowledge of river gear and wait to create a clean, serviceable system. You'll learn how to inflate and rig your raft, where to stash accessories, and how to seat passengers and paddlers. You'll even learn what it takes to keep your raft properly balanced to maximize its performance. This is your next step along the path from gear pile to put-in.

Inflating Your Raft

PUMPS

Since rafts float better and hold more weight when they have a lot of air in them, let's start out by inflating the raft. Pumps specially suited to rafting range from powerful 110-volt AC electric blowers to affordable hand and foot pumps. The big AC blowers are wonderful timesavers, but you've got to have an electrical outlet or generator nearby to tap their benefits.

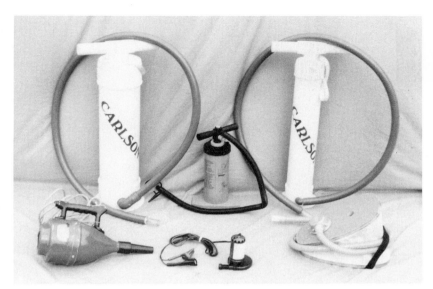

A variety of manual and electric pumps. Back row: three hand pumps. Bottom row, from left: big blower, LVM, and foot pump.

ing goes, "Size isn't everything." Some small pumps blow out air on both the up and down stroke of the handle, making inflation fast and easy.) Any raft pump should have a durable hose and a nozzle sized to fit your raft's valves perfectly. Also, some pumps work in reverse and can actually suck air out of a raft. This handy deflation feature helps get the last bit of air out of your raft before you store it.

INFLATING THE RAFT

Before you blow up your raft, remember two things: (1) don't exceed your raft's recommended air-pressure rating (usually 2 to 3 pounds per square inch); and (2) blow up the chambers slowly and evenly. By adding air evenly around the raft you'll avoid overpressurizing—and possibly damaging—the delicate baffles that separate each chamber. The addition of the *proper* amount of air makes the raft perform at its best. Overinflated rafts tend to tear more easily and can even become permanently distorted. Underinflated rafts, on the other hand, can be real slugs. They wobble through rapids and are more prone to wrapping, twisting, and flipping.

To properly inflate your raft, first put just enough air in each chamber to give the raft its normal shape. Next, go around again and top off the raft by adding air to each chamber until the raft is fully inflated. (Don't exceed its recommended psi!) When you're

Twelve-volt DC-powered air pumps, on the other hand, attach to your car's battery and put out about 1.5 to 2.5 pounds per square inch (psi) in air pressure.

No matter what type of electric pump you have, use it only to give the raft its full shape and then use a hand or foot pump to top off the raft with the final bit of air. Topping off the raft with a manual pump increases the lifespan of your electric pump and will make your raft much stiffer on the river.

Hand- and foot-powered pumps come in a variety of sizes. Hand pumps with large, wide-diameter barrels let you pump up rafts fast and efficiently, while smaller hand pumps are easy to carry on your raft. (As the say-

WHEN INFLATING YOUR RAFT . . .

(1) First use an electric or manual pump merely to bring the raft up to shape, inflating all chambers evenly.
(2) Top off the chambers evenly to prevent undue stress on baffles.
(3) Check pressure periodically by hand or with a gauge, especially on hot, sunny days.
(4) To prevent floor damage, never put hand or foot pumps on the floor when the raft is on the ground.

done, look at the tubes. Smooth-surfaced, identically sized tubes will tell you that you've blown up your raft correctly, while a crease in any tube above a baffle means that the chambers aren't equally inflated. Figuring out if your raft is properly inflated takes a little bit of experience, and can be done with an air gauge or by feel. A raft is usually fully inflated when a struck fist bounces firmly off the tubes.

Rigging the Frame

If you're going to be rowing, the next item on your preriver agenda will be to strap the frame to the raft. If the frame needs to be assembled, do that outside the raft to avoid pinching the fabric. Also, put the raft in the river before you add the frame. That way you won't find yourself 50 feet from the shoreline trying to muscle an overweight pile of raft material and steel across rocks, grass, or dirt.

Most raft frames are designed to sit right in the center of the passenger compartment, and for good reason. Saddled with little more than a central rowing frame and an oarsperson, a raft floats like a giant bowl, its pivot point directly over its midline. By placing the oars over the middle of the raft, the rower can easily spin either end of the raft with single- and double-oar turning strokes.

I like to strap down the frame after I've already inflated the raft, especially if the frame will hinder easy access to the valves. However, some rafters prefer to top off the raft after the frame has been strapped down so that the straps will be extra taut. If you fit in the latter category, take care not to overstress lash points such as D-rings and thwarts.

Loading Accessories

SPARE OARS

On anything except short roadside raft trips, rafters should carry one or two spare oars. Firmly lash the spare oars to the frame's siderails with short straps or quick-release buckle systems high above the waterline so they won't snag on rocks or hydraulics. While most rafters prefer to lash the spare oars to the frame with the blade facing the bow, this could actually cause the oar to swing wildly if the front strap loosens or fails. Try mounting the spare oar with the blade facing the stern.

SPARE PADDLES

Spare paddles can be strapped crosswise onto thwarts and held firmly in place by a strap looped once around the shafts, then once around the thwarts. Do your best to keep the blades and handles out of the way of shins and knees to prevent injuries when the going gets rough. Although you can also store paddles at an angle in the stern or even lash them to the outer tubes, never lay them on a standard floor. Rocks can snag the paddles, damaging the floor and injuring paddlers' feet.

BOWLINES

A bowline—about 50 to 75 feet of rope tied to the raft's front D-ring—comes in handy in many situations. You'll use it to tie the raft to shore, for lining difficult rapids, and for tying up your rolled raft to store it.

LASHING DOWN FRAMES

When selecting straps to hold down the frame:

(1) use straps that are barely longer than the minimum length needed to secure the frame;
(2) use enough straps to hold the frame firmly in place; and
(3) adjust the straps so that the free ends face the rower. (That way the rower can quickly tighten loose straps without leaving his or her seat or missing many strokes.)

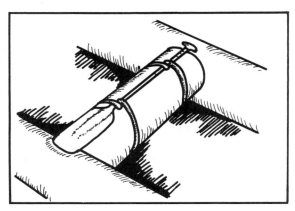

One way to carry spare paddles is to strap them across the back thwart. Loop straps around handles to prevent loss or excess movement.

When not in use, keep the bowline neatly coiled and safely stowed to avoid entangling passengers.

There are three basic ways to store a bowline. Perhaps the easiest way is to clip a *bowline bag* (which looks like an oversized throwbag) to the bow D-ring. This bag retains the rope in loose coils when not in use and seals shut with a pull closure so the rope won't snake free. (A loose bowline is a hazard to crew members and can jam between rocks.) Two more innovative ways of storing the rope in a safe coil are found in the Appendix.

HANDLINES

If your raft is equipped with a full set of exterior D-rings, a handline can be threaded through each D-ring around the perimeter of the raft. The handline provides a grab point for swimmers and makes pulling the raft ashore easier. Like any loose rope, the handline is considered a safety hazard by some rafters—especially if it hangs loosely—since it can entangle limbs or snag on lifejacket clips. Other rafters like the security it affords.

When rigging an exterior handline, use nylon or polypropylene line at least ½-inch in diameter, or use 1-inch-wide nylon tubular webbing. Tie one end of the line to the stern D-ring with a half hitch, leaving about 2 feet of extra line hanging from the knot. Then, starting with the next D-ring, pull the rope as tight as possible and wrap it once around the D-ring before moving to the next D-ring. Continue this process until

the rope can be tied back to the loose rope at the stern with a square knot.

BAIL BUCKETS

I have yet to figure out where to put a bail bucket to keep it from getting broken or endangering passengers! However, most rafters prefer to hang the bucket away from passengers in the stern of a paddle raft (near the guide) or in the center compartment of an oar boat (near the rower). Always keep the bail bucket securely stowed on a short leash, yet readily available for those all too frequent moments when your raft begins to resemble your bathtub.

ADDITIONAL GEAR

In later chapters we'll learn to properly pack and load rafts for overnight expeditions. But in this chapter we're concerned with keeping the raft trim and performing at its best. Gear, like passengers, adds a lot of weight to the raft and makes it more difficult to maneuver. Accordingly, it is just as important to load gear so that it won't hinder your raft's performance. To accomplish this, keep three things in mind: (1) don't overload the ends of the raft, (2) keep the heaviest gear low in the raft, and (3) leave enough open floor space for passengers' feet and for bailing standard-floor rafts.

If you're carrying only yourself and one or two days' worth of gear, loading an oar raft is pretty easy. You can lash down all your gear in the stern without worrying much about doing wheelies all the way down the river. But as you add more gear for extended river trips you'll want to give more consideration to gear placement. Don't just randomly toss your gear in the stern. Keep in mind the three points just mentioned.

In paddle rafts gear placement becomes a bit more challenging. Since lots of space must be left for paddlers' feet and legs, less room is left for gear. There are a number of ways to overcome the disadvantages of paddle rafting. First, consider leaving some of your gear at home. Not only will that make life on the river less complicated but it will also make your raft lighter and more maneuverable. Next, consider leaving some of your paddlers at home. If you pick the right raft, and have enough paddle power to handle the river, the extra paddlers will just take up valuable gear space. Finally, think of the most compact and efficient way to store your gear. This means taking a few extra minutes to compress your gear tightly into dry bags and tying them into the center of the raft where they'll rest over the pivot point.

Passengers in Oar Rafts

NONPADDLERS

In an empty oarboat, one or two passengers can sit in the bow compartment without upsetting the raft's balance. But by the time the third passenger climbs aboard, it's time either to move the frame back a bit or to start drawing straws for the back seat. The more body weight the raft has to carry, the more important it is to spread that weight around evenly.

Most guides will find that a few intrepid volunteers will leap into the bow compartment before the river trip, while the more apprehensive members of the crew will crawl towards the stern. The end result of this type of natural selection is that you'll obtain a happy medium in both seat selection and weight dis-

tribution without having to ruffle anybody's feathers.

Keep in mind that you'll need to leave plenty of room to operate the oars. Forewarn the passengers that you'll be leaning forward and backward frequently to maneuver the raft and that they should be prepared to give you some extra space if necessary.

PADDLE ASSISTS

Stern-mounted rowing frames are frequently used on commercial trips when a paddle captain needs extra leverage to guide the crew through difficult rapids. Also known as *hybrid* rigs and *paddle assists,* the stern-rowed raft lets the guide shout commands forward to the paddle crew while reaping the powerful benefits of a set of long, sturdy oars. In a clutch, the guide can override an uncooperative crew and make an important move. The stern frame's drawback is that when the crew isn't paddling, the raft's pivot point is so far back that the raft becomes more difficult to turn than a center-rowed raft. Also, the oarsperson sits on a veritable catapult seat that can toss him or her forward when the raft hits big holes or slams to a halt at the base of steep drops.

The same paddle-assist concepts that work with stern frames can be applied to center frames. By seating a cou-

Passengers can relax and let one oarsperson do all the work.

Stern-mounted rowing frames let guides combine the power and control of rowing with the thrill of paddling.

A SOLID FOUNDATION

Since paddle strokes use every muscle in the body, all the paddlers have to lock into the raft by pressing their legs against thwarts, slipping their feet into footcups, or using friction and balance to stay aboard. Paddlers should seat their buttocks far enough out on a tube so they can reach the water, but not so far out that they'll fall overboard when the first wave or rock hits. Sitting on the thwarts or floor—though it seems safe and comfortable—simply won't do. It puts the main tube between the paddler and the river and makes paddling impossible.

Legs and feet should stay inside the raft. This not only puts most of the paddler's body weight inside the raft but also places a tube between limbs and bone-crushing rocks or logs. On large, obstacle-free rivers, some paddlers prefer riding *cowboy style* with their outer leg dangling in the river. Though acceptable when there are no rocks present, this style of paddling places more of the paddler's body weight outside the tube and makes it easier to fall out.

Once you're comfortably seated, lean the lower part of your legs against a tube or thwart. If the raft lacks

ple of paddlers in the front compartment, the rower gains some extra power, ballast, and flexibility. This helps on all types of rivers. In steep, technical rivers, where narrow chutes or big boulders frequently interfere with rowing, paddlers can take over and help execute critical maneuvers. On large-volume rivers, where big haystacks or breaking waves are common, the bow paddlers add paddle power and can throw their weight forward in big hydraulics. This takes some of the workload off the rower and makes the raft stronger overall.

Paddle Teams

Shed that frame, ditch the oars, and grab some paddles! Paddle rafting is the ultimate in team-oriented adventure. In this section we'll discuss the things you need to teach passengers about where to sit and how to brace their feet and legs in the raft.

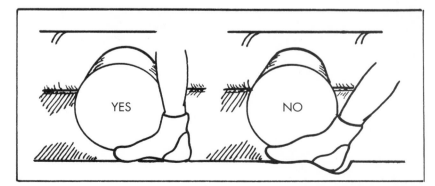
If your raft doesn't have footcups, brace your feet and shins against tubes or thwarts. However, never wedge your feet all the way under thwarts.

footcups, push your feet halfway under a thwart. (*Never put your whole foot or leg under the thwart since that increases the risk of entrapment or compression injuries.*) If a footcup *is* available, slip your foot far enough into the cup to get a solid grip, but not so far that your foot won't easily slide out in an emergency. With feet, legs, and butts properly planted on the raft, you'll be ready to tackle the rapids.

SEATING ARRANGEMENTS

On gentle rivers, guides can be hard pressed to give their passengers a really exciting ride. On some easy rivers I've gone so far as to stack all the passengers in the stern compartment and paddle into small, deep rapids with the bow riding high in the air. With each passing wave, the bow would bounce higher and higher until it finally flipped backward, sending us all into the drink. It made for a great laugh on warm, gentle rivers, but gave us a quick lesson in how improper weight distribution affects your rafting success.

Three considerations go into positioning members of your paddle team: (1) *even strength distribution,* (2) *even weight distribution,* and (3) *adequate room to paddle.*

Even strength distribution begins with the most important member of the crew: the paddle captain. In North America, the paddle captain sits in the stern compartment. From there the captain can watch oncoming rapids and crew members, call out paddle commands, and execute the powerful rudder strokes necessary to guide the raft.

Using a five- or six-person team as an example, the next most important passengers are the bow paddlers: They set the pace for the rest of the crew (under the watchful eye of the paddle captain), control the front of the raft, and take charge of the bowline. In a well-balanced paddle raft, the bow paddlers should be the strongest and most capable paddlers in the team—able to react quickly to commands and willing to paddle fearlessly in the midst of difficult rapids. (If the strongest bow paddler is seated *diagonally* opposite the guide, the guide and that paddler can sometimes maneuver the raft when everybody else is too nervous to move!)

The last two or three paddlers should be seated as follows: Two paddlers should sit near the middle of

A six-person crew properly seated in a 14-foot raft.

the raft and the last passenger can sit in the stern next to the guide. (Keep in mind that all paddlers need enough room to move around or the crew's strokes may get tangled up.)

VARYING THE SIZE OF THE PADDLE TEAM

The same concepts that apply to five-person teams work with any odd-numbered team: If you have three paddlers, seat the guide in the stern and the other paddlers in the bow or center compartment. If you have seven paddlers, seat the guide in the stern and spread the other paddlers evenly throughout the raft. In large, even-numbered paddle teams, the last paddler can sit next to the paddle captain since proper guiding technique keeps the guide's paddle on *one side* at all times. However, if the raft is only half full (half empty?), make the stern the captain's private domain so that he or she has plenty of room to move around.

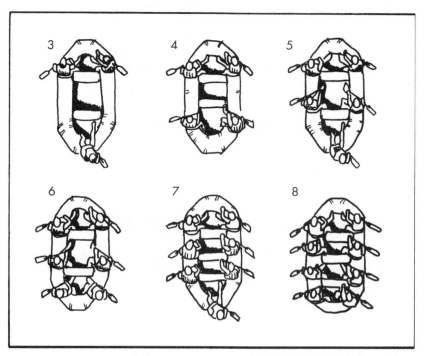

Different ways to seat paddlers: Strive to balance the paddlers' strength and weight evenly throughout the raft while allowing adequate space to paddle.

5
RIVER MORPHOLOGY
THE DYNAMICS OF RUNNING WATER

From my boyhood days in eastern Massachusetts to my most recent adventures on the steep rivers of the Sierra, Cascade, and Rocky mountain ranges, I've been enthralled with moving water. As a child, I'd dash outside during spring freshets to watch water collect and flow through small roadside gullies. Tossing tiny sticks into these meager currents I'd stare transfixed as my make-believe rafts descended the miniature pebble-strewn rapids. Even today, standing high atop a rocky precipice to scout a new rapid, I feel the same inspiration that roused my imagination many years ago.

To the ordinary landlubber, whitewater rapids are a primal source of fascination. Flowing like unbridled liquid avalanches, rapids are breathtaking in their beauty and awe-inspiring in their power. But to an experienced river runner, rapids are predictable and orderly. Obstacles, constrictions, and changes in volume or gradient have definite and reliable effects on the river's surface. The seasoned rafter knows these effects intimately and can anticipate how currents and rapids will affect a raft.

In this chapter we will disassemble and examine rivers. Before we look at the big river picture, we'll dissect rapids into tangible components like pieces of a puzzle. Then, once we've gained an understanding of how the pieces work and fit together, we'll reassemble the puzzle and form real live rapids much like the ones you'll see on your next river trip.

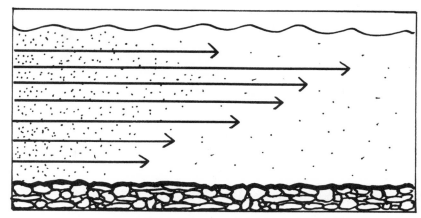

In this example of laminar currents, the longer arrows represent faster currents and appear just below the surface. The currents near the riverbed are slowed by friction.

A Look Beneath the Surface

WATER MECHANICS

Ask the average river runner how water moves and in what state, and he's likely to respond, "It moves downhill in West Virginia." Well, yeah, that's a correct response. But ask hydrologists about water movements and they'll mention three very different states: *laminar,* *turbulent,* and *chaotic.* Each state describes a different pattern of currents and appears at different places within the river system.

LAMINAR FLOWS

For many rafters laminar flow is the most comfortable type of current to experience because it is the safest and most predictable. Laminar flows show up on smooth, straight riverbeds where, if we were to slice the river from bank to bank, we would find some distinct patterns. As the accompanying diagram shows, rivers contain multiple sheets of water, each moving at a different speed. The small circles and long arrows represent the fastest-moving sheets and are located near the center of the river below the surface. Large circles and short arrows represent slower sheets, their downstream progress hampered by friction from the riverbed, banks, and air. Between each sheet there's a zone of mild shearing, better described as an interface between two laminar

sheets moving quite independently and at different speeds.

To *feel* the differences between laminar sheets, let your raft glide freely across the river surface. If you plant your paddle deep in the river, you will feel a forward tug. That tug is caused by subsurface laminar sheets moving forward faster than the sheets on the surface. If you've ever fallen out of your raft in a big, powerful river, you may have experienced a *tunnel effect,* as if you were trapped inside a giant horizontal tube that wouldn't let you go. That is because the core of the river (just below the surface) is an independent laminar sheet totally separated from its surrounding

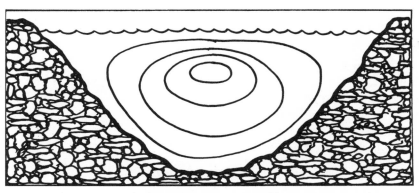

In this cross section view of laminar currents, the smaller circles represent the faster flows.

sheets. Once you are in the tunnel, the shear zones hold you inside until your lifejacket finally propels you back toward the surface.

TURBULENT FLOWS

Turbulent flows arise wherever obstacles (like boulders or narrow cliffs) obstruct the current. These obstacles force too much water into too little space, which in turn forces one laminar sheet into another. When this happens, the laminar sheets begin to break up, leaving smaller ribbons of current that seek their way independently through the neighboring currents.

Rafters should look for turbulence at places like

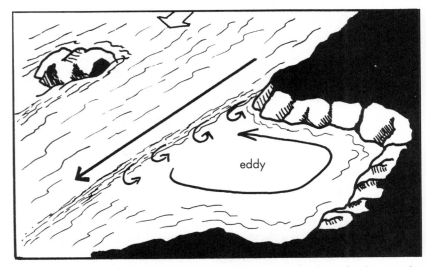

As the main current slips past an obstacle, the straight lines (laminar currents) begin to shear off and rotate behind the obstacle (turbulent currents). In this case, the result is an eddy.

A hole: When current plunges over a boulder or ledge, some of it sneaks downstream beneath the surface while the rest of it recycles upstream to fill in the cavity. You can judge the intensity of some holes by the size and power of the backwash: The bigger the meaner! Small holes are fun to crash through, but giant holes can flip rafts or even trap swimmers.

chutes, where the independent ribbons slip free and create ripples or waves on the river surface. Turbulence also appears in eddies, where the laminar sheets are pressed together as they slip around an obstacle. The turbulent zone appears behind the obstacle where the laminar sheets break up. The eddy is separated from the passing laminar sheets (the main current) by an abrupt boundary that rafters call an *eddy line*.

CHAOS

At the extreme end of water behavior patterns—just as with many rafters' behavior patterns—there is chaos. Simply put, chaos is a state of utter confusion. The river's normal flow lines disintegrate and bounce around randomly. Interestingly, all of this commotion cancels itself out, leaving little real movement at all. Probably the best example of chaos is the

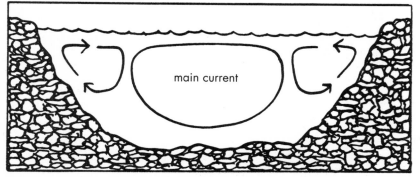

Helical currents flow away from the bank on the surface, meet the main current, then dive. Next, the water works its way back to the bank, then rises along the shore to repeat the cycle.

ordinary hole (discussed in detail later in this chapter): At the base of a steep slide (like at the back of a rock or ledge) too little water tries to fill too large a space and settles on trying to be everywhere at once . . . chaos. Though the water explodes randomly throughout the hole, the hole itself ends up being stationary.

HELICAL CURRENTS

Within any river, other universal patterns emerge. *Helical currents* flow outward from the bank along the surface until they collide with the main current, where they spiral downstream, dive, and work their

way back toward the bank under the surface.

If you have ever swum a river, you may have noticed that the last few feet to the shore seemed harder to swim than anywhere else. That's because the helical currents were pushing you away from the bank, out toward the center of the river.

MEANDERS

In the main current you'll find *horizontal* and *vertical meanders.* In horizontal meanders, the main current weaves back and forth across the river trying to make a complete trip from one bank to the other and back again in a distance equal to 11 times the channel width. In vertical meanders, the main current climbs from deep pools to shallow riffles and back again within a downstream distance of 3 to 7 times the channel width.

Bending the Riverbed. Since meanders can be confusing, a couple of examples are in order. Let's start off with horizontal meanders. First, pick a bend in the river. Next, measure the river's width. Finally, multiply the river's width by 11. If you proceed downstream that distance, theoretically you will find another bend in the river where the current completes a horizontal

Horizontal meanders work back and forth across the river, continually pressing against the outside bank. Left to its own accord, the meander will erode the outside bank until the riverbed takes on the same shape as the meander.

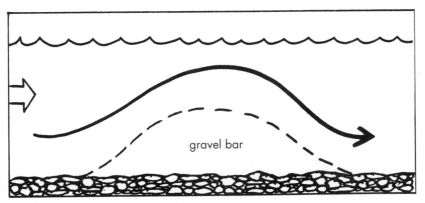

Vertical meanders rise and descend as the current flows downstream. Eventually, this action creates alternating shallow sandbars and deep pools.

meander. For vertical meanders, measure the distance across the river at a pool, multiply it by 3 to 7, float that distance downstream, and—voilà—another pool. (Now, before you go try out these experiments, I've got to add a disclaimer: Currents don't always get their way. Banks are constantly eroding and rerouting the main channel, so it's a constant battle between hydrodynamics and the impediments of new boulders.)

Shaping the Riverbed. What does all this scientific mumbo jumbo mean for river runners? Well, water's intense desire to meander influences the shape and feel of rivers in ways that rafters can see and understand. The river leans against any bank that gets in its way, using its erosive power to gradually carve out a new bend. At the same time, the current's linear motion causes the current to pile up on the outside of the bend, where it has to travel faster than the water on the inside of the bend to reach the same point downstream. Finally, the flows along the outside of bends dive down and creep along the bottom toward the slower currents at the inside of the bend.

The net effect of all this activity is that the fast-moving water on the outside of the bend keeps gnawing at the outer bank and slowly pulls part of the bank into the river itself. At the same time, the slow water along the inside of the bend loses its ability to support the eroded particles and deposits them on shallow bars. As the process continues, deeply undercut cliffs, exposed roots, and overhanging trees begin to appear along the outside of the bend, while the inside bend becomes shallower and drier with each passing year.

River Characteristics

Outwardly rivers display a broad range of emotions—at times calm and soothing, at other times angry and riotous. But inwardly, rivers are lazy by nature. Water

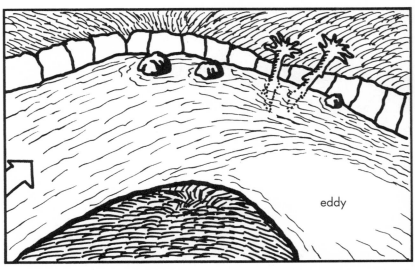

The current flows deep and fast around the outside of the bend (top), eroding the outer bank. The current along the inside of the bend (bottom) is slow, allowing sediment to settle out and create shallows.

can be compared to a train running along a track: It just keeps rolling in the same direction unless something comes along and knocks it off course. Water, just like a train, follows a path of least resistance as it is pulled downhill by its natural engine, gravity. So, then, why do rivers and rapids look so different from one another?

There is much more to whitewater rivers than water's natural tendency to follow a course of least resistance. Obstacles clutter the main channel, riverbeds descend more steeply in places, and water levels fluctuate with seasonal rains, snowmelt, or droughts. In the end, three factors have a profound effect on the intensity and character of whitewater rivers: *volume, gradient,* and *changes in river structure.*

VOLUME

River volume is measured in cubic units per second. In the United States, the foot is used for the cubic unit, and the correct term is *cubic feet per second,* or *cfs.* In metric countries, the meter is used in place of the foot, so river volumes are measured in *cubic meters per second,* or *cms.* Simply stated, cfs and cms measure the amount of water that passes a specific point each second. However, the proper formula is the river's width, times its depth, times the current's velocity. For example, a river 20 feet wide by 10 feet deep, with a current flowing 5 miles per hour, has a flow of 1,000 cubic feet per second (20' x 10' x 5 mph = 1,000 cfs).

Volume Versus Velocity. Using this basic formula, you can see that the addition of more water—say, from a recent rain or a tributary—to the same 20-by-10-foot river will increase the speed of the current. For example, double the flow of the river, making it 2,000 cfs instead of 1,000 cfs. Since the river's depth and width haven't changed, the additional water must move *twice as fast* to make the formula work. Instead of moving 5 miles per hour, the velocity jumps to 10 miles per hour (20' x 10' x 10 mph = 2,000 cfs).

Changes in volume or river velocity have some important effects that rafters need to understand. Since water is *heavy*—weighing 8.33 pounds per gallon, or 62.4 pounds per cubic foot—the addition of a few cfs or an increase in river velocity causes a huge increase in the amount of force that water exerts on a raft or a swimmer.

Water Weight. Let's look at this by going back to the cubic foot of water. Instead of using just one cubic foot of water, slice a long rod of water out of the river 1 foot wide by 1 foot high. Now, make that rod the same length as the river's flow in cfs. For example, if the river is flowing at 1,000 cfs, make the rod 1 square foot by 1,000 feet long. The weight of that long pillar of water flowing past a designated point in the river doesn't have a force of just 62.4 pounds; it is backed by the force of 1,000 cubes of water, or *62,400 pounds!* Fortunately, the fluid properties of water let much of that force flow around a raft, rock, or body unnoticed. However, a raft held in place against the main current—during a wrap, for example—can prove just how powerful and heavy the river really is. The wrapped raft is held tight by thousands of pounds of pressure, making it very difficult to remove.

Ever-Changing Velocities. Up until now, we've assumed that rivers move downstream at a constant rate of speed. However, as you will soon discover, rivers flow upstream in places and at differing speeds within the same section of river.

In an eddy, reverse currents can flow upstream toward an obstacle just as fast as the main current flows downstream. When the two currents slide by each other, powerful *rotational* or *twisting* forces are created. Rafters caught on the interface between the currents have to fight the current's desire to spin their raft wildly.

Rotational forces are also found where fast and slow currents meet. As the faster currents pass the slower currents, friction pulls pieces of both currents free and causes them to rotate. The interface between the two currents is not as dramatic as those found in eddies, but it is still enough to spin your raft around unless you fight to keep it straight.

A change in velocity—whether from an increase in gradient, a narrowing of the river, or an increase in flow—changes the river's force significantly. It works like this: For every doubling of the current's velocity, the force exerted by the water quadruples. This added force can exert itself on anything in the water's path, or it can be used to support debris suspended in the river's

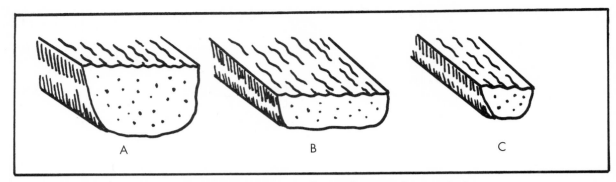

This diagram shows three cross sections of one river at different places. In diagram A, the river is broad, deep, and flowing slowly. In diagram B, the river is the same width, but shallower, forcing the river to flow faster. Finally, in diagram C, the river is both shallow and narrow. Here, the river must flow the fastest.

current. (That is why flooded rivers can displace boulders and transport giant logs like overgrown corks.)

Volume Versus River Size. Without even looking at a river up close, rafters can get some idea how *big* it is by looking at its average flow. In a very general sense, rivers can be categorized as small, medium, or large. Small rivers can be from a few hundred cfs up to about 1,000 cfs, medium-sized rivers can range from 1,000 to 6,000 cfs, and some large rivers can exceed 100,000 cfs! Still, this type of description is pretty subjective. One rafter's *small* may be another rafter's *big* depending on their points of view. Also, rivers grow and shrink in size and power with seasonal water fluctuations or dam releases.

Gauging Volume. Many government agencies monitor river flows. In turn, rafters can obtain water-level information by contacting the agency that monitors the river they plan to run. If you're not quite sure which agency to call, check out the Water-Level Information section of the Appendix.

One problem I've run into with gauges is that many agencies monitor water levels on a *gauge-height* basis. Rather than simply announcing the flow in cfs or cms, the agency will give you a gauge height in feet or meters. All this tells you is how high a river has climbed up an oversized ruler placed in the river at a set location. To use this information you'll have to know the river intimately or be able to correlate the gauge height with river flow. Many of the guidebooks

explain how to do this. If that doesn't work, the agencies themselves usually maintain a correlation table.

Volume Versus Difficulty. Trying to correlate changes in water volume with the river's difficulty rating is nearly impossible. On many rivers, rapids become more difficult as water levels rise. On others, rapids disappear beneath gentle blankets of swift water at higher flows. No matter what happens to the river you plan to run, remember that larger volumes and faster currents can turn gentle rivers into powerful hazards.

GRADIENT

In North America, gradient is described in *feet per mile* (fpm) or *meters per kilometer* (mpk). Both ratings measure a river's average descent over a given distance.

To figure out a river's gradient you will first need to know three things: the elevation at the put-in, the elevation at the take-out, and the distance between the two points. Here's an example of how these numbers work: If the put-in is at an elevation of 3,000 feet and the take-out is at 1,200 feet, the river drops 1,800 feet in that section. If the section to be rafted is 36 miles long, the river drops 50 feet per mile (1,800 ÷ 36 = 50). Here's the formula: (put-in elevation − take-out elevation) ÷ miles = gradient.

Rapids appear where the gradient of one section of river exceeds the river's average gradient, and pools form where the gradient dips below the overall average. If a river descends evenly over its entire length, the

Pool-drop rivers like the one shown here alternate between calm pools and plunging rapids. Continuous rivers, on the other hand, descend gradually down an evenly tilted riverbed. (Notice that the rafter is getting ready to punch straight through the unavoidable hole with momentum. That's the way to do it.)

rapids might be long and constant, but if the river alternates between pools and drops, the rapids might be short but intense. The most severe example of a *pool-drop* river would be one that descends very little in its placid stretches, then plunges violently over giant waterfalls.

Like the other descriptive factors, gradient gives you some clues about the character of a river. Most whitewater rivers have an average gradient of 10 to 100 feet per mile. However, it is becoming quite common to see rafters boating rivers with gradients upward of 200 feet per mile. Still, one rule of thumb should be kept in mind, especially when exploring new rivers: The steeper the river, the more difficult the whitewater.

Surface Features

River structures are seldom uniform. Riverbeds descend more steeply in some places than in others, cliffs narrow and confine channels, and obstacles clut-

ter and obstruct the main current. Each of these structural changes has profound effects on the river, some of which we have already discussed. If a certain amount of water is forced into a smaller space (between two cliffs, for instance), its velocity will increase dramatically; if the main current descends down a steep slide, the gentle laminar currents will gradually give way to turbulence or chaos; and if the river travels around a bend, the currents along the outer banks will move faster than those along the inside of the bend.

Since rafters like to spend most of their time above the river's surface (after all, the majority of rafters rate their whitewater success in terms of avoiding submarine adventures and close encounters with aquatic creatures), it is the *surface* effects of changes in river structure that we are most interested in. So let's step away from the river, scramble to a point high upon the bank, and start looking at the river's surface features.

We'll begin with a calm, straight river—one that flows freely over an unobstructed channel—and then

GO WHEN IT FLOWS

Let's start off with a basic premise: River running is a lot of fun when there's enough water to float your raft. Now you're probably thinking, "Great. I just spent a bunch of money on this dumb book so Jeff can tell me I need water to go rafting." Well, yeah. Sort of. Just try showing up at a river at the wrong time of year and you'll see what I'm saying.

Rivers obtain water from three sources: snowmelt, rainfall, and springs. Plus, if a horde of engineers arrived with blueprints and bulldozers sometime before you did, your river might also receive water released from dams and big conduits. Planning river trips involves some understanding of how these water sources affect rivers.

Snowmelt rivers typically inhabit the foothills of grand mountain ranges like the Rockies, Cascades, Sierras, and Alps. After a few days of hot spring weather, the snow liquefies and surrenders to the tug of gravity. As it trickles downhill, the flow of water collects in ever-growing rivulets until it is finally large enough to be called a creek or river.

Rain-fed rivers work in the same way, except that falling rain replaces melting snow as the system's driving force. In rain-fed watersheds it frequently takes a few days of rain before the ground stops absorbing all moisture. (This is why summer rains rarely fill rivers quickly.) Once the ground is saturated, the surplus water flows downhill and the millions of tiny raindrops collect to form streams.

By looking at a river's flow history you can tell whether it is fed by rain or snow. If its flow peaks during the warmest days of spring, it relies primarily on snow for its water; a river that peaks in the middle of the region's rainy season is rain fed.

This information is important for selecting the best time of year to go rafting. Since rivers are dangerous at peak and flood stages, the optimal time to run a river is usually before or after it has reached its peak. On small streams with limited watersheds, peak flows might only last a day or two after a heavy storm, but some larger rivers subside slowly after hitting their peak water levels.

To learn about any river's optimal season, first consult some local guidebooks or call one of the government agencies listed in the Appendix. Then check with guidebooks and other boaters to obtain recommended levels for river running and plan your trip for the time that the river reaches those levels considered the safest and most fun for rafting.

we'll make some changes. As obstacles enter the picture, rapids will begin to appear. We'll find chutes, waves, holes, and eddies . . . the things river runners call *fun*— at least if they're not too large or too dangerous.

TONGUES

At the top of many rapids, the main current enters a slick, smooth-surfaced ramp called a tongue. Tongues are typically V shaped, with the tip of the V pointing downstream. These *downstream tongues* form between rocks, cliffs, or shallows, and point out the deepest, least-obstructed channel. There may be just one large tongue, or there may be many tongues of different sizes. When there's more than one tongue—as when there are large boulders or islands dividing the river into many channels—the safest and deepest tongue will usually be either the largest or the one that begins dropping the soonest. The reason for this is that channels that wait longer before they begin to drop lose water to deeper channels, so by the time the smaller channel reaches the base of a rapid it may consist of boulder fans barely wet enough to float a raft.

UPSTREAM Vs

Another type of V is the upstream V. A V whose tip points upstream is a shockwave created by obstacles

Tongues (A and B) show deep, clear channels, while upstream Vs (C and D) show subsurface hazards. Rafters should stay on the tongues and avoid the upstream Vs.

that pierce or lurk just beneath the surface. Unlike a tongue, an upstream V is a warning sign—a signal to rafters to steer clear or else risk damaging their boats on the obstacle.

You can make your own miniature version of an upstream V by sticking your finger in a swift current. Chances are, a V-shaped shockwave will spread out from the downstream side of your finger.

STANDING WAVES

Standing waves are some of the most fascinating and entertaining of all river features. From the small erratic riffles of your local creek to the giant haystacks of large-volume rivers, standing waves provide rafters with the ultimate aquatic roller coaster ride.

River Waves Versus Ocean Waves. No discussion of river waves would be complete without some comparison to ocean waves. Although ocean and river waves may look similar, there are distinct differences. First, river waves are stationary—they remain at the same location as the forces or obstacles that form them. Ocean waves, on the other hand, travel toward shore

where they dissipate or crash as they roll up the beach. Second, water travels *through* river waves, releasing its energy as it goes, while the water inside an ocean wave hardly moves at all, retaining its energy until it rolls onto the beach.

How Standing Waves Are Formed. Many things form waves: subsurface boulders, changes in gradient, converging currents. Ultimately, most waves are created by a change in water speed.

One common place to find standing waves is at the terminus of an obstacle-free, downward-sloping section of riverbed. The potential energy stored in fast-falling water turns into lively kinetic energy at the bottom of the slope. The standing waves—which can line up in series of waves known as *wave trains*—are just the river's way of getting rid of all that excess kinetic energy. The first wave in the train is usually the largest, with each successive wave diminishing in size. (*Tailwaves* are wave trains that begin at the base of a rapid.)

Standing waves also appear when cliffs, shallow gravel bars, boulder piles, or other obstacles force a broad river into a narrow channel. Because water can't

River and ocean waves have a lot in common—just ask the surfer. This photo was shot in the heart of Idaho's river country.

Standing waves form when the current slows down at the base of a sloping riverbed.

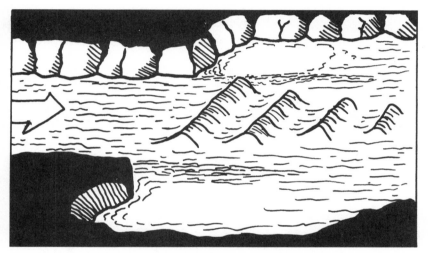

Standing waves form where the fast current of a chute meets the slower-moving water below.

be compressed like air, it moves faster when confined by narrow streambeds or obstacles. You'll find this happening whenever currents are squeezed *horizontally* between banks or boulders or *vertically* over rocks or river bottom. The moment the channel reopens, the energy stored in the fast-moving water dissipates in the form of standing waves.

Submarine boulders or ledges can also form waves. The current picks up energy as it travels faster over the top of the obstacle, then releases it downstream in a series of waves. A hump or cushion—not a standing wave—forms above the obstacle, followed by standing waves downstream. Since waves formed by rocks and boulders frequently stand alone, their solitary presence gives warning of an obstacle beneath the surface.

Still another cause of standing waves is converging currents. *Convergence waves* often form where two channels meet, or where a tributary spills its current into the mainstream. Water piles up and gathers energy at the convergence, then releases the excess energy grad-

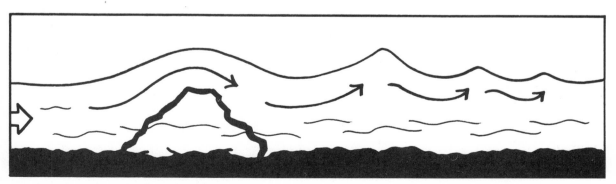

Standing waves forming after a boulder.

Convergence waves forming where two currents meet.

waves, they're actually formed by converging standing waves, each contributing its energy to force the haystack higher than its surroundings. With all this energy packed into one wall of water, haystacks are rarely stable—they tend to dance around on the river's surface and surge randomly.

BREAKING WAVES AND STOPPERS

When a wave becomes too large to support its own weight and shape, the uppermost water starts spilling down the wave's upstream face. Whether they're called *curlers, curling waves, breaking waves,* or *reversals,* these waves can be very power-

ually in the form of standing waves. If the convergence is caused by a deflection of the main current back upon itself by cliffs or steep banks, the waves that bounce off the cliffs are sometimes called *reflection waves.*

DIAGONAL WAVES

When a submerged ledge or boulder cuts diagonally across the main channel, surface waves won't line up perpendicular to the main current. Instead, the first wave or two below the ledge will lunge upward at an angle to the main current, forming diagonal or *lateral* waves. Diagonal waves also appear wherever cliffs, submerged boulders, converging currents, and constricted channels deflect waves at an angle to the main current. No matter what forms the diagonal waves, the waves following the first few diagonal waves realign themselves to be perpendicular to the main current just like other standing waves.

Diagonal waves can form after a submerged diagonal ledge or ricochet off boulders, islands, or cliffs. After the first couple of waves, the tail waves realign themselves perpendicular to the current.

HAYSTACKS

Haystacks are the mountain peaks of the riverscape. Although they look like towering, peaked standing

When a standing wave becomes too large to support its own weight, the crest falls down the wave's upstream face. This rafter is wisely avoiding the powerful breaking wave across the river.

ful. If enough water is falling down the upstream face, it can carry sufficient force to stop and flip your raft—hence the name *stopper.*

PILLOWS

When the current collides with an obstacle, some of the current flows vertically against the obstacle's upstream side and forms a mound of water called a pillow or cushion. These mounds stand higher than the surrounding river and disclose the presence of boulders and other obstacles. As pillows grow, they eventually become too large to sup-

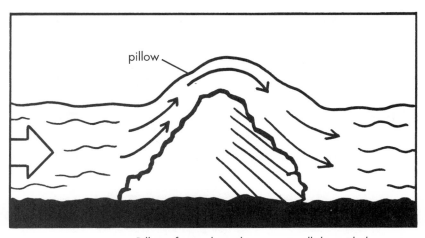

Pillows form where the current collides with the upstream side of an obstacle. The current rises upward against the obstacle, forming a cushion, then settles back down as it slips around the sides of the obstacle.

port their own weight. When that happens, the highest water spills down the upstream face, creating a hydraulic much like a breaking wave.

UNDERCUTS

A pillow—or, rather, the lack of a pillow—also reveals a major river hazard: undercuts. To spot an undercut from your raft, watch the river. Whenever the current collides with an obstacle without forming a pillow, beware! It is a certain indication that the obstacle is undercut, and that the current is diving under it—just where you don't want to be! Since powerful currents can drag rafts and swimmers under ledges, banks, and boulders, undercuts must be treated as some of the worst hazards to be found on whitewater rivers.

ROOSTER TAILS

Rooster tails are pillows gone berserk. Like pillows, rooster tails form when a fast current piles into the upstream side of a rock or boulder. However, rather than letting the water build smoothly on the shoulder

of the rock, the rock slices through the current and deflects water into the air, creating a fountain in the shape of a rooster's tail.

If the rock is tilted upstream, it produces an *upstream rooster tail,* which is identified by the fan of water deflected through the air in an upstream direction. A *downstream rooster tail* fans water through the air in a downstream direction.

Rafters should avoid any kind of rooster tail because the exposed rock and fast-moving currents can combine to tear or wrap the raft in an instant.

BOILS

Boils are upswellings in the river current created when such things as underwater boulders, undercut ledges, and converging currents cause the river surface to roll and bubble like a giant pot of boiling water.

Small boils—common features on many rivers—can be annoying when you line up for a rapid. They'll throw you off course when you're casually drifting and slow you down when you're trying to gain momen-

This paddle captain is giving the "thumbs up" because his team avoided the dangerous undercut rock in the upper left-hand portion of the photo.

The upstream rooster tail (left) and the downstream rooster tail (right) pose serious hazards to rafters and should be avoided.

tum. Still, they're rarely dangerous. Giant boils, on the other hand, can lift and tilt your raft, or even flip it over if they're big enough.

HOLES

Take a moment to refer back to the diagram on page 44. As the illustration shows, when water pours over a rock or ledge, the water plunges down a *falls* toward the riverbed and then flows downstream along the bottom of the river. A deep cavity appears in the river surface just downstream of the falls. In an effort to fill this cavity, the river grabs surface water from downstream and pulls it in a reverse direction back into the cavity. (This zone of upstream currents is called the *backwash*.) Viewed from the side, the hole's currents rotate like a wheel, with the surface rolling upstream and the bottom rolling downstream. This rotating liquid vortex goes by many names, including *hole, reversal, souse hole,* and *stopper.*

Holes, like waves, come in all shapes and sizes. Large holes—sometimes called *keepers*—can hold and flip a raft with ease; small holes can be crashed with momentum. Knowing the difference between friendly and unfriendly holes is one of the most important skills any rafter can have. Fortunately, there are four factors that reveal the intensity of a hole: (1) the *height, angle,* and *volume* of the falls; (2) the *shape* and *width* of the hole; (3) the hole's *depth;* and (4) the *length of the backwash.* These factors mix and match in countless ways, but understanding how they work together will reveal a lot about a particular hole. Let's start by looking at the falls.

The Falls. Water plunges downward at the upstream side of a hole. Generally, the steeper and taller this falls, the more severe the hole. In vertical falls—often called *pourovers*—water plummets toward the bottom of the river and can create a deep hole with a small pocket of violently opposing currents, especially if the pourover is more than a few feet high. Sloping falls, on the other hand, can create long zones of backwash—a perilous hazard for rafters.

Falls with a lot of water usually create stronger holes than do low-volume falls. In a tight, constricted channel, the whole river might plunge over a sharp ledge. This can create a nearly impenetrable hole that will easily trap and hold rafters. On the other hand, a small boulder in the middle of a broad stream might create a barely noticeable hole, or one just big enough to splash your crew. In any case, the addition of more water to the falls generally makes for a more powerful hole.

Hole Shapes. There are four different shapes that describe almost any hole: *smiling, frowning, horizontal,* and *diagonal.* Each shape describes the hole's appearance from an upstream perspective.

In a smiling hole, the middle of the hole is the farthest upstream and the hole's outer edges curl downstream and away from you. This lets some of the current—and anything floating on it—escape laterally out of the hole, making smiling holes the safest to run.

Frowning holes, whose edges curl back at you, focus much of the current's energy toward the middle of the hole, creating a powerful magnet for anything stuck in its grasp. This can spell disaster for rafters. Large frowning holes can hold rafts and swimmers indefinitely, making lateral escapes nearly impossible.

Horizontal holes show up in two places: at the bases of artificial dams and river-wide ledges. If the volume of water flows evenly over the ledge all the way across the river, the resulting hole forms a foreboding bank-to-bank obstacle for rafters. Like frowning holes, these holes can be powerful and dangerous, making escape very difficult.

The final type of hole—a diagonal hole—appears

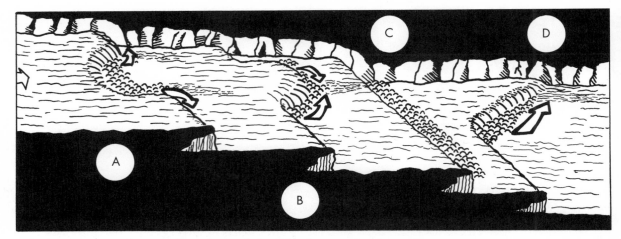

Holes have a variety of personalities. Smiling holes (A) kick outward and provide an escape route for rafts while frowning holes (B) kick inward, creating a powerful trap. Some horizontal holes, like the one shown here (C), have no escape route and can trap a raft. Diagonal holes (D), on the other hand, kick toward their downstream ends where rafts can safely escape.

wherever an obstacle or ledge cuts across the channel at an angle to the current. Diagonal holes have one side farther upstream than the other so that the current slides downstream across the face of the hole. If the rafter moves to the downstream end of the hole, the raft will eventually slip free and back into the main current—hopefully upright.

Hole Width and Depth. Hole width and depth are the next factors that indicate the strength and danger of any hole. Hole width is measured perpendicularly across the current. Wide holes are much more difficult to exit than are narrow holes and should usually be avoided. Hole depth describes how far beneath the surface the recirculating current extends, and is determined by the speed and volume of the falls. In deep holes, the falls forces water all the way down to the riverbed. From there, the current climbs back toward the surface and repeats the cycle without letting much water escape. On large-volume rivers, a rafter trapped in the grasp of a deep hole

could be in real trouble. Not only can the downward current behind the rock slam swimmers against the river bottom, there is only a narrow zone of escape directly on the bottom of the river.

Shallower holes don't extend all the way to the bottom of the river and are usually much safer for rafters, all other factors being equal. Since the hole's rotating

In this shallow hole, the downward current only extends partway to the river bottom and allows easy escape under the backwash. In deep holes—especially those in which the falls plunges all the way to the riverbed—escape is much more difficult.

currents only reach part of the way to the riverbed, swimmers can easily escape from under the upstream currents by diving down into the free-flowing downstream current.

The Backwash. The term *backwash* describes the zone of upstream current that forms downstream of a hole. In some holes, an object floating on the surface 20 or more feet downstream of the falls can travel back upstream on the backwash, only to find itself caught in the maelstrom yet another time. Rafters can follow an easy rule of thumb: The longer the backwash, the more difficult and dangerous the hole.

Spotting Holes. Even though holes can appear anywhere a ledge or boulder lurks beneath the surface, the hole itself might be hard to spot from upstream. Fortunately, recognizable signposts reveal the hole's presence to observant rafters. If you're in a rapid, look for the calm, smooth hump formed by water gliding over a submerged obstacle. If you can see beyond the hump, look slightly downstream for the foamy backwash. Gradually you will get better at spotting holes, and eventually you'll be able to discern fun, runnable holes from hazardous holes just by looking at them from upstream.

LOWHEAD DAMS AND WEIRS

Lowhead dams and weirs include a variety of artificial structures. Many lowhead dams were originally designed to divert water into grain mills or irrigation networks. These days, they are built for everything from flood control to power generation.

Fabricated from cement, asphalt, rebar, and riprap, most lowhead dams are installed straight across the river channel, with walls rising out of either end of the dam. As the water drops over the top of the dam, it slides down a smooth face and spills onto a flat or angled apron. As the water plummets into the pool below the dam, the currents form *incredibly dangerous* holes.

Holes below lowhead dams often extend all the way across the river, are very straight, contain a lot of power, and have a long zone of backwash. Any one of these factors could create a very dangerous hole in its own right, but when combined they form one of the most hazardous obstacles known to whitewater enthu-

To spot holes from upstream, look for a smooth hump in the river's surface, or for the backwash that forms at the base of the hole. Both can be seen in this photograph.

siasts. In fact, a great number of river-related fatalities are due to lowhead dams.

For rafters, I've got only two words of advice: *Steer clear!* Even runnable-looking lowhead dams conceal dangerous currents, and many contain nasty piles of submerged rebar, trapped logs, and construction debris.

When you're on the river, watch for artificial structures and smooth, riverwide horizon lines. These signs can tell you that a dam is coming up and it's time to pull to the bank!

WATERFALLS

When holes get too big for their britches, we call them waterfalls. To me, waterfalls include pourovers, slides, and any type of drop that's high and steep enough to make me think twice before I raft it. In many ways, waterfalls are no different from holes. Every waterfall has a downward-plunging current and a zone of back-

Weirs and lowhead dams contain dangerous keeper holes. Don't run them.

wash, and can be any of a number of shapes or sizes. Accordingly, everything we just learned about holes applies to waterfalls.

Waterfalls can be detected from upstream by their distinctive horizon lines. When you first start rafting, keep a keen eye downstream. If the river seems to disappear suddenly without going around a bend, pull over and walk downstream. It may be simply that the gradient has increased, or it could be that the river is about to plunge over a waterfall. As you start to discern the differences between rapids and falls, clues like nearby trees and large boulders, or even the sound of the water, will tell you whether the river is about to pour over a dangerous waterfall.

EDDIES

I've waited until the end of this chapter to discuss eddies for two reasons. First, eddies combine almost everything mentioned so far about currents and river features. They have oppositional currents, they appear behind obstacles, and they contain both laminar and turbulent currents. Second, eddies are the most impor-

tant hydraulic formations rafters can know and understand. They provide gentle parking zones for loading and unloading rafts, and safe havens for scouting or resting before the next drop; they can even make cross-river maneuvers easier.

Eddies are found behind any obstacle that deflects the main current—boulders, bank protrusions, even bridge abutments and logs. No matter what the obstacle is, it has the same effect: When the main current collides with the upstream face of the obstacle, it works its way around the obstacle and accelerates. This leaves a depressed zone of low pressure behind the obstacle. Water from downstream actually flows *upstream* toward the obstacle to fill in the gap, creating a pocket of current moving in the opposite direction to the main current. (For an example, see the accompanying diagram.)

A feature called an *eddy line* marks the narrow divide between the eddy's upstream currents and the main flow's downstream currents. The currents of the eddy and the main channel mix, swirl, and jet along the eddy line. On large, powerful rivers, the eddy and the main current might even rise to two different levels and wrestle violently along the transition zone. When there is a visible wall of water blocking the entrance to or exit from the eddy, rafters call the eddy line an *eddy fence*.

Two factors affect the intensity of an eddy: (1) the size and shape of the obstacle and (2) the velocity of the current. If the obstacle has chiseled, well-defined edges, it will sharply sever swift currents and create crisp eddy lines and stable eddies. Rounded obstacles and slow currents, on the other hand, allow currents to mix, weaken the eddy, and melt the eddy lines.

Shallow obstacles can create

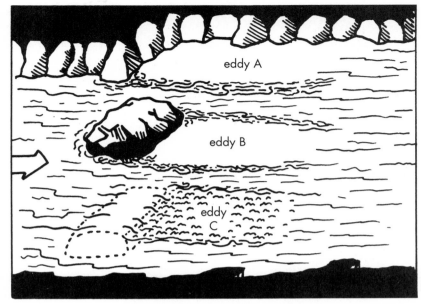

A solid green eddy forms behind a peninsula (A) and the exposed midstream boulder (B). An aerated white eddy forms behind the partially submerged boulder (C).

eddies even if they don't pierce the river's surface. As the river slides over the top of the obstacle, it loses its momentum and swirls in an aerated pocket. The foamy eddy that is formed behind the obstacle is called a *white eddy*. More solid eddies are called *green eddies* or, because they contain powerful, vertically boiling currents, *boiling eddies*.

The Big Picture

The thing that makes rafting so exciting is that no two rapids are alike. The river features we've discussed in this chapter not only vary in size and intensity from river to river, but also mix and match in myriad combinations. Some rivers contain long series of gentle waves interspersed with calm pools, others display steep boulder gardens punctuated by steep holes, and still others have giant haystacks bordered by vicious eddy fences.

As you move from one river to another, the same distinctive hydraulics will be found again and again, and their distinguishing characteristics will become

Waterfalls are like holes . . . just a lot taller.

comfortable and familiar. You'll soon associate solitary waves or pillows with submarine boulders, strange water fountains with surface-piercing rocks, and smooth humps of water or foaming backwash with holes. Eventually, each feature will direct you to safer channels or forewarn you that any attempt at running some rapids is at your own risk.

The Rating Game

There are two universal systems used by rafters to classify the difficulty and intensity of rapids. The most popular system is the *International Scale of River Difficulty*, which grades rapids on a scale of I to VI. In the southwestern United States, another system, known as the *Deseret Scale* or *Grand Canyon System,* is sometimes used. This system rates rapids on a scale of 1 to 10. Unfortunately, neither system is perfect. Rapids change constantly and are affected by water-level fluctuations and shifts in the riverbed. Rafters might rate rapids differently depending on their attitudes or skill levels. Also, the pursuit of more difficult whitewater has resulted in a downgrading of many rapids. Rapids that used to be considered Class VI (extreme) have been downscaled to Class V after many successful descents. So river classifications are little more than a starting point for finding out about any river. You should gather as much additional information about rapids as you can.

THE AWA RIVER-RATING SCALE

The American Whitewater Affiliation (AWA) has published the leading version of the International Scale of River Difficulty. Here it is:

This is the American version of a rating system used to compare river difficulty throughout the world. This system is not exact; rivers do not always fit easily into one category, and regional or individual interpretations may cause misunderstandings. It is no substitute for a guidebook or accurate firsthand descriptions of a run.

Paddlers attempting difficult runs in an unfamiliar area should act cautiously until they get a feel for the way the scale is interpreted locally. River difficulty may change each year due to fluctuations in water level, downed trees, geological disturbances, or bad weather. Stay alert for unexpected problems!

As river difficulty increases, the danger to swimming paddlers becomes more severe. As rapids become longer and more continuous, the challenge increases. There is a difference between running an occasional Class IV rapid and dealing with an entire river of this category. Allow an extra margin of safety between skills and river ratings when the water is cold or if the river itself is remote and inaccessible.

Class I: *Easy. Fast moving water with riffles and small waves. Few obstructions, all obvious and easily missed with little training. Risk to swimmers is slight; self-rescue is easy.*

Class II: *Novice. Straightforward rapids with wide, clear channels which are evident without scouting. Occasional maneuvering may be required, but rocks and medium-sized waves are easily missed by trained paddlers. Swimmers are seldom injured and group assistance, while helpful, is seldom needed.*

Class III: *Intermediate. Rapids with moderate, irregular waves which may be difficult to avoid and which can swamp an open canoe. Complex maneuvers in fast current and good boat control in tight passages or around ledges are often required; large waves or strainers may be present but are easily avoided. Strong eddies and powerful current effects can be found, particularly on large-volume rivers. Scouting is advisable for inexperienced parties. Injuries while swimming are rare; self-rescue is usually easy, but group assistance may be required to avoid long swims.*

Class IV: *Advanced. Intense, powerful but predictable rapids requiring precise boat handling in turbulent water. Depending on the character of the river, it may feature large, unavoidable waves and holes or constricted passages demanding fast maneuvers under pressure. A fast, reliable eddy turn may be needed to initiate maneuvers, scout rapids, or rest. Rapids may require "must" moves above dangerous hazards. Scouting is necessary the first time down. Risk of injury to swimmers is moderate to high, and water conditions may make self-rescue difficult. Group assistance for rescue is often essential but requires practiced skills.*

Class V: *Expert. Extremely long, obstructed, or very violent rapids which expose a paddler to above average endangerment. Drops may contain large, unavoidable waves and holes, or steep, congested chutes with complex, demanding routes. Rapids may continue for long distances between pools, demanding a high level of fitness. What eddies exist may be small, turbulent, or difficult to reach. At the high end of the scale, several of these factors may be combined. Scouting is*

Class III whitewater.

mandatory but often difficult. Swims are dangerous, and rescue is difficult even for experts. Proper equipment, extensive experience, and practiced rescue skills are essential for survival.

Class VI: *Extreme. One grade more difficult than Class V. These runs often exemplify the extremes of difficulty, unpredictability and danger. The consequences of errors are very severe and rescue may be impossible. For teams of experts only, at favorable water levels, after close personal inspection and taking all precautions. This class does* not *represent drops thought to be unrunnable, but may include rapids which are only occasionally run.*

FINE-TUNING THE SCALE

The International Scale's six classifications work well for making basic comparisons between rivers or rapids, but rafters have had to fine-tune the descriptions to keep up with the vast spectrum of rapids being run today.

Pluses and Minuses. With the addition of mathematical signs and decimals, the International Scale explodes into a long list of highly descriptive ratings with smaller increments between classifications. With plus and minus signs, a rapid that spans a gray area between Class III and IV ratings can be rated *Class III+* (slightly harder than Class III) or *Class IV-* (slightly easier than Class IV). By the time all the potential ratings are tallied, the International Scale's six classifications multiply into 15 (Class I-, VI-, and VI+ are rarely used).

The Class V Decimal System. At the upper end of the whitewater scale, a decimal system has emerged that helps distinguish one Class V rapid from another. Similar to the numerical system used by climbers, the Class V rating system classifies rapids Class V.1 (easy Class V) to V.10 (extremely difficult). This system keeps occasional Class V rafters from get-

Class V.1 or Class V.10? You be the judge. (Photo by Julie Prange)

ting into something above their skill level.

Remember that any rating system is subjective and that as time goes by, rafters will keep getting better. What was rated Class V ten years ago may be rated Class IV today, and today's Class IVs may be the Class IIIs of the next decade. Also, rafters are still trying to perfect the upper end of the rating scale (decimal system). Rely on your own skills and judgment, and don't let anyone—or any system—tell you what you can or can't do!

6

PROPULSION BASICS
DIFFERENT STROKES FOR DIFFERENT BOATS

Steering a raft through whitewater involves two very distinct activities performed in harmony: reading rapids and executing the proper set of maneuvers. Watching a skilled oarsperson or finely tuned paddle team running a difficult rapid reveals both the simplicity of individual oar and paddle strokes and the complexity of combined whitewater maneuvers.

This chapter provides the most critical tools for learning how to maneuver rafts through whitewater: basic oar and paddle strokes. From the fundamentals of backrowing to the intricacies of forward paddling, this chapter gives you the first glimpse of the tech-

niques you'll need to run rivers successfully. It is your opportunity to put your hands on the wheel and feel what it's like to drive a raft on the river.

Oar Strokes

BACKROWING

Backrowing—or pulling on the oars—is the foundation of many raft maneuvers for two reasons: It slows the raft down in relation to the current and provides the starting point for the ferrying techniques discussed later in this chapter.

Before you take your first backstroke, let's talk about the four phases that make up any stroke: the *reach, catch, power,* and *recovery phases.* In the backstroke, the *reach phase* pushes the oarblades backward and the handles forward. Make your reach by leaning comfortably forward, arms outstretched, and pressing the handles downward. This will lift the blades clear out of the river behind you. In the *catch phase,* lift your hands, dipping the blades back through the river's surface until they just barely disappear. Now it's time to pull the oars through the water in the *power phase.* Pull straight back on the handles, dragging the blades through the water until your hands come close to your chest. The stroke ends with the *recovery phase,* which begins with pushing the handles down again, popping the blades free of the surface. The oars are recovered by pushing your hands forward, which sets up the oars for another cycle.

So, there it is . . . the basic backstroke. Now let's make the backstroke more powerful and effective by adding a little leverage. First, make sure one or both feet are planted squarely on the footbar. This will give you a solid platform to brace against as you begin pulling back on the oars. Next, concentrate on using the powerful muscles of the legs and back, and think of your arms and hands as little more than giant gaff hooks connecting your torso to the oars. Finally, focus on moving the oars in level planes either below or above the river

To backstroke, plant the oar blades in the water behind you, and pull your hands toward you. The blades will swing forward while your raft moves backward.

surface. Don't let the oars dive in huge submarine arcs, and avoid lifting the oars too far out of the water. This will save a lot of energy and add to the effectiveness of your strokes.

In the portegee, or push stroke, you plant the oar blades in the water in front of you and push your hands away from you. The blades will swing backward while your raft moves forward.

PORTEGEE

The portegee—or *push stroke*—is just the opposite of backrowing. In fact, a more descriptive word for the portegee would be *frontrowing*.

In the portegee, the rower leans back, pulls the oar handles close to the torso, and lifts the handles. This plants the blades into the river toward the bow. The rafter then begins the stroke's power phase by leaning forward, pushing the handles outward, and straightening both arms.

The portegee is less effective than backrowing because it relies on the weaker muscles of the front torso. However, it is very useful in gentle rapids and is frequently used to give a raft the last bit of push up a steep wave or through a strong hole. To make the stroke a little stronger, put one foot on the floor close to your body and push with your legs.

TURNING

Single-Oar Turns. Oar turns are based on a simple theory: *One-legged ducks swim in circles.* Pull on one oar and the bow will turn toward that oar. Push on the same oar, and the bow will turn away from it. Whether you pull or push this oar, the raft is going to turn.

Double-Oar Turns. Whenever you need to execute faster, more powerful turns, push on one oar while simultaneously pulling on the opposite oar. This tech-

Shipping your oars forward (as shown here) or backward will prevent them from catching in narrow slots.

nique, called the double-oar turn, causes the bow to spin quickly toward the oar being pulled without any loss of forward motion.

SHIPPING

In narrow or rocky channels there will be times when there will be more rock than water lapping against your oarblades. Sometimes, just lifting the blades out of the water will protect your oars, but at other times you'll have to pull the oars inboard to avoid hitting rocks. (This really only works if you're using oarlocks—you'd have to reset the oars if you were using pins and clips.)

Another technique rowers use to keep their oars out of harm's way is called shipping. Oars can be *shipped forward* by tucking the blades against the side of the bow, or *shipped backward* by tucking the blades against the side of the stern.

ROWING SWEEP BOATS AND PLOHTS

Sweep boats and plohts use long, sturdy oars (often called *sweeps*) mounted paral-

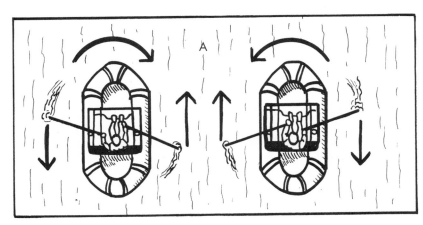

You can turn your raft with single-oar turns but double-oar turns (shown here) are more powerful. Either way, the bow will always spin toward the backstroking oar.

MORE ROWING TIPS

There will be times when shipping an oar gives the river carte blanche to push your raft wherever it desires. However, if you ship your oars with the blades forward, you can still control the raft with subtle sculling motions.

When the blades are tucked close to the sides of the bow, one blade can be lifted out of the water, replanted a foot or so from the tube, and pulled back to the tube. This ministroke moves the raft sideways toward the oar. To move the raft away from the oar, just start with the blade near the tube and push it outward a foot or two. If you're using oarlocks, try sculling the blades in a figure eight pattern just beneath the surface, pushing them toward and away from the bow. You'll soon be amazed by the amount of control you can gain over your raft in tight chutes.

Rafters using oarlocks can also *feather*, or rotate, the oars by twisting their wrists to and fro. If you twist the oar handles until the blades are horizontal to the river's surface it will be easier to draw the oars through the air on windy days. Also, feathering the blades under water will give you a better feel for submarine currents.

To avoid jamming your oars in shallow or technical rapids, keep an eye on your downstream oar and use your upstream oar to maneuver. You'll catch fewer rocks that way. Finally, if you're making maneuvers around big boulders, drop the blades into passing eddies to bolster the power of each stroke.

—Gary Stott, Cascade Outfitters

lel to the raft's long axis (over the bow and stern). This is quite different from regular oar rafts, which mount the oars sideways over the left and right gunnels.

A sweep boat floats with its long axis parallel to the current and the guide standing in the center of the raft. To move the raft back and forth across the river, the guide pulls or pushes the oars and relies on ferry angles. Since these craft are *steered* more than they are *rowed*, they are designed for use on rivers with consistent currents. On pool-drop rivers, or rivers with very slow stretches, it is difficult to propel these rafts downstream unless they're turned sideways.

Rowing sweep boats and plohts requires a solid stance, with the whole body leaning into or away from the oar to create long, smooth, powerful pushing and pulling strokes. In larger plohts and sweep boats, it is common to have two or more guides controlling the oars. The extra body weight and strength of the additional rowers can generate a tremendous amount of power. Finally, since it is nearly impossible to slow the descent of these types of craft without first turning them sideways, it is important to anticipate maneuvers and follow less-drastic routes.

Paddle Strokes

For team-spirited whitewater adventure, few experiences compare to paddling rapids with a finely synchronized crew. Working in unison, paddlers can achieve the same degree of success in rapids as do their oar-wielding brethren while giving every crew member a chance to get involved.

The paddle strokes used in rafting have evolved significantly over the last decade. Traditionally, rafters paid little attention to the subtle yet effective techniques used by other whitewater paddlers, such as open canoers. But following the advent of competitive raft racing, rafters began to take a closer look at their paddling techniques. Today, many of the same strokes that power canoes and C-1s (one-person decked canoes) are used in paddle rafting with little or no modification. Only the raft's large tubes and difficult seating positions alter the paddling techniques.

In this section we will look at a variety of paddle strokes, from basic forward and backstrokes to advanced strokes like *cross draws* and *farback strokes*. We'll build upon the seating configurations learned in Chapter 4 and explore all the basic strokes that paddle teams use to run rapids.

GET A GRIP

Good paddling techniques start with proper hand grip and hand

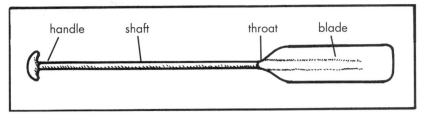

A typical paddle.

position. The accompanying diagram shows that a paddle consists of a handle, a shaft, a throat, and a blade. On a typical rafting paddle, the handle is shaped like a hot dog or a T.

The *T-grip* is designed to let you wrap your fingers over the top of the handle with your thumb underneath. (As easy as that sounds, you'd be amazed how many people wrap both hands around the shaft—just look at some outfitters' brochures or in your favorite river magazine!) Keeping the upper hand on the T-grip is very important: It stabilizes the paddle, con-

trols the blade angle, and lessens your chance of dropping the paddle. On the other hand, you don't need a white-knuckle grip on your paddle. If your forearms are screaming, loosen up! The handles are designed to work with a gentle grip to save your hands from fatigue.

The lower hand, or *shaft hand,* wraps around the shaft with the palm facing forward (toward the bow). If possible, place your shaft hand 2½ to 3 hand widths up the shaft from the throat for maximum effectiveness.

MOTORIZED RAFTS

Giant motorized rafts can provide more splashes, bigger bounces, and a safer trip than some oar- or paddle-powered rafts. They also let people see in two or three days what would ordinarily take much longer to explore.

Outboard motors help accelerate J-rigs, G-rigs, and other inflatable behemoths down high-volume rivers. This breaks the tubes free of the current's grip and makes all sorts of downstream maneuvers possible. When big cross-river maneuvers are necessary, the guide can swing the raft around, point the bow upstream, and ferry around islands, boulders, and holes.

—Bernie Fandrich, coauthor, *Rafting in British Columbia*

Motorized rafts have their own specialized sets of river-running techniques.

THREE TYPES OF PADDLE STROKES

All paddle strokes fall into one of three categories: *power strokes, turning strokes,* and *braces. Power strokes* (forward and backstrokes) move the raft forward and backward. *Turning strokes*—which are used to spin your raft—range from basic forward and backstroke combinations to advanced turning strokes such as *pry, sweep,* and *draw* strokes. These last three strokes can be used near the bow and stern to control the speed and direction of the raft's spin. (When they're used just to drive the raft laterally they aren't technically turning strokes, but they'll be included in the same section to keep matters simple.)

The final category—which doesn't *really* fit the definition of strokes—is *braces.* Rafters are only beginning to discover how useful canoe-style braces are in rafting. Whether you're on a technical creek that wants to flip your boat as it squeezes through a steep, narrow slot, or on a giant river that threatens to dislodge you from your raft with each passing wave, braces provide a way to stay upright and in the raft when the topsy-turvy world of whitewater takes control.

BASIC POWER STROKES

The Forward Stroke. The forward stroke—the most important stroke in the paddler's arsenal—uses the powerful muscles of the torso. To execute the basic forward stroke, lean forward and thrust the paddle toward the bow. The lower arm becomes straight as the paddle reaches its maximum comfortable extension, and the upper arm remains slightly bent at eye level. From that position, keep the blade at a right angle to the tube, pull it toward you with your lower hand, and push forward with your upper hand. End the stroke just forward of your hips and start over again. (If you let the blade pass your hips, you might get thrown off balance.)

The Backstroke. The backstroke is, for the most part, just the opposite of the forward stroke. You hold the paddle in the same manner as for forward strokes, but you plant the paddle behind your hips and drive it toward the bow.

During the backstroke's reach and catch phases, you rotate your outside shoulder backward and plant the paddle in the water slightly behind the hips. Starting there, move through the power phase by rotating your outside shoulder and waist forward. The recovery phase starts with the blade just in front of your hips.

A full backstroke can take both power and finesse in heavy hydraulics. The tendency of many paddlers is simply to leave the paddle where it was planted and lean against the current rather than to finish the stroke. If you need more power, use your hip as a fulcrum: Lean the shaft against your outside hip and rotate your

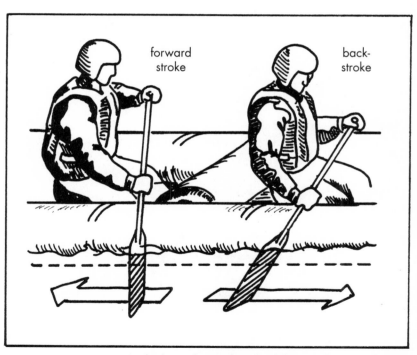

In the basic forward stroke (left) you plant the blade ahead of you, then simply pull your shaft hand toward your hip while pushing away with your upper hand. To backstroke (right), plant the blade behind you and rotate forward while pulling your upper hand toward you. You can use your hip as a fulcrum, but beware of submerged rocks and powerful hydraulics.

outside shoulder forward while pulling the inside shoulder and arm backward. This creates more power than with arm strength alone, and works great in situations where the raft must be slowed suddenly. However, when you use this technique, rocks, eddies, and strong hydraulics can pole vault you out of the raft or injure tender joints—so *be careful!*

ADVANCED POWER STROKES

The Advanced Forward Stroke. Few paddlers will find it necessary to perfect their forward stroke beyond the simple technique just described. However, racers and advanced rafters can add power and efficiency to their forward strokes by using the techniques developed by world-class canoers.

The advanced forward stroke is beautiful and fluid when properly executed, but actually consists of four phases: the *reach, catch, power,* and *recovery* phases.

Start the *reach phase* with your blade held perpendicular to the raft. Raise the paddle and extend it toward the bow, keeping your lower arm straight and your upper arm slightly bent at eye level. At the same time, rotate your outside shoulder forward. At full extension, your upper body leans forward 15 to 20 degrees for a little extra reach, but your hips stay stationary and your lower back straight. Now, your torso is *wound up* in preparation for the catch and power phases of the forward stroke.

Begin the *catch phase* by planting the paddle in the river close to the side of the raft. To get a good catch, keep your paddle nearly vertical, at an angle of about 70 degrees to the river surface.

Now comes the heart of the stroke—the *power phase.* Pull the paddle by rotating your shoulders and waist back without bending your lower arm very much

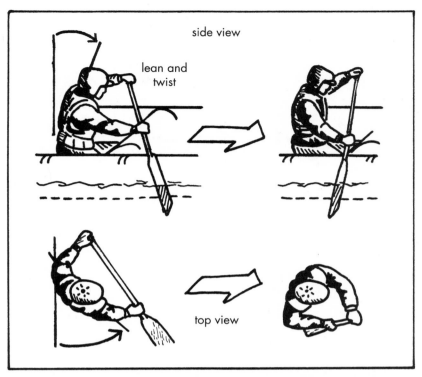

side view

lean and twist

top view

The advanced forward stroke: "Wind up" your torso by rotating your waist and thrusting your outside shoulder forward, and hold the paddle vertically out over the tube (left). During the stroke's power phase, rotate your torso back to its starting position (right). You'll need to drop your top hand to help finish off the stroke, but your torso, not your arms, will provide most of the power for the stroke.

(keep it comfortably straight, not stiff). At the same time, keep your hands close to the outside of the tube with the paddle as vertical as possible. This paddle posture captures energy that would be lost if the paddle were pushed down into, rather than pulled through, the river.

The *unwinding* of the torso during the power phase provides an enormous amount of power during the first 5 to 7 inches of the stroke, but the power quickly diminishes before the paddle reaches the hips. Accordingly, short, fast strokes work much better than longer, less-efficient strokes.

Start the final phase of the forward stroke—the *recovery phase*—just forward of your hips. (Continuing the power phase past your hips causes the paddle to

THE FORWARD STROKE

Most rafters can make it down whitewater rivers using casual forward strokes, but seasoned rafters know how to get the most from every stroke. Here are some tips to help improve your technique:

1. Pretend you're planting your blade in cement at the start of the stroke, and pull your body forward to the paddle, not vice versa.
2. Concentrate on your torso rotation rather than relying on your arms for power.
3. Dig your paddle into solid water and oppositional currents to maximize your pull.
4. Time your strokes so that you don't misfire between waves.
5. Select a paddle length that lets you sink most (not all) of the blade in the water.

shovel or lift water, and pulls the raft imperceptibly downward rather than driving it forward.) Slice the blade out of the water by twisting your wrists slightly, then lift the paddle and return it to the catch position. If you rotate the paddle so that the blade is parallel to the water, you can move it forward with very little wind or water resistance.

The Farback Stroke. The farback stroke is a rarely used advanced stroke that can come in handy when shooting for a tight eddy or executing quick turns around obstacles. Basically, it's just a forward stroke in reverse: You rotate your torso so you're looking toward the stern, plant the blade behind you, and pull the paddle toward you. The farback stroke will work with conventional paddle rafts, but it really comes in handy in paddle cats where open frames and customized seats give you lots of flexibility and freedom to experiment with strokes on either side of the tubes.

Cross and Hybrid Strokes. When paddling between the tubes of a cataraft, you can perform strokes that mimic the outside strokes. Try a *cross forward* stroke by thrusting the paddle forward to the catch posi-

tion inside the tubes. Plant the blade so that the shaft tilts about 20 degrees from vertical, and keep your shaft hand about 6 to 10 inches forward of the upper hand. Use more of a pelvic thrust than a torso twist during the power phase. Move your hips forward and straighten your torso upward until the blade reaches a point between the knees and torso. (Don't let your hands pass behind the front of your body.) Finish the stroke by twisting your wrists, unlocking the paddle, and slicing the blade forward underwater.

Farback strokes (left) and cross-forward strokes (right) are just two of the advanced paddle strokes borrowed from canoers.

TURNING STROKES

The Basic Paddle Turn. Turning a raft with paddles works the same way as with oars: The bow always turns toward the side applying the backstroke. Backstroke on the right and the bow goes right. Backstroke on the left and the bow goes left. Of course, if you forward paddle on either side, the bow will spin away from your strokes.

Paddlers can add speed and power to their turns the same way rowers do, by paddling in opposite directions on either side of the raft. To turn the bow to the right, the right side back paddles while the left side forward paddles; to turn the bow to the left, the right side forward paddles and the left side back paddles.

Advanced Turning Strokes. Since forward strokes and backstrokes are all it generally takes to turn a raft, *turning stroke* is a misnomer. Fortunately, rafters learned to borrow true turning strokes from canoers when they were looking for ways to maneuver their rafts. A whole slew of strokes specially developed to control the speed and trajectory of the canoe's spin survived the transition from raft to canoe. It turns out that the canoe

strokes work equally well in rafting, especially when they're used by bow or stern paddlers.

Keep in mind that this book describes how strokes *ought to look*, not how they're going to look when you try them on the river. So even though it's good to know how each stroke works in theory, don't expect to pull it off exactly as it's described here. Rapids will inevitably force you to use variations of every stroke, and you're likely to devise an infinite number of combinations to get you where you want to go.

The Sweep Stroke. The sweep stroke carves a broad arcing path along the side of the raft. Properly executed, it turns the raft *and* moves it forward (*forward sweep*) or backward (*reverse sweep*).

To do a forward sweep stroke, hold your upper hand lower than usual so that the paddle shaft angles downward, across the tube, and into the water at a 45-degree angle. (This position allows maximum extension in the reach phase of the stroke while keeping the paddler safely inside the raft.) In the catch phase, plant the paddle as far forward as possible with the blade parallel to the tube. With your shaft arm comfortably straight, start the power phase by pulling the paddle through an arc away from the boat. If you're sitting on the right side with the paddle in front of you, at 12 o'clock, trace the paddle through a path from 12 o'clock to 3 o'clock or 4 o'clock before beginning the recovery phase. Remember to rotate at your waist and use the powerful muscles of the torso, not your arms! If you have executed your stroke properly the bow will turn *away* from you.

Stern and center paddlers will discover that their forward sweeps have little effect on the raft. For stern paddlers, the reverse sweep stroke is a powerful tool. As you may have guessed, the reverse sweep is the same as a forward sweep, but in reverse. The crit-

You can turn a raft by forward or back paddling on just one side, but it's faster to get everyone in on the action. The raft on the left is executing a right turn, the raft on the right, a left turn.

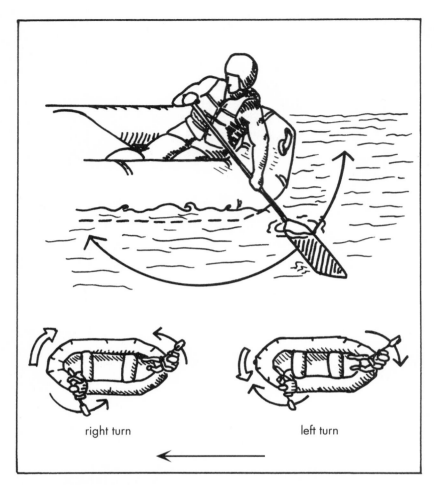

Forward or backward sweep strokes are used to turn the raft. A wide arcing paddle path is essential.

right turn   left turn

draw strokes while remaining in position to forward stroke.

To start the draw stroke, rotate your torso outward (toward the river) until you're facing 90 degrees away from the raft. Next, reach both hands out and plant the paddle parallel to the raft; pull the blade directly toward you and the side of the raft while keeping the shaft as vertical as possible. If the stroke is done correctly, the raft will actually move toward the paddle. Finish the stroke before the paddle hits the tube by twisting your wrists to release the blade and lift the paddle from the water.

The Cross-Bow Draw. The cross-bow draw is another stroke borrowed from canoeing; it has survived in rafting circles as both a stroke and a team maneuver. A well-tuned paddle team can use cross-bow draws to dramatically slow their descent while moving their raft laterally.

The basic stroke is really called a *cross draw*, which is simply a draw stroke on your *off* side (the side opposite the one you'd usually draw on). In a cross-bow draw, a bow paddler scoots toward the bow and draws *across* the bow of the raft. The rest of the team kicks in with their own strokes to make the cross-bow draw maneuver work.

If you're not following me yet, no sweat. Here's an example: To move a five-person paddle team quickly to the right, the left bow paddler does a cross-bow draw, both right-side paddlers make draw strokes, the paddle captain draws to the right or back upstream, and the back left paddler pries or backstrokes. If everyone balances the timing and strength of their strokes, the raft will slow down and move to the right. To get it to move to the left, just reverse each paddler's role.

ical difference between the two strokes is in paddle position. During the reverse sweep, the catch phase begins at 6 o'clock (directly behind you) and ends at 3 o'clock or 2 o'clock. Also, the reverse sweep spins the bow *toward* the paddling side.

The Draw Stroke. Draw strokes excel in difficult rapids when you have to move your raft laterally without turning it. They can be used in a fix when there isn't enough time to get around an obstacle, or when the raft's path has to be diverted sideways on steep, sliding rapids. Draw strokes also help in big, heavy water when rafts get knocked off track. Bow paddlers can turn rafts quickly into oncoming waves and holes with

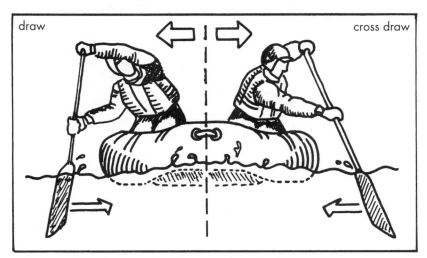

To draw stroke (left), reach directly out to the side of the raft and pull the blade back toward you. Keep the paddle vertical throughout the stroke and finish the stroke before the paddle hits the tube. The cross draw (right) works the same way, but you reach across your body before planting the paddle.

The Pry Stroke. A pry stroke is just the opposite of a draw stroke: Plant the blade close to the tube and move it away from you by pulling the upper hand inward and pushing the shaft hand outward. When properly done, the pry stroke moves the raft sideways away from the paddle. Since raft tubes interfere with the pry stroke, it is not as effective for rafters as for canoers, but it provides an excellent turning stroke for paddle captains. If you need to *supercharge* a draw stroke, just add some pry strokes on the opposite side of the raft.

The paddle captain, sitting on or near the stern, can execute the pry by twisting the waist and shoulders around, planting the paddle in the river behind the raft, then uncoiling the torso while pushing the blade away from the raft. If the pry is executed off the captain's right hip, the bow will turn to the right; a left-sided pry will turn the bow to the left. For more power, the paddle captain can use one hip as a fulcrum. (When using the pry stroke, beware of submerged rocks that could catch your paddle and throw you off balance.)

BRACING

It is the definitive image of *yahoo* rafting: a crew of slack-jawed, wide-eyed rafters holding their paddles over their heads and screaming "Whe-e-e-e-e-e!" I call this *gaping* or *air bracing.* Most of the time, these paddlers are paying an outfitter good money to let them do that. But some of the time, paddle captains are nursing ulcers as they try to guide uncontrolled rafts through whitewater rapids.

It takes a while to convince paddlers that paddling actually increases their likelihood of staying aboard in medium-sized rapids. First of all, you are more atten-

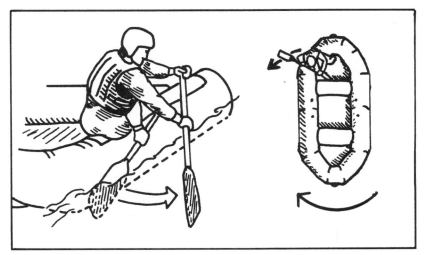

The pry stroke works best in the stern, and is often used by paddle captains to turn the raft. Pull your upper hand inward while pushing your shaft hand outward. If it's easier, feel free to use your hip as a fulcrum. If you're doing a pry on the right side of the raft, the bow will turn to the right.

tive when you're paddling, so you are usually better attuned to changes in the raft's direction. Also, the upward pressure the river exerts on your paddle blade during strokes can actually push you into the raft. This upward thrust, in a very basic way, is the foundation of bracing.

There are two basic braces for rafters: the *low brace* and the *high brace*. Each has its own time and place.

The low brace (left) is used as a last resort to stay aboard a bucking raft. To low brace, slap the surface with the back side of the paddle blade, push down with your shaft hand, and lift up with your upper hand. At the same time, shift your weight inboard. The high brace (right), is like a draw stroke, but is used to keep a raft from flipping.

The Low Brace. It's time for a low brace when your raft bucks or tips violently, sending your side of the raft dipping precariously downward and exposing you to the grasp of an overly amorous river surface. If your tube sinks low enough, not even a powerful sphincter will help you maintain your grip on the seat. What you need to do is low brace.

Think of low bracing as using your paddle as an outrigger. Start out by cocking both your wrists and knuckles downward so you can slap the river surface with the back side of your paddle blade and hold the shaft almost horizontal to the river's surface. As your paddle hits the water, push down with your shaft hand while lifting up at the T-grip. Keep your body weight low and shift it horizontally into the passenger compartment, bringing the paddle in with you as you go. If your raft doesn't flip, the low brace might provide just enough leverage to keep you high and dry.

The High Brace. The high brace comes into play when the river has shot your side of the raft skyward.

Before you lose your seat or go for a swim, lean way out over your tube and do something akin to a draw stroke. Hold your paddle with your knuckles pointed upward, elbows bent slightly, and the shaft pointing almost underneath the raft. Rather than *drawing,* try to *shovel* some water back toward you. You'll probably end up drawing no matter what you think you're doing, but that's OK. If all goes well, the extra weight and downward pull will settle the raft back down on the river.

7

PADDLE CAPTAINING
THE ART OF WHITEWATER CHOREOGRAPHY

Team rafting straddles a line between shared elation and communal frustration. When a paddle crew perfectly executes difficult maneuvers in intense whitewater, the feeling is incomparable. But when the team falls out of sync and lets the raft ricochet off of rocks and hydraulics, paddle rafting can be a nerve-wracking endeavor.

The paddle captain provides the critical link between the raft and its engine—the paddlers. Equal parts coach, choreographer, cheerleader, and drill sergeant, the paddle captain strives to balance paddlers' strokes, translate maneuvers into understandable commands, and provide the necessary inspiration to complete a successful descent. All the while, the paddle captain picks the course through rapids and executes turning and rudder strokes to keep the raft moving along a safe course.

The Pretrip Lecture

Effective guiding begins long before paddlers ever board the raft. Good paddle captains immediately break the ice and open up cordial lines of communication with their crew. They also explain all the rafting techniques that will be used and all the emergency procedures that must be followed. What the guide says in this speech—and how funny or foreboding the lecture sounds—depends on the river, the types of rafts being used, and the caliber of the day's crew.

No matter what river you're paddling, and what crew you have, there are some basic points you ought to bring up in any introductory lecture:

1. Introduce the guides, the equipment, and the river.
2. Give passengers some idea of what to expect during the trip (e.g., rapids, scenery, photographic opportunities).
3. Assign passengers to oar or paddle rafts depending on the available equipment, their personal preferences, and their capabilities.
4. Outline safety precautions such as keeping lines tightly stored, rafts bailed out, and lifejackets securely fastened. Also note the importance of proper riverwear to make the trip more safe, comfortable, and enjoyable.
5. Go over the paddle commands, being sure to include unique commands such as *highside, dig in,* or *get low.*
6. Discuss emergency procedures, highlighting what to do in the event of a flip or swim.
7. Include anything else that will make the river trip safer and more enjoyable for your crew.

Seating the Captain and Crew

THE CAPTAIN'S CHAIR

In North America, paddle captains usually sit as close to the stern as they can get. The stern seat provides

The guide's pretrip lecture gets passengers ready for a day of rafting.

Big, breaking waves and powerful holes do funny things to rafts. When the bow crashes into the hydraulic, the stern snaps skyward but quickly regains its shape. The guide has to anticipate that snap or risk getting catapulted into the middle of the raft. Lift your butt off the stern tube and stay low on your feet just before smashing into boat-stopping hydraulics and you'll spend more time safely nestled *behind* your crew than flailing around in the *middle* of your crew.

extra clearance and adds reach to guiding strokes, which translates into better leverage on the water and more power for turning the raft. If you find yourself paddling abroad you may discover that not everyone agrees on where the guide ought to sit. In some countries paddle captains sit in the bow, and sometimes there are paddle captains in both bow and stern.

Short or heavy bodies, elevated stern kicks, and undersized tubes can make it tough to sit all the way back in the stern. These situations can prop you too high above the water to stroke effectively or dip you so close to the river's surface that you're constantly flopping around the back of the raft just struggling to stay aboard. If you're confronted by any of these problems, just slide your butt a little forward and sit on a side tube just like everyone else. Don't worry . . . everyone will still know who the captain is!

SEATING THE CREW

Take a moment to refer back to the seating configurations suggested in Chapter 4. Because paddle rafting relies heavily on the forward stroke, it is best to place the strongest, most experienced paddlers in the bow. Good bow paddlers respond quickly to the guide's commands, set a good example for the rest of the crew, and provide some muscle where it is needed the most. The weakest paddlers should be seated in the middle of the raft, with moderately strong paddlers seated toward the stern. Also strive to balance the strength of the paddlers on both sides of the raft.

Guiding Strokes

THE STROKES

Paddle captains can use all of the strokes discussed in Chapter 6, but the *turning* strokes—such as the sweep, pry, and draw—are the most useful. These strokes change the raft's angle quickly, setting the raft up so that the crew can assist in making maneuvers.

The only new stroke to add to the paddle captain's repertoire is the *rudder stroke*. In this stroke, the paddle captain places the paddle behind the stern, at 6 o'clock, with the blade parallel to the raft's axis. As the raft

Guides often use rudder strokes to steer the raft through whitewater.

moves forward, the paddle can be turned slightly in either direction to change the angle of the bow.

EXPERIENCE IS THE KEY

It's easy to get confused the first time you sit in the captain's seat. Since many strokes have a reverse effect on the raft, guiding is something like rubbing your tummy and patting your head. Here's what I mean: A draw stroke on the right side will turn the bow to the left, while a pry stroke will turn the bow to the right. A right-side forward sweep carried past 3 o'clock will turn the bow to the left, while a reverse sweep initiated at 6 o'clock will turn the bow to the right.

Experience is the key to overcoming these paradoxes. Practice guiding in easy rapids every chance you get, and soon the raft's movements will feel natural.

CHOOSING SIDES

One common urge among novice paddle captains is to switch sides with their paddles—ruddering with the paddle on the right hip one moment and on the left hip the next. Since the raft is unguided whenever your paddle is out of the water, it is better to learn to guide and stroke from just one side. Right-handed paddle captains usually keep the paddle on their right side, and only paddle on their left in extraordinary circumstances.

Paddle Commands

Paddle commands are nothing more than one- or two-word descriptions of strokes, maneuvers, and techniques. The paddle captain bellows these commands like a crazed aerobics instructor, and if all goes well the paddle crew responds with the appropriate strokes.

BASIC COMMANDS

The basic paddle commands are *forward paddle, back paddle, left turn, right turn,* and *stop* (or *drift*). Each describes a stroke of the same name; *stop* and *drift* just mean *stop paddling.*

To get the crew to respond appropriately, you should explain each command and the corresponding set of strokes ahead of time. Then, in the pools above the first rapids, the crew can practice responding to the

commands, starting with the easiest ones first (forward paddle, back paddle, and stop). As the paddlers get better at executing the correct strokes, you can start giving turn commands, eventually building into complex commands like *draw right* (paddlers on the right side execute draw strokes), *dig* (bow paddlers execute big forward strokes through large waves or reversals), or *get down* (crew sits low in the raft to avoid falling out).

ADVANCED COMMANDS

Get 'em Psyched. Big rapids—chock-full of boat-eating holes and menacing obstacles—have a way of turning novice crews into flailing maniacs. To get your crew psyched up and ready to perform, explain how hydraulics are going to affect the raft, what an unexpected collision with a rock could mean, and how to handle all of the situations they can expect to encounter. At the same time, tailor different commands to evoke an appropriate response from the crew. If you get them psyched up and tuned in ahead of time, they'll do much better when they get on the river.

Get Down. If there's a chance of getting pounded by big falls, holes, and breaking waves, add some comments to your pretrip discussion about holding on and getting low in the raft. This move—which is discussed in greater detail in Chapter 10—can help keep your paddlers aboard and your raft upright by keeping the center of gravity low.

To make "hold on and get low" commands easy, give the command a short name like *get down* and have the crew practice leaning into the raft so they will respond automatically when you give the command.

Dig. Digging means jabbing your paddle all the way through the backwash of a big breaking wave or hole, grabbing the green water downstream, and pulling yourself through the hydraulics. The paddle captain can call out a *dig* command to get the bow paddlers to dig their paddles deep into the solid water while the rest of the crew forward paddles strong and fast to prevent a stall.

FINE-TUNING

Be flexible in your choice of commands, and match them to the requirements of the river. Keep in mind that commands should be easy to understand, should sound different from one another, and should roll off your tongue quickly. The shorter and faster your commands, the more effective your crew's response will be.

HANDLING LAG TIME

Since there is always some lag time between commands and strokes, paddle captains have to anticipate moves and talk fast. Any hesitation on the part of the captain is intensified by the delay in paddlers' reactions. By anticipating the next move, paddle captains have a chance to form their thoughts before translating them into verbal instructions. Still, in fast-moving whitewater, some commands must be given and changed within a split second. If a guide thinks about the command too long ("Hmm, does a draw stroke turn the bow right or left?") the raft might get eaten by a hole before the answer emerges. Sometimes it is better to say something and be wrong than to say nothing at all. If you choose a wrong command, at least you'll see the negative effect right away and be able to fix it, rather than trying to figure it out in your mind.

Lag time also affects how the team paddles together. Many times, one bow paddler starts paddling a moment before the other bow paddler. Since the middle and stern paddlers follow the strokes of the person in front of them, the whole raft falls into a syncopated rhythm that makes it wiggle like a beaching walrus. Tell paddlers to keep their heads up to see what everyone is doing, not just the person in front of them. That way, the whole raft will work together as one synchronized unit.

HANDLING OVERSTROKING

Another delay phenomenon seems to happen after paddlers start stroking. Rather than stopping on command, excited paddlers keep on paddling . . . usually until your screams or a friendly whap on the shoulder gets their attention.

One of the easiest ways to cure overstroking is to limit the number of strokes in your command. Rather than just yelling, "Forward paddle," say, "Forward two strokes." If your crew listens to you carefully, you'll have gained the upper hand over the chronic overstrokers. If you need more strokes, you can add a few more in the next command.

YOUR VOICE

Many things influence paddle teams, including the intensity and decibel level of your voice. If you really want to see your crew paddling, raise your voice and shout something like, "Paddle faster! C'mon!" (Don't yell, "Oh no! We're doomed!" Everyone will freak out and head for the floor.) If power strokes aren't necessary, save your vocal cords for the big rapids downstream. Also, offer helpful criticism to weak paddlers in order to balance the team's strength. Remember that *you* are the captain. Don't let paddlers do what *they* want; teach them to do what *you* say!

THE SEASONED TEAM

The longer a paddle team works together, the more harmonious their actions become. Rather than constantly responding to guiding commands, team members develop a feel for when they are paddling in sync, or when their strokes are unproductive. Teams that have paddled many rivers together require few, if any, commands other than comments about route selection. With this type of team it is easier to explain which path you want the raft to follow ("Let's go to the left of the first rock, then back to the right to get around the hole") and let everybody feel what it is they're supposed to do. Occasional commands like "Straighten the raft up," or one or two of the standard commands, will keep things moving smoothly.

8

WHITEWATER
RUNNING THE RAPIDS

Although high-quality whitewater rafts are delightfully buoyant and stable in gentle water, they are little more than mindless inflatable vessels, subject to the whims of currents and oarstrokes. In severe whitewater an unguided raft follows the same course as other flotsam, sometimes into the heart of danger, sometimes avoiding obvious obstacles.

By now you've learned the oar and paddle strokes that boaters use to harness a raft's capabilities. Now it's time to combine those strokes into definite maneuvers, to expand your knowledge of river features, and to learn the fundamental techniques necessary to run

rapids. This is your next big step toward becoming a whitewater rafter!

Five Types of Maneuvers

Amazingly, every maneuver known to whitewater rafters falls within one of five categories: (1) maneuvers that keep you *parallel* with the current, (2) *ferries,* (3) *turns* and *pivots,* (4) *sideslips,* and (5) *eddy turns* and *peel outs.* Each of these either moves the raft in a new direction or rotates it around its pivot point.

As you begin to learn about these techniques, think of how they'll work when they're done on moving currents, and visualize the two components that make up each one: the raft's *momentum* and its *angle* in relation to the current. Some maneuvers—like ferries and eddy turns —rely heavily on current to drive the raft across the river's surface. Others—such as turns and sideslips—rely little on currents but have to overcome them to be effective. The same current that assists one maneuver may hinder another.

River Directions

Rivers have descriptive directions, just as maps are labeled north, south, east, and west. There are four terms used to describe river directions: (1) *upstream* is where the current is coming from; (2) *downstream* is where the current is flowing to; (3) *river left* is to your left as you face downstream; and (4) *river right* is to your right as you face downstream. These terms will help you understand the movement of the rafts in the accompanying diagrams and will make your descriptions of rapids understandable to fellow river runners.

Staying Parallel with the Current

The first technique any river runner should learn is how to keep the raft parallel with the current. This not only helps when it's time to slow the raft down, but it continually expands your understanding of river currents and provides a solid basis for most other river-running techniques.

Since rivers rarely flow in a straight line, keeping

River directions: the river is flowing from the bottom of the diagram to the top. A is upstream; B is downstream; C is river left; and D is river right.

your raft parallel with the current can be trickier than it sounds. There are bends to contend with, eddies and slack water that try to spin your raft, and obstacles that interfere with your strokes. However, you can start with a straight, obstacle-free section of river where it will be easier to work on your river-running techniques.

To slow a raft on a straight section of river, line up the raft's long axis with the current lines using subtle adjustment strokes. Once properly aligned, the raft can be slowed or accelerated with back and forward strokes. If there are no obstacles downstream, leave the raft on the main current, relax, and enjoy the scenery.

As illustrated in the next diagram, the current slows down as the main current flows from a deep channel onto a shallow shoal. As the raft crosses the interface between faster and slower currents, the slower current drags on the bow while the faster currents push on the stern. If the raft turns even slightly to the current the river will try to twist it sideways; to avoid this the rower or paddlers must turn the raft in the opposite direction with well-gauged turning strokes.

Eddies have the same raft-twisting effect as changes in the current, only worse: Eddies flow in the opposite direction of the main current! The added force of these oppositional currents can frustrate even the best rafters. If it becomes impossible to turn the raft back in the direction of its original course, just let the eddy spin it, then complete the spin with a turning stroke and realign the raft with the current.

Ferrying

HISTORY

Today's ferrying techniques date back to days when cable-guided ferry barges transported people, horses, and wagons across swift rivers. Attached to a cross-river cable by one or two strong chains, these barges could be turned at an angle to the current either by turning a rudder or by changing the length of one of the chains. Once the barge was turned at an angle, the current would push on the barge's upstream side and force it cross-river to the opposite bank.

Modern rafters pull against the current with oars and paddles instead of cables, but they use the same angles and forces to help move their rafts across the river. Carrying on with the tradition of ferrying, rafters now use these historic techniques to maneuver their craft around riverborne hazards and into safe channels.

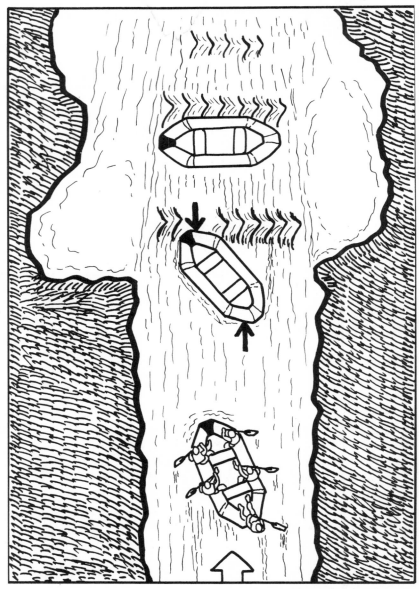

This raft is emerging from a fast chute at a slight angle to the current. As the bow hits the slower water flowing through the waves, the fast water of the chute is still pushing on the stern. As a result, the raft spins sideways as it meets the waves. If the waves are tall enough, the raft might flip.

OAR RAFTS

There are two types of ferrying techniques: *back ferrying* and *forward ferrying*. In a back ferry, start off with your bow pointed downstream and align your raft parallel to the current. From this position, begin backrowing; you will feel the raft's descent slow down significantly. Now, begin ferrying toward the left bank by turning the bow 30 to 45 degrees to your right. If you continue backrowing while maintaining that angle, the raft will either slow or cease its descent (depending on the power of the current) and will move sideways toward river left. To reach the right bank, simply point the bow towards the left bank and use the same backstroke.

If back ferries sound confusing, just think of one easy concept: *Pull away from the danger.* If you want to get away from the left bank, point your bow toward it and pull away . . . you'll move to river right. If you want to move away from a rock as you approach it, point your bow toward it and pull away. You'll ferry away from the rock in the direction of your stern.

It takes a little practice to really get the feel of back ferrying; stick with it until it becomes second nature. As you become more attuned to proper angles and trajectory, start experimenting with your oar strokes. Do long, slow strokes work better? Or are short, fast strokes better for you? Also try adjusting your cross-river speed. The more angle the raft maintains in relation to the current, the faster the boat will move across the current, but the faster it will also proceed downriver.

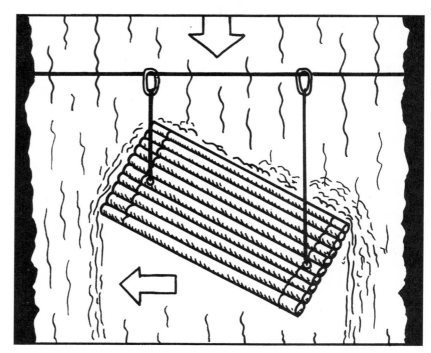

Old-time ferries relied on strong cables and river currents to move back and forth across the river. By increasing the length of one cable, currents would build up on one side of the barge and push it to the opposite bank. Rafters use the same techniques today as the basis for ferrying.

Now, I hate to disappoint you, but the forward ferry is not very complicated. In fact, the only difference between the forward ferry and the back ferry is the direction of the bow. In the forward ferry simply turn the bow upstream and portegee (push on the oars) to push against the current. Keep in mind that the portegee, or forward stroke, is not as powerful as the backstroke, so the forward ferry is more energy-consuming and difficult to maintain than the back

FERRYING

Don't be overwhelmed by the techno-garble you're reading about ferrying. Just head for the river and try it. If you pull on the wrong oar or set a wrong angle, you'll know right away: your raft will take off in the wrong direction. In a split second you can switch oars or angles, pull again, and take off on a perfect ferry.

The two rafts on the left are back ferrying and the two rafts on the right are forward ferrying.

ferry. Also, forward ferries can leave the raft broadside at bad times as the oarsperson rotates it through one or two 180s to turn the raft into the forward ferry and back downstream again.

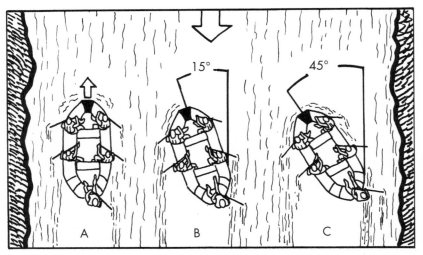

To learn to ferry, first line up your boat parallel with the current (A), then begin to angle toward one bank. A narrow ferry angle (B) slows your descent but moves you slowly sideways. A wide ferry angle (C) speeds you across the river but isn't as effective at slowing your descent. Experiment with different angles to learn how to match them to different situations.

PADDLE RAFTS

Ferrying is a dynamic pursuit, where fickle currents do their best to frustrate rafters' efforts. In an oar boat, the rower can feel the changes in current and adjust the raft's ferry angle immediately. Paddlers, on the other hand, must work in unison while ferrying. This makes paddle-raft ferries more challenging—but also more exciting.

Ferrying a paddle raft cross-river is identical to oar-boat ferrying. Again, begin the back ferry by aligning the raft parallel to the current, bow facing downstream, and slow the raft's descent with synchronized backstrokes. (Paddlers should stroke in unison and concentrate on the river and their course rather than looking at their paddles.) It is up to the paddle captain to turn the raft 30 to 45 degrees to the current. As the team continues backstroking against the current, the raft will move in the direction the stern is pointing.

The forward paddle ferry starts with the bow fac-

THE ZIG-ZAG APPROACH

Rafts are the albatrosses of the whitewater world: clumsy, oversized beasts that perform best when just gliding on invisible currents. Expert rafters, on the other hand, can dart from eddy to eddy, picking their way down difficult rapids, and displaying an enviable amount of prowess and control.

Next time you're on the river, break a long rapid down into bite-sized pieces. Drop over a ledge and catch an eddy. Peel out and ferry to another heady. Take 4 or 5 minutes to descend what used to take you 60 seconds. Ultimately, you—not the river—will command where and how fast your raft moves.

ing upstream and uses the powerful forward stroke to counteract the current. The paddle captain steers the raft and points the bow in the direction he wants the raft to go.

APPARENT VERSUS REAL COURSE

The first few times you try ferrying your raft across a strong current, you're likely to notice that it takes a stroke or two to stop the raft's downstream momentum and that it takes a moment before the raft even starts moving across the river. The reason lies in the raft itself—fat, heavy rafts *drift* or sideslip more than other whitewater craft, even when you execute a ferry properly.

Your raft's slow, drifting nature often means that the route you imagined your raft *would* follow won't be the same as the route your raft actually *will* follow. By anticipating the difference between your raft's *apparent* and *real* course, you can adjust early and make the moves you desire.

FERRYING AROUND BENDS

Back in Chapter 5 you learned that currents don't curve around bends but flow in a straight line from the inside to the outside of the bend and accelerate around the bend's outside. To compensate for the river's tendency to slam your raft toward the outside of the bend, you should enter bends from the inside corner. From there it will be much easier to follow the current to the outside of the bend than to fight the current back to the inside.

Since the current flows straight at the outer bank, you'll have to turn the raft at an even greater angle to the inside bank than you would expect.

(Remember, you're staying parallel with the current, not with the bank!) First work against the current to slow down, then begin ferrying to the inside of the bend to avoid being dragged toward the outer bank. Oar rafts can make this ferry by tucking the stern toward the inside bend and using powerful backstrokes, but paddle rafts might want to turn their bow inward in order to use the crew's more powerful forward strokes.

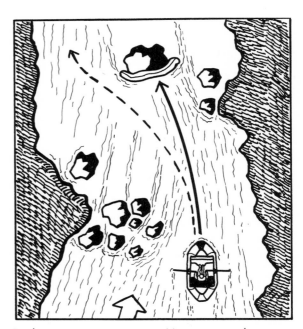

Real versus apparent course: Momentum and current will carry your raft further downstream than you might expect when you are trying to execute a maneuver. This raft forgot to account for drift when it tried to move to the left and wrapped on a rock.

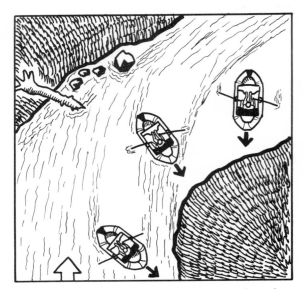

Ferrying around bends: Remember to angle the raft to the current, not to the bank. If there are no obstacles present, start along the inside of the bend and keep pulling toward the inside bank. If there are obstacles there, it will be easier to move toward the outside of the bend quickly.

Turns and Pivots

Turning a raft in whitewater rapids differs little from turning a raft in flat water. In fact, the same turning strokes that were discussed in Chapter 6 are used to turn the raft here. Unlike ferrying, turning doesn't call upon river currents for assistance; it just requires some powerful oar and paddle strokes. The only time current becomes a factor is when it is piling up on the wrong side of your raft and counteracting your attempted turn.

Rafters should remember that the raft's inertia will keep it turning after the strokes have ended, resulting in a spin. Most turns require little more than one or two quick strokes. As the accompanying diagram shows, pivots are sharp turns that are usually used to straighten and narrow a raft's profile when approaching a tight slot, to align the raft with oncoming hydraulics, or to free a partially snagged raft from exposed obstacles. Front pivots (turning the bow downstream) and back pivots (turning the stern downstream) are shown.

Sideslips

In some boulder- or hole-riddled rapids there simply isn't enough time to execute a turn or ferry around an obstacle. Some rapids will wrap or flip any raft that lets itself turn broadside. In this kind of situation, a quick horizontal sideslip may be the only way to find safe passage.

The fastest and most efficient sideslipping strokes for paddle rafters are the draw, the cross-bow draw, and the pry stroke. If performed correctly, each of these paddle strokes move rafts laterally across the river in a hurry. Oar rafts can sideslip by planting one blade against the bow and pushing it away from the tube (to move the raft away from the oar), or by planting it a foot or two from the bow and pulling it toward the tube (to pull the raft toward the oar). Since these oar strokes are limited in their application, good rowers

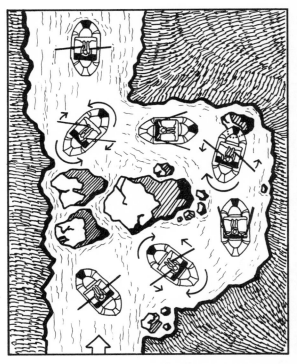

As this raft enters a tricky rapid, a front pivot narrows its profile so it can squeezes through a narrow slot. A back pivot then helps it slide off a rock. One last front pivot lines up the raft with the current again.

Though this crew looks like they're about to run straight into a boulder, they're getting ready to sideslip toward the bottom of the picture by executing draw strokes on the left side of the raft.

recognize their shortcomings and try to avoid getting themselves into tight situations in the first place.

Eddy Maneuvers

PUTTING ON THE BRAKES

A raft floating along on the main current has a lot of inertia. It carries not only its own weight but also the force of the main current, so to stop that raft in its tracks takes at least the same amount of braking force working in the opposite direction. One example of incredible braking forces are midstream boulders. If a boulder hasn't been moved for a while, chances are it isn't going to let some measly raft push it out of the way. Another example of braking forces are big holes or reversals, where the surface current is moving upstream at the same rate as the downstream current. A raft hitting this surface current broadside might find its downstream progress violently arrested.

What *you're* looking for are user-friendly braking forces—something that will let you stop without wrap-ping, flipping, swimming, or losing your composure. What you're looking for is an *eddy*.

Eddies are one of the most important features on the river. Their upstream currents can provide enough braking power to gently—or violently—stop a raft. A mild eddy provides a calm haven for weary rafters, a parking area for loading and unloading boats, and a placid platform from which rapids can be scouted. Conversely, large, tumultuous eddies can trap and flip small rafts and can make any trip across an eddy line difficult.

ENTERING EDDIES

High and Deep. The best way to enter an eddy is to paddle or row into it *high* (upstream, where the maximum current differential is located) and *deep* (directly behind the center of the obstacle). In fact, it is even OK to barely skim the obstacle while entering the eddy. Entering high and deep brings into full effect the river's friendly forces—upstream currents that will brake the raft's momentum and bring its descent to a halt.

If you're wondering why you shouldn't enter eddies low, here's an answer: The powerful upstream currents found higher in the eddy begin to disappear downstream. So a raft entering an eddy low is left with nothing more than its own oar or paddle power to stop its descent and may blow right past the eddy. Somewhere between the eddy's high and low point, the currents are grabby yet forgiving. This midway point can be a nice spot to aim for if you're trying to beach a heavily laden raft, since the stronger upstream currents high in the eddy might drag you past your landing spot.

Speed and Angle. There are two things to think about when entering an eddy: the speed of the raft and the angle of entry. Both concepts tie into one goal: to get across the eddy line quickly!

The most important step in entering an eddy is establishing a good *ferry angle* upstream of the obstacle. Since currents jet along eddy lines faster than they do

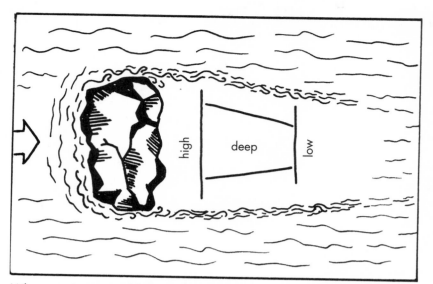

When entering most eddies, aim both high and deep. That is where the eddy is the strongest.

into a forward ferry and use the more powerful forward strokes to drive the raft, bow first, at a 45- to 90-degree angle across the eddy line. (Oar rafts can do this by portegeeing.)

Speed is one of those vague terms that varies in meaning from person to person, and eddy to eddy. The key to entering an eddy is to get across the eddy line—fast! The slower you try to cross an eddy line, the more likely you are to miss the eddy altogether. Then again, if you enter a small midriver eddy too fast you're likely to blow out the other side. So the key to eddy success is to match your speed with the eddy's power and to choose an angle that will quickly expose your raft to the eddy's upstream current and drag it to a halt. (Note: In weak eddies, a few extra paddle or

either inside the eddy or out in the main current, eddy lines create hydraulic shields that deflect any raft approaching the eddy with too little angle. On the other hand, any raft that approaches the same eddy line with too much angle will succumb to the main current before it has a chance to cross the eddy line.

To enter an eddy in an oar raft, start your maneuver far upstream by rowing wide of the obstacle. At the same time, angle the stern so that it will point 45 to 90 degrees upstream of the obstacle when you get there. Now begin back ferrying toward the eddy and keep this angle as you pull across the eddy line. Once you are in the eddy, the upstream currents will pile against the raft, drag it to a halt, and begin pushing it upstream along the eddy.

Paddle rafts can enter eddies the same way as oar rafts by using backstrokes, or they can turn upstream

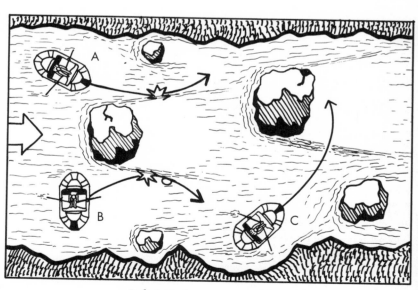

Raft A tried to enter an eddy with too little angle and was deflected downstream by the eddy line. Raft B came in too sideways and missed the eddy because it was caught on the main current. Raft C approached the eddy with about a 45-degree angle and made a perfect entry.

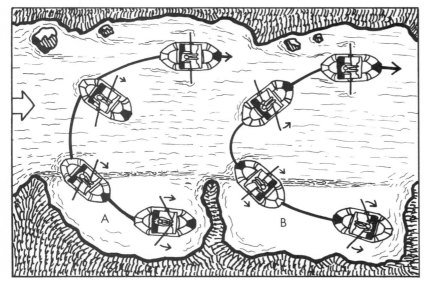

Raft A is ferrying out of its eddy and across the river. Raft B is executing a peel out.

oar strokes might be necessary to drive the raft upstream and bring it to a halt.)

STAYING IN EDDIES

Once you've made it into an eddy, look around. Are you at a standstill or are you still moving? Since an eddy has its own set of currents, it will carry your raft upstream toward the confluence with the main current. Because this confluence marks the most powerful transition point between the eddy's current and the main current, you'll probably want to relax in the calmer waters deep in the eddy. To stay in the heart of the eddy, use small correction strokes or lean the raft against the wall or

boulder that formed the eddy and hold on.

EXITING EDDIES

There are three ways to exit an eddy: (1) ferry across the eddy line, (2) *peel out,* and (3) exit downstream. Downstream exits are only used in mellow eddies with weak currents—all you have to do is paddle or row downstream until the eddy releases your raft. The first two exits—ferries and peel outs—take a little bit of know-how, and some finesse.

Ferrying Out. Ferrying out of an eddy is little different from ferrying across the main channel, except that the transition between currents tends to take novices by surprise. The moment the bow or stern hits the main current, the raft will try to spin downstream. To avoid spinning out when you're trying to ferry, anticipate the main current, build some upstream momentum as you work the raft to the top of the eddy, and cross the eddy line pointing more upstream than usual (10 to 25 degrees to the main current). When the raft enters the main current, use some extra-powerful strokes to drive the main-current side of the raft upstream. Once you're totally free of the eddy, you can ferry across the river as usual.

Peeling Out. A *peel out* is an exciting maneuver that spins the raft downstream as you exit the eddy. To start

MORE EDDY TIPS

To prevent traveling all the way through a small midstream eddy, enter it extremely wide. Keep maneuvering with your oars or paddles until your raft stops, or turn within the eddy to get your whole raft inside. Although 45-degree-angle entries work fine, wide entries (60 to 90 degrees) get you into the heart of the eddy and slam the raft into its strongest upstream currents.

If you need to cross a giant eddy line into a huge, boiling eddy, stroke across at full speed to keep up your momentum. Don't stall out on the eddy line or you'll get munched!

your peel out, accelerate the raft upstream and across the eddy line just as in the ferrying exit, but point the upstream end of the raft 30 to 45 degrees to the main current. As the raft crosses the eddy line, the main current will pile against the upstream tube and spin the raft to face downstream.

CAPSIZING FORCES

Whether ferrying or peeling out of an eddy, rafters have to contend with strange currents swirling about the eddy line. The overlapping currents found here not only slide horizontally past each other—speeding up and throwing off your maneuvers—but they also drive downward, building within themselves strong capsizing forces. On large-volume rivers, giant eddy fences can generate enough capsizing force to suck down one side of the raft and flip it.

Even on mild rivers these capsizing forces can wreak havoc. When a raft exits a fast-moving eddy, its upstream tube is exposed to the main current. The main current drives against the upstream tube, then *under* the raft, trying to drag the upstream tube under with it. Unsuspecting passengers can be tossed overboard as their tube plunges downward, and powerful currents can be strong enough to flip the whole raft.

Whether entering or exiting eddies, rafters can avoid tilting and flipping by shifting their weight to the far side of the raft, away from the diving current. In other words, shift passenger weight *upstream* when entering eddies, and *downstream* when exiting eddies. Once a vulnerable tube has been unweighted, the river has little chance to do any harm.

Heading Downriver

The philosopher Heraclitus once said, "You cannot step twice into the same river, for other waters are continually flowing on." Few words capture the mystique of river running as eloquently as these. With each bend in the channel, rivers reveal new facets of their personalities—sometimes tranquil, sometimes tumultuous. Even the personality of an individual rapid is transformed as water levels rise and fall or as streambeds

erode and shift. Although rapids shift freely from one mood to another, the skills and techniques needed to read and run them remain constant.

READING RIVERS

To novice rafters unfamiliar with the distinctive components of rapids, whitewater rivers epitomize nature in chaos: liquid furies. But to the seasoned river runner, rapids share common features, each one a road sign to routes of safe passage. Reading rivers is the art of interpreting those signs, recognizing the pitfalls of ill-chosen routes, and envisioning the maneuvers that will be necessary to float rapids safely. You've already learned all the road signs and maneuvers rafters use to read rivers; now it's time to apply them.

THE TWO Cs

While you read the rest of this chapter, keep in mind the Two Cs: *currents* and *contingency plans*. First, think of rowing and paddling as the means of changing your raft's speed and direction in relation to the current, not in relation to solid obstacles such as rocks and cliffs. Second, always have a contingency plan in case you miss a stroke, bounce off a rock, or pop an oar loose. Finally, remember that whitewater is ever changing and that your ability to *adapt* is more important than learning the name or category of each technique. If you keep these mental footnotes handy, the following techniques will make more sense and your boating success will increase.

The SAFE System

Rafting is a surprisingly systematic endeavor, with regular routines that simplify the way we run rivers.

On your first outing you may find yourself preoccupied with all facets of rafting technique. Oars may feel awkward, paddle commands might make little or no sense, and currents may drag you unwittingly toward obstacles. However, these fledgling frustrations will soon disappear, leaving your mind open to the real task at hand . . . *reading the river.*

Before running any whitewater rapid, rafters can follow a preset game plan called the SAFE System. The

SAFE system is an easy way to evaluate any rapid, and provides a safe and simple approach to whitewater travel. It is based on four steps:

1. **S**COUT rapids fully before entering them. This can be done from either bank or, if there is an eddy or slow pool, from your raft. Make sure that every trip member observes the entire rapid from a variety of angles, looking both upstream and downstream. Also, select visual guideposts—such as uniquely shaped boulders—that will guide you as you're running the rapid. Finally, remember that rapids look different when you're floating toward them in a raft than when you're standing alongside them on the bank.

2. **A**NALYZE the rapid and your group's ability to run it. Where are the obstacles? Where are the safest channels? Is there a safe line through the rapid? Which way will you swim if you fall out? Are your team and equipment capable of running the rapid safely?

3. **F**ORMULATE a plan. Which route will you follow? What is your backup plan? What maneuvers will you have to execute? Should you portage instead? Should a rescue team be stationed along the banks?

4. **E**XECUTE your plan. Run the rapid, carry the raft along the bank, or line the raft to safety.

SCOUT

Unless you know what's around a bend or over a horizon line, or you feel that you have the skills to pull to shore in an emergency, scout! Pull ashore well above the lip of rapids and long before strong currents drag your raft places you don't want to go.

Starting from your landing point, walk all the way to the base of a rapid, or all the way around a bend, so that you can see the entire section of river you'll be running. A lot of times it may take some scrambling to reach the best vantage points, but the clear lines of sight are usually well worth the extra effort! While scouting, make mental notes of easily recognizable landmarks and distinctive hydraulics—if you decide to run the rapid, you can use them as signposts to tell you where you are and where you need to turn.

Remember that rapids are areas of *falling water* and that your landmarks might not be visible from upstream. Keep looking over your shoulder as you walk back to the raft to see if your landmarks disappear. If they do, walk downstream again and pick new ones.

ANALYZE

By now you have learned to recognize the hydraulics and obstacles you'll see in a typical rapid. You learned that tongues and wave trains signify safe channels, while sharp ledges, rooster tails, and undercuts are hazards to be avoided. It's now time to apply your knowledge of river features—together with your knowledge of raft maneuvers—to analyze the rapid before you.

When scouting a rapid look for two things: obstacles and safe routes. On smaller rivers the hazards will probably be solid obstacles such as rocks or logs. Large-volume rivers, on the other hand, might not have any solid obstacles to cause you concern but can have minefields of keeper holes and menacing haystacks that could spell the demise of raft and crew.

To find safe routes, try walking upstream from the bottom of the rapid and play connect the dots. Can safe routes be connected, or are they broken up by major hazards? (The more broken and twisted the route is, the harder the rapid will be.) Your goal is to discover at least one *clean line* through the rapid—one that you can maneuver without putting yourself or your crew in serious danger. If you are scouting a particularly difficult rapid, note where you can exit the current if you flip, and where *not* to be if you find yourself swimming.

Once you find a runnable line through the rapid, ask whether your team's skills and equipment are up to the demands posed by the river. If not, take a look at the bank and figure out a way to portage or line the raft.

FORMULATE

If you think you *can* run this rapid, run it mentally first. Imagine each move you'll make as your raft descends the rapid from top to bottom. Again, keep in mind the landmarks you scouted out before, and correlate them with moves you'll make in the rapid. As you visualize each maneuver, think of what could go wrong and what you'll do in the event of a

When you are on the river, be SAFE: Scout, analyze, formulate, and execute your run through rapids.

mishap. Finally, discuss your plan with your fellow rafters, especially those who will be in your raft. If there's any chance that you'll have problems, station rescuers at key points along the bank to assist you. (More on that in Chapter 9.)

EXECUTE

By the time you get back in your raft, you have already run the rapid in your mind. Now it's time to do it for real!

The entry into the rapid is often the most critical maneuver. Unless you have to punch a big hydraulic right at the top of the rapid, consider approaching the lip as slowly as possible to catch a last glimpse downstream. It might even be helpful to stand up in the raft in order to gain a better view. Remember that the rapid is going to look quite different from your new vantage point—especially if the rapid is steep—and that you'll probably have prerapid butterflies.

As you enter the rapid, relax and look around. It is amazing how many rafters experience tunnel vision in whitewater, emerging wet and excited in the pool below but totally unable to remember what just happened upstream. Run the rapid methodically, sticking to your main plan and adjusting it whenever the river proves to be too cunning a foe. Make each move by adjusting your raft's momentum and angle just as you learned earlier in this chapter, and be ready to celebrate your trip when you reach the safety of the pool downstream. If all goes well, you'll have plenty of reason to rejoice!

The Added Edge

BAILING

Standard-floor rafts hold an amazing quantity of water. Whether it all pours in from one giant wave, or accumulates after many splashes, the extra water

Bailing helps keep standard-floor rafts light and maneuverable.

makes the raft heavier and less maneuverable.

Every standard-floor raft should have at least one bail bucket securely stored and available for quick use. In pool-drop rivers (rivers with calm pools following short, steep rapids) it is usually easier to wait for a calm eddy than to bail the raft in the middle of a rapid. On rivers with continuous whitewater, on the other hand, stopping may be difficult or impossible, making fast, effective bailing very important.

In an oar raft, it's nice to have a *swamper* along—someone who will bail while the rower concentrates on the oars. Without a swamper, the rower has to set the oars down in order to bail out the passenger compartment. In paddle rafts, the bow paddlers should be the *last* people selected to bail out a raft since they are important to the overall control of the raft. Appoint the middle paddlers to handle the task. Make sure that each time the raft is to be bailed the swampers securely store their paddles, push the buckets toward the floor to fill them as quickly and full as possible, and hold them tight when they dump the water back into the river.

HIGHSIDING

Highsiding can give your raft an edge over boulder-cluttered rapids. Many rafters call highsiding *rock siding,* which is perhaps an easier way to visualize this technique.

Highsiding Obstacles. When a raft rides up onto a small rock or a shallow boulder, the crew can usually free the raft by shifting their weight to the side of the raft that will swing free, pushing off the rock with their feet, bouncing up and down, or using pivot strokes to loosen the raft. If the current is strong enough, though, the raft may keep sliding up the obstacle while the lower tube dives deeper into the main current. Left to its own devices, the river will bury the lower tube and pin the raft against the obstacle, causing a *wrap*.

This raft has slid up onto a rock and the upstream tube is about to dive underwater. To avoid a wrap, the crew is highsiding.

To avoid a wrap, the entire crew highsides by leaning on the downstream tube (the tube riding up on the rock). This unweights the upstream tube, allowing its tremendous buoyancy to lift it free of the river's currents. The crew can then pivot the raft off one side of the rock before the river has a chance to pin it in place.

Highsiding Hydraulics. Highsiding works equally well when a raft gets caught in a large hole. In holes, the upstream surface currents combine with the downward current of the falls to try to flip the raft upstream. To avoid flipping, crew members can lean over the downstream tube and high brace. Then, while keeping their center of gravity low in the raft, the crew can try paddling the raft laterally out of the obstacle. (The crew's low center of gravity helps them stay in the raft if it bucks wildly or spins suddenly. If the raft does spin, all crew members will need to scamper quickly to the downstream tube again.) If the raft is caught in a wide, powerful hole, it can take considerable patience and fortitude to bust free!

DIGGING

Powerful hydraulics—like holes and breaking waves—can halt, spin, and flip a raft before you even knew what hit you. If you can't avoid such traps you need to punch them straight, hard, and fast! In an oar raft, this means that the rower should portegee all the way through the hydraulic, or turn the raft downstream and backrow through. Paddle teams can get the edge on big hydraulics by putting their strongest paddlers in the bow. The bow paddlers should reach deep into the backs of breaking waves, or over the tops of curling holes, and dig their blades into the solid body of water downstream. This will give the bow paddlers a firm grip on the current that can pull them through the hydraulics. Also, if all paddlers lean slightly forward, throwing their weight at waves and holes as if these watery bodies were tackling dummies, the raft might gain just enough extra momentum to bust through some of the biggest hydraulics.

LOWERING YOUR CENTER OF GRAVITY

Some rivers generate waves and holes of mind-boggling proportions. Rafters seated high on a tube are in a precarious position—just one giant splash away from a swim. On occasion, the only way to stay aboard the raft is to keep your body well inside the passenger compartment with your weight low.

This crew is entering a huge hole. To make sure no one falls out, the guide has had the paddlers lean in and get low.

Back in Chapter 7 we talked a little bit about "getting down." Now its time to turn what looks like a cowardly maneuver into a genuine technique.

There are three important elements of getting paddlers low in a raft. First, when dropping your weight toward the bottom of the raft, don't let your legs slip under the thwarts, and don't sit or kneel on a standard floor—these moves are an invitation to injury when the raft bucks or hits rocks. Next, use your outside hand to hold the paddle, and keep your paddle low and toward the outside of the tube—this will stop the paddle from swinging wildly and hitting your neighbor. (Tall rafters can still paddle even when seated low in rafts.) Finally, turn your inside shoulder—not your head—into the raft. This will prevent heads from knocking together, and will keep your vision clear so you can anticipate your next move.

BEACHING

Rafts must be pulled ashore when bank scouting, stopping for lunch, portaging, or taking out. Knowing how to stop and secure the raft to shore is as important as maneuvering the raft on the river.

In a one-person oar raft, beaching can be quite a feat. Unless the river is calm near the bank, the rower must slowly approach the shore, free up a line, and tie the raft off before it gets away. In paddle rafts, beaching is usually handled by an agile bow person who can stow her paddle and deftly jump ashore.

Proper beaching technique involves these *six steps*:

1. The crew maneuvers slowly toward shore so as not to bounce off the bank and keeps stroking to counteract the current once at the bank.
2. Paddles or oars are securely stowed.

3. One person grabs the bowline and unravels it.

4. The bow paddler or rower jumps ashore with the rope just *before* the raft hits the bank (not *after!*).

5. If the person now on the bank is strong enough, and the raft is not too heavy or moving too quickly, she can simply pull back on the rope to get the raft to pendulum into the bank. A superior alternative is to belay the raft by quickly wrapping the bowline once or twice around a rock, a tree, or some other solid object. (*Never* wrap the rope around your wrist, back, or any other part of your body!)

6. If the raft simply won't stop, one person should quickly reboard the raft, recoil the rope, and store it safely so that it doesn't pose a hazard downriver. In paddle rafts, the belayer can also release the rope and follow the raft downstream along the bank.

Honing Your Skills

In time, such things as oar strokes, whitewater maneuvers, and reading rapids will become second nature. As your basic skills improve, you may find yourself longing for wilder rapids or contentedly returning to the gentle rivers you have become accustomed to. No matter what your aspirations, you can vastly improve your rafting skills by looking at the river you're on *right now* in a very different light.

Until now you have been taught to look for the safest, easiest routes through rapids. At the same time, you learned that many rapids have several runnable channels. Now it's time to shun the obvious passages and test your skills by *using* the river to challenge yourself.

Rather than taking the cleanest line through a Class II or III rapid, look for an imaginary slalom course, using boulders, holes, or logs to mark your serpentine route. Ferry back and forth around boulders and try to connect the eddies behind rocks, stopping in each one as you go. Soon you will be able to put the raft exactly where *you* want to go, rather than just wherever the *river* carries you. With a little bit of practice, your skill level will skyrocket, preparing you for greater challenges to come.

9

SAFETY AND RESCUE
KEEPING YOUR HEAD & GEAR ABOVE WATER

Risk is a constant companion in whitewater travel. Nonetheless, many veterans scoff at danger, bragging about how few times they have flipped or swum in their careers. That would be like a skier saying, "I've skied for 17 years and I've only fallen once!" Sounds pretty silly when you think about it.

Today's rafters find themselves in a unique paradox. Equipped with top-quality equipment and a wealth of intellectual know-how, modern rafters are able to tackle rapids that would have sent previous explorers scurrying toward the riverbank in search of portage routes. Also, the techniques that took our predeces-

sors many years to learn can now be acquired by zealous novices in just a few weeks or months.

The rush toward more exciting and difficult whitewater has carried with it greater risk and increased peril. The difference between a Class III and a Class V swim can be astounding, yet many newcomers find themselves on expert runs without ever having flipped a raft in whitewater before. And fundamental rescue skills—such as those necessary to retrieve a wrapped raft or a pinned swimmer—frequently elude the eager novice while he moves on to harder and harder rivers.

As in any outdoor sport, uncontrolled risk invites

SAFETY AND RESCUE

Safety and rescue procedures—like rivers themselves—change from moment to moment and from one situation to another. This book doesn't attempt to describe every technique you could ever call upon in a river emergency, but it takes a big step toward ensuring safe, responsible boating.

Before attempting more challenging rivers, enroll in a swiftwater rescue course and read such books as *Whitewater Rescue Manual* by Charlie Walbridge and Wayne Sundmacher (Ragged Mountain Press, 1995) and *River Rescue* by Les Bechdel and Slim Ray (Appalachian Mountain Club Books, 1989). Follow the basic guidelines you learn in this chapter and practice newfound safety skills at every opportunity. You'll soon find that proper skills, knowledge, and judgment will keep your river outings safe and enjoyable.

calamity. Accordingly, safety should be the primary concern on any river outing, whether it involves a peaceful scenic float or a heart-pounding Class V descent.

Having What It Takes

PRETRIP PREPARATION

One of your most important pretrip considerations is selecting a river that every member of your group is capable of running. Using the weakest members of your party as a reference point, pick a river that is within your *entire* group's skill level. This may sound silly at first—after all, many outfitters carry paying passengers down rivers they would never get to paddle or row by themselves—but it really isn't. Outfitters know their rivers intimately, can anticipate most hazards, and have adequate rescue provisions for the less-lucky members of their trips.

There are scores of outstanding guidebooks, maps, and other resources to assist you in your search for the ideal river. Be sure to adequately research the location of and distance between put-ins and take-outs, the time it will take to run the river, the classification and location of major rapids, and the recommended water levels for safe trips. Pay particular attention to road access and shuttle information—important factors on any trip since shuttles frequently consume a lot of valuable time and daylight. Also keep in mind that any guidebook is only a reference, and that rivers change

constantly. Seek out the recommendations and advice of more experienced rafters—their firsthand knowledge of a particular river will exceed that of any guidebook author.

The next step in your pretrip agenda is to survey water levels and local weather forecasts. Even gentle streams become angry, dangerous torrents at high water, and bone-chilling winds or driving rains can dampen even the liveliest rafting spirits. A number of government agencies provide prerecorded river-level readings and weather reports over the phone. Another source of information is your local whitewater shop or an outfitter located near the river. Finally, check the Appendix for the names of national agencies that monitor river levels and ask them how to contact the agencies nearest you. Keep this information handy for future outings.

TIME ON THE RIVER

Rivers flow—dams notwithstanding—on their own schedules. Still, veteran rafters can *guesstimate* how long a trip will take by comparing the current's average velocity to the distance between the put-in and the take-out. Beginner-to-intermediate rafters can avoid this kind of guesswork by simply consulting a guidebook or a knowledgeable rafter to find out how long a particular trip usually takes.

Once on the river, rafters can try to beat the clock by paddling faster than the river's average flow, but that expends a lot of energy and cuts down on the quality of the rafting experience (unless, of course, you're rac-

SHUTTLES

The river shuttle is one of those necessary evils that accompany every river trip, and no matter how many times you do a shuttle, there will be room for screw-ups. Yessiree, shuttles have been botched by novices and veterans alike!

Plan your shuttles well in advance. Consult a guidebook for directions, and double-check your information against any maps you can find: AAA road maps, National Forest maps, U.S. Geological Survey maps . . . whatever. If you're not going to be doing the shuttle personally, give the real drivers the right directions, and make sure they understand them. (You'd be amazed how many times shuttlers turn the wrong way, get lost, and wind up asking directions at the nearest minimart!)

Add shuttle time to your river time when planning trips. Some rivers might have only 10 miles of water between put-in and take-out but require a full day of shuttle driving. I call the comparison of road miles to river miles the shuttle-to-fun ratio. Unless you're a hard-core road tripper, pick rivers with low shuttle-to-fun ratios, such as a river that carves a serpentine canyon while the road beelines for the take-out. Also, take into account time-consuming factors like mountainous terrain and stop signs. What looks like a fast and easy shuttle route on a map might be slower than a mule train once you're actually on the road.

Pay special attention to your gear: Strap your raft tightly to the trailer and take extra care to prevent chafing. Unless you've got lots of passenger space, you should also check the local weather forecast. If it predicts cool evening weather, have some warm, dry clothes waiting at the take-out and find some shelter for the nonshuttling members of your group.

Last, but not least, figure out what you're going to do with your car keys. As one possessed of little, if any, short-term memory, I can attest to leaving car keys in the dumbest places imaginable. But now my misadventures can become your lessons. Don't put your keys in an ammo can or a dry bag; if you flip, your keys could end up on the bottom of the river. Don't hide the keys under a rock or a car bumper; clever crooks know this trick and will spend a half-hour searching around your car. And don't give your keys to your best friend, girlfriend, or spouse; you'll be blaming each other for months if they get lost. Leave nonessential keys at home and keep your car keys on your person in a zippered or Velcro-sealed pocket. That way, whether you flip, wrap, or tick off your best friend, you'll still have your keys.

If all this seems too complicated, you might be able to hire someone to worry for you. That's right . . . there are people who make a living on running shuttles. Government agencies, outfitters, chambers of commerce, and local paddlers can tell you where to find professional shuttle drivers; they're usually pretty reliable.

Well, drive safely, and I'll see you at the minimart!

ing). Also, rivers tend to hold time-consuming surprises for the wary and the unwary rafter alike—an unseen snag can puncture a tube and delay your take-out, or an unexpected rise in water level might increase the river's difficulty and call for more scouting or portaging.

To make sure you have enough time to enjoy your whitewater trip safely, *expect the unexpected* and leave enough time to handle ordinary mishaps. Start early enough to assure your arrival at the take-out in daylight, and leave enough time to run your shuttle.

PRETRIP DISCUSSION

Before leaving the put-in, take some time to gather the group and select a group leader. Discuss the day's itinerary, expected hazards, what order the group should travel in, and the signals that will be used to communicate between boats. (See the accompanying diagram for suggested signals.)

Equipment

Top-quality equipment often makes the difference between an enjoyable river excursion and a whitewater fiasco. On the other hand, you don't have to dump all your hard-earned money into the finest gear available—it is simply important to use equipment that is designed to withstand the rigors of whitewater use.

In addition to the gear and equipment described in Chapter 3, rafters should carry an assortment of essential safety gadgets: *carabiners, knives, whistles, prussiks, pulleys, throw bags, static ropes, web slings,* and *first aid kits.* If you're fortunate, they'll just collect waterspots while you enjoy the river, but if an emergency arises their presence will bring you peace of mind.

Carabiners. Aluminum-alloy carabiners are truly the river runner's *multipurpose tool:* They can be used to clip in gear and attach lines to rafts and can be substituted for pulleys in rope rescues. Experienced river runners often carry one, two, or three carabiners clipped to the shoulder or waist of their lifejacket so that they'll be readily accessible when needed. However, it is important to keep the carabiners tucked flat against the lifejacket with the gates *facing inward* to prevent injury or accidental clipping onto stray ropes or branches.

Knives. It is not at all uncommon for knife-wielding river guides to get some nervous stares from first-time

Stop   Help/Emergency

Go Right   Go Left

All Clear   O.K.

Some common river signals. Whatever signals you use, discuss them before the trip so that everyone understands them.

rafters. I mean, it sort of makes the guide look like some kind of semipsychotic Rambo-wannabe. Nevertheless, the river knife is another essential safety tool for guides and recreational rafters alike. It can be used to cut the floor out of a hopelessly pinned raft or to sever a rope quickly before it puts anybody in danger.

Good quality river knives have solid sheaths of plastic or stiff leather and can be worn on the chest or shoulder of your lifejacket for quick access. If you have a thumb-release sheath, check the release frequently to make sure your knife will still be there when you need it.

Whistles. It is encouraging to see and hear more whistles in use today than ever before. They are real attention-getters in almost any situation and can be used to signal an emergency with three short blasts.

Prussiks. A prussik is a short loop—about 4 or 5 feet long—made of 5- to 7-millimeter kernmantle rope. It can be used to tie off rafts or to set brakes in Z-drag rescue systems (discussed later in this chapter).

When you make your own prussik you may decide to wear it around your waist like a belt. Simply measure your waist with your lifejacket and rafting clothes on, then double your waist width and add 1 foot to get the length of rope you'll need. Tie the ends together

with a double fisherman's knot to form the loop (see the knot-tying section of the Appendix). Now the prussik is ready to be worn around the waist and can be clipped together with a carabiner.

Pulleys. A pulley is one of those items you'll be really glad to have the first time you wrap your raft. Pulleys reduce rope friction in Z-drag rescues and increase the efficiency of any rope-rescue system. For river use, select sturdy aluminum-alloy pulleys designed to accommodate ½-inch (11-millimeter) rope.

Throw Bags. Throw bags—also known as *throw ropes*, *rescue ropes*, and *rescue bags*—are remarkable rope-retaining tools designed to spool out rope freely when the bag is tossed to a swimmer. They simplify rope throwing and make it easier for swimmers to see the rope coming—especially when the bag is filled with brightly colored, high-flotation rope. When not in use the throw bag neatly stows rope out of harm's way.

Rescue gear: make sure that you have everything you need to make your rafting trips safe and enjoyable.

Static Ropes. Wraps and entrapments are two of the greatest perils facing whitewater rafters. Either situation demands a rope with superior strength and minimum stretch. High-quality static lines have incredible tensile strength—far more than found in most throwbag ropes—and very little stretch. Rafters should carry at least 100 feet of neatly stored ½-inch (11-millimeter) static rope for unwrapping rafts and freeing stranded or trapped swimmers.

Web Slings. Web slings—made of 1- or 2-inch-wide nylon webbing—will serve all sorts of purposes. They can be used as anchors in Z-drag systems and rappels, and can even be used to make seat harnesses for vertical extrications. Carry a few slings of varying lengths (10 to 20 feet long) in your rescue kit and you'll be prepared to set up anchors in most any type of canyon environment.

First Aid Kits. A first aid kit should be standard equipment on any river trip. Minor injuries are inevitable, even on easy rivers, but can often be treated immediately by someone trained in first aid. Take the time to consider the type of trip you're undertaking and the location of the nearest medical assistance when you assemble the first aid kit. Consult the Appendix for a list of suggested items to include.

Group Travel

LEAD AND SWEEP RAFTS

River trips are safer when two, three, or more rafts join in. The extra rafts and passengers can provide assistance in emergencies, and often make the difference between a successful rescue and a disaster. In groups of three or more rafts it will be helpful to choose a *lead* boat to run at the front of the pack and a *sweep* boat to bring up the rear. The lead raft usually contains the most experienced and knowledgeable rafters, acts as a scout or probe in rapids, and renders assistance to other rafts when they pull over to scout. The sweep boat also contains highly experienced rafters but lags slightly behind the pack so it can keep an eye on the other rafts and help out if a problem arises.

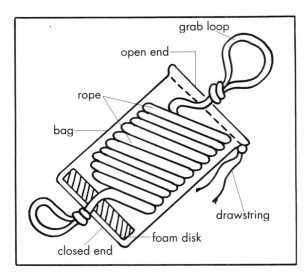

A throw bag is an important rescue tool. It usually contains sturdy, brightly colored, high-flotation rope, and is much easier to toss than a coil ropes. The rope feeds out gradually when a rescuer throws the bag.

GROUP SCOUTING AND RESCUE

It is best to scout rapids together as a group, and to follow the SAFE plan (Scout, Analyze, Formulate, and Execute). Try to get everybody involved and listening to the group discussion even if only one or two individuals may be responsible for many of the decisions. If any rafter is unwilling to try a rapid, let that individual walk, line, or portage around it.

In easy rapids a rescue plan is rarely needed, but more difficult rapids demand extra precautions. Position a couple of rafters with throw bags at key points along the rapid to render assistance if a flip or swim is possible. If the rapid is too difficult to be run safely, scout out the riverbank for a portage route or a lining route. Practice *redundant safety,* which simply means having both a main plan and a contingency plan for everything that could go wrong.

Portaging and Lining

Rapids evoke a broad spectrum of emotions—from excitement to outright fear. Your mind's inner voice usually provides a good gauge of your chances of suc-

It is helpful to have the whole group scout rapids together. That way, each member of the team can decide whether to run the rapid or walk around it, and everyone can agree on a game plan.

cess. Those of us who like to ignore our *mind's* inner voice can listen to our *bodies*—a sudden need to urinate or an inability to spit are pretty good indicators that the rapid's going to present a heck of a challenge.

Always keep in mind that portaging and lining are commonplace on difficult rivers and are viable options whenever rafters choose to avoid running a particular rapid.

One of the key considerations in running versus portaging rapids is how *everybody else* in the group feels. If you're rowing your own raft you can usually run a rapid without upsetting anybody else. But if you're a paddle captain you'll have a tough time avoiding a mutiny if you decide to *go for it* in a marginally runnable Class V+ rapid against your crew's wishes.

Before you line your raft around a rapid, secure or remove any gear that might break loose. Next, attach long ropes to both the bow and the stern and scout out a foot path along the bank that won't snag the rope. When you're ready to go, give the raft a slight push out toward the current. With two people controlling the ropes, adjust the raft's angle just as you would if you were riding it. If it will be running steep falls or sticky holes, keep the raft moving fast and pull hard on the downstream line to prevent it from being held. In long, powerful chutes, try tying a length of rope to the bow only. Have one person hold the raft in place above the chute while the belayer walks the end of the rope downstream to the midpoint of the chute. When the belayer is ready, the upstream person can let the raft go. As the raft zips through the channel, the belayer runs down-

When confronted with a difficult rapid, you may have the option of lining or portaging around it.

stream until he reaches a point where he can pull the raft to shore.

Because there are so many complexities involved in lining rapids, portaging can be a less-strenuous option for lightly loaded rafts. Terrain permitting, all the team has to do is hoist the raft and carry (not drag) it to a safe pool below the hazards.

Self-Rescues

River-based rescues fall into two categories: *self-rescues* and *assisted rescues*. In self-rescues, rafters are essentially left to attend to their own well-being; in assisted rescues, land- and water-based rescuers contribute to the relief efforts with throw lines, extra boats, and physi-

cal support. In both types of rescue, one aspect of river safety reigns supreme: People come first!

SWIMMING

Swimming a rapid, much to the surprise of many beginners, is nothing like swimming in a lake or a pool. Strong currents can overwhelm and quickly fatigue even experienced swimmers. However, once swimmers have become familiar with the forces involved—either by swimming easy rapids or from prior experience—they can relax and rationally set about swimming to safety.

Unless you intentionally jump into the river, your first reaction to swimming will be one of surprise. Most of the time you'll pop back to the surface instantly, cussing the cold and aiming your lips toward the sky. Survey the river and banks the moment your

Your first swim can come as quite a surprise!

vision clears and look downstream for calm pools and major hazards. Hold onto your paddle unless releasing it increases your chances of a quick rescue.

If you are near your raft and it is still upright, pull yourself back into it from the upstream side to avoid getting caught between the raft and an obstacle. (Sometimes it is better just to get into the raft as fast as you can without worrying whether you're on the upstream or downstream side!) Overturned rafts can be mounted and paddled back to shore in easy rapids; but it is important to beware of the danger of holding onto a raft when you are swimming. Although it provides tremendous flotation and high visibility for rescuers, the raft could pin and crush you against an obstacle. Be prepared to abandon your boat if you will be better off swimming to safety.

RERIGHTING RAFTS

If your raft is equipped with *fliplines*, a bowline, or a stern line, it is possible to climb atop the overturned boat and reright it. One type of flipline is a small bag containing 10 to 12 feet of thick nylon rope. The bag attaches to a D-ring or to the rowing frame and is sealed with a Velcro closure when not in use. The moment you need it, just open the bag, pull out the line, and throw it across the raft's floor. Swim around to the opposite side of the raft and use the rope to climb onto the floor, then stand up on the raft's edge, pull on the flipline, and lean backward until the raft flips over.

In serious whitewater you might want to prerig a 1-inch nylon-webbing flipline tightly across the floor underneath the raft. (Secure the webbing to the rowing frame or to D-rings with a cord that will break free if you hit a snag.) With the prerigged flipline you won't waste precious time getting the line in place or risk letting it float off the floor before you swim to the far side of the raft. Instead you can simply grab the line, pull yourself up onto the floor, and continue just as you

Practice self-rescue techniques before you tackle difficult rapids.

would with a bagged flipline.

One way to reflip a self-bailing raft is to insert your paddle's T-grip into the floor lacing or floor hole. You won't have as much leverage as you would with a flipline, but this technique will work fine on small self-bailers.

What happens if your raft doesn't have a flipline, it isn't a self-bailer, and you're not paddling? Well, you can loosen a bow or stern line and tie part of the rope to a side D-ring or the rowing frame. Once the rope is tied in place it can be used in the same way as a flipline. Keep in mind, however, that the extra rope is a real hazard. Do everything possible to avoid becoming entangled in the loose coils!

Before you reflip a raft, be prepared to fall right back into the river when you pull on the line or paddle. Be careful not to fall backward into rocks, and consider staying aboard if this would be safer than swimming the next rapid. Finally, unless there's a big pool just downstream, be prepared to reboard the raft quickly before the next rapid.

Fliplines tied across the far side of the raft can be used to help pull it back over again. If the raft is heavy, it may take many people to flip it upright.

ACTIVE SWIMMING

If you find yourself too far from rafts or rescuers, you should be prepared to actively find a way to the safety of an eddy or the bank. Start off by getting yourself to the surface. (Now, I don't really expect you to ask yourself what the first goal is—your lungs will remind you in a hurry!) In violent hydraulics it can be pretty difficult to find the surface. Relax for a second and look around. Head toward the light or follow the bubbles. When you know you're moving in the right direction, keep a cool head and tight lips until you can breathe again.

Once back at the surface, aggressively spot and avoid hazards and prepare to swim toward shore when an opportunity arises. Swimmers in shallow, boulder-strewn rapids should lie on their backs, feet held high and pointed downstream. By assuming this *human shock absorber* position you can fend off rocky collisions with your feet and use backstrokes and kicks to ferry yourself toward safety.

With your feet floating ahead of you, a new hazard presents itself: foot entrapment. To avoid this peril, never try to stand up in rapids. Instead, wait until the current has subsided or you are in the calm of a gentle eddy.

In any swimming situation, let the river dictate your actions. In deeper, more powerful rapids you may be better off turning onto your stomach and swimming aggressively toward shore. In steep, bone-bruising rapids, the *cannonball* position—knees pulled into your chest—may be a good short-term way to protect your limbs (and other vital parts) from injury. Always strive to keep enough air in your lungs—breathe only in the calm troughs between wave crests and turn your head to the side to avoid inhaling any spray or foam.

When swimming a rapid, you can use your legs like giant shock absorbers to avoid painful collisions with obstacles. Keep your legs and feet near the surface, but ball up if you're going to go over a steep drop. When an opportunity arises, swim actively toward safety.

HOLES AND DAMS

The upstream surface currents of large holes and low-head dams can recirculate swimmers indefinitely, and once you are caught in such a trap your lifejacket might not have enough flotation to buoy you above the aerated water. Accordingly, holes and dams sometimes demand special techniques for quick escapes.

Keep in mind that most holes are too small to be keepers. If you find yourself stuck momentarily in the backwash, relax for a second, breathe when you can, and try to swim sideways out of the hole. If you can't escape sideways, remember that the falls contains a powerful downcurrent that can be used to push you under the hole and out. Swim right into the falls, curl up in the cannonball position, and hang on for the ride. If you come up on the boil line, be sure to swim aggressively downstream before you start to get recirculated.

Lowhead dams contain the deadliest of all holes and are the most difficult to escape. *Don't run them!* If you ever *do* find yourself swimming a dam, you may recirculate in the backwash many times. Try to save your energy and work your way toward shore. Swimming into the falls may be enough to push you out under the backwash, but be prepared to make many attempts at self-rescue. Above all, *don't give up!*

STRAINERS AND SWEEPERS

Some of the worst hazards facing swimmers and rafts are downed trees (sweepers) and boulder sieves (strainers). These obstacles work like giant gill nets by letting water pass through freely and capturing solid objects (swimmers and rafts) in their grasp.

If you find yourself heading toward a strainer or a sweeper, try to swim around it with all the power you can muster. If a collision is inevitable, turn onto your stomach and face downstream, concentrating on the

SWIMMING

I've heard seasoned guides vigorously debate the best way to swim rapids: feet downstream and hands out to your side, rolled over on your belly and swimming toward shore, balled up and protecting your limbs. No matter what you hear, there's only one rule for every swimming situation: do whatever the river demands!

If there's a huge waterfall coming up, get to the first safe, dry spot you can find. If canyon walls have locked you into a quarter-mile of non-stop, bone-chilling rapids, try to reboard your raft. Sometimes you might even have to wait a while, conserve some energy, then make a powerful attempt to swim into a single eddy.

There is no *best way* to swim every rapid. Don't let guide chatter clutter your judgment. Save yourself!

approaching log or tree. A split second before you reach it, kick your legs and pull yourself over it *head first* using any handholds you can find. Give it all you've got! If you can't make it over the log, try hanging on until you can be rescued. If you absolutely have to go under it, first feel for snags with your feet and legs. Remember, swimming under a strainer is the last thing you want to do! Do this only as a last resort!

PULLING SWIMMERS INTO RAFTS

When a strong rapid bounces just one or two passengers out of an upright raft they usually surface nearby. If the swimmer can be rescued without endangering the rest of the crew, follow these simple guidelines:

1. Act fast! Get the swimmer into the raft before the situation gets worse.
2. Have the swimmer move upstream of the raft so that it won't pin him against a rock. (It may be safer to get the swimmer aboard fast than to move him to the upstream side of the raft.)
3. Have just one or two passengers assist the swimmer. Keep everyone else paddling or rowing to maintain control of the raft.
4. The rescuer should stand up in the raft in front of the swimmer with her knees braced against the main tube for support. Then, with the swimmer facing the raft, the rescuer should grab the shoulders of the swimmer's lifejacket and lean back into the passenger compartment and pull, lifting him out of the water. (It is usually much easier to pull the swimmer in if he kicks his feet underwater and pulls on an available rope or strap.)
5. Keep rowing or paddling—don't gloat over the rescue. There may be more rapids just downstream.
6. If a quick rescue imperils the rest of your crew, wait until it is safe before trying to help the swimmer.

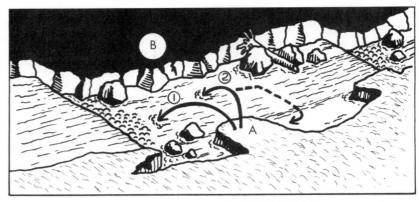

Position rescuers where they'll do the most good. Here, rescuer A can toss a throwline 45 degrees upstream toward the swimmer after a flip (1), and can get in a second toss (2) before the swimmer heads downstream. Plus, rescuer A can pull the swimmer into a safe eddy (dotted line). Rescuer B, on the other hand, is in a bad position. There's no eddy nearby, and a rope rescue is likely to pull the swimmer into the dangerous boulder sieve.

Rope Rescues

THROW BAGS

A throw bag can become a life-saving umbilical cord linking a swimmer with a rescuer, but it takes a lot more than just aiming and tossing to carry out a good rescue. It takes frequent practice to land a throw rope right where a swimmer can reach it, and it takes keen knowledge of currents and river forces to finish off a rescue once the swimmer actually grasps the rope.

GETTING ROPES TO SWIMMERS

Eye Contact. Before throwing a rope to a swimmer, evaluate the situation. The most effective rope rescues are those that were anticipated before the swim. If the rescuers are stationed where the swimmer actually has an opportunity to see a throw bag coming, they have a chance to establish the *first goal* of rope rescues: eye contact with the swimmer. If a rescuer stands slightly downstream of where a flip might occur, the swimmer has a chance to get back to the surface and clear his vision before the rope toss is made. Then, with a

Toss the throw bag the best way conditions allow: Underhand and overhand often work best, but you can even throw sidearm.

The Toss. The rescuer's *third goal* is to actually get the rope *to* the swimmer. Depending on your dexterity and on surrounding obstacles like overhanging cliffs or branches, your best toss may be underhand, overhand, or sidearm. Though it helps to be adept at all three types of throw, most rescues are done with an underhand toss. Just use the best throw you can and aim to land the rope *at or just downstream of* the swimmer so that he can reach the rope even if it is a few feet away. (If you aim upstream of the swimmer, the slower surface current will slow the rope's descent while the swimmer accelerates downstream in the deeper, faster currents.)

strong yell from the rescuer ("ROPE!"), the swimmer has a chance to look at the rescuer and see the rope coming.

Bank Positioning. The rescuer's *second goal* is to establish proper bank positioning, taking into account the power of the main current, the shape of the bank, and the location of downstream obstacles. Position the rescuer close to the water's edge (if she's too high above the river, the working length of the rope will be shortened) so that her first toss angles *45 degrees upstream* toward the swimmer. From that point the current can actually help push the swimmer toward the rescuer as the rope is pulled in. (Also, by throwing the rope upstream to the swimmer, the rescuer may have a chance at a second toss if the first one misses the mark.) If there are calm currents or gentle pools below a likely flip spot, the rescuer can use the rope to pendulum the swimmer in to shore. Never pull a swimmer into a worse situation than he's already in. Make sure the rescue pool is free of boulder sieves, sweepers, and other hazards.

The Helpful Swimmer. A swimmer has to be able to help himself just as much as the rescuer helps him. The swimmer must be prepared to grab the rope with one or both hands and turn onto his back, face up. (It is important to grab the rope, not the bag!) In this position the swimmer's body will plane toward the surface and offer less resistance to the current. The swimmer should never wrap the rope around his hands, limbs, or body!

The swimmer should hold the rescue rope over his shoulders and lie on his back. That way, he'll plane toward the surface and keep an air pocket over his face. Never wrap the rope around your wrist, arm, or body!

BELAYS

Once the rescuer and the swimmer are holding each end of the rescue rope, it is time to work the swimmer toward shore. Both people should pull the slack out of the rope and prepare for a powerful jolt as the rope pulls tight. There are two ways to pull the swimmer ashore: The rescuer can pull the swimmer in from a stationary position with a *static belay*, or she can run downstream with the swimmer in a *dynamic belay*.

Rescuers can use a static belay (left) or a dynamic belay (right) to assist the swimmer. In case a dynamic belay becomes necessary after a static belay has already begun, never wrap the rope more than one turn around an anchor.

Static Belay. In a static belay, the rescuer pendulums the swimmer toward the shore from a stationary point on the bank. The rescuer can step on the end of the rope if she's worried that it will pull free or she can

use a belay anchor, such as a tree stump or a boulder. To use a belay anchor, wrap the rope one-half to one full turn around the object. If you wrap the rope more than once around the anchor, it will take longer to unwrap it if a dynamic belay becomes necessary.

Dynamic Belay. In strong currents, a dynamic belay may work better because it reduces the counteracting forces that could jerk the rope from the swimmer's hands. In a dynamic belay, the rescuer walks or runs down the bank alongside the swimmer, pulling him in gradually with light rope tension. This technique, as you can imagine, works only if there is an open corridor along the river bank.

River Crossings

It is sometimes necessary to walk rafters across a shallow river without a rope. This can be done solo in gentle currents or as a team in stronger currents. No matter which technique is used, the same basic concepts apply: All shallow-water crossings are premised on maintaining *three points of contact* with the river bottom, and they must be done slowly and methodically to avoid foot entrapment. One crossing method may

When doing a solo crossing, use a long paddle, oar, pole, or sturdy branch to brace yourself. The pole and your feet provide three points of contact with the riverbed. By leaning forward and moving just one point of contact at a time, you are much more stable than you would be without a brace.

outweigh another, depending on the speed of the current and the depth of the river.

SOLO CROSSINGS

When crossing a river by yourself, use a long, sturdy paddle, oar, pole, or tree limb as a brace; this, together with your two feet, provides three points of contact. Face upstream, jam one end of the pole into the river bottom, and tilt it 30 degrees back toward your shoulder. At the same time, brace your shoulder against the pole and lean your body 30 degrees upstream against it. Now, maintaining this 60-degree triangle, you can slowly sidestep your way across the river, moving one point of contact at a time.

GROUP CROSSINGS

The most basic group crossings are mere variations of solo crossings: The solo crosser carries someone *piggyback* from one bank to the other, or one person leads the way across the river with the second person pressed tightly against his back and the back of his legs.

If more people are to be added to the group, each new person can step toward the outboard shoulder of the person in front of him, effectively making a *wedge* formation. In a *line astern* crossing, additional people follow directly behind the point person and press down on his shoulders to increase the stability of the system.

If there are three people in your group, arrange yourselves in a triangle and lock your arms around each other's shoulders. The heaviest person stands on the downstream point of the triangle, facing upstream, and the group leans into each other to form a pyramid. With one person moving his feet at a time, the group can work its way across the river.

Another way to shuttle people across the river with-

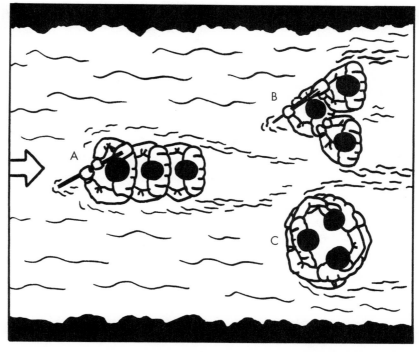

Three ways to cross a river with a small group: Group A is standing in a line astern formation, group B is using a wedge formation, and group C is using a triangle formation. Each technique relies on the downward pressure exerted by each individual to stabilize the entire group.

out a raft is with a *fixed horizontal line*—a rope stretched taut just a foot or so above the river. The crosser simply stands upstream of the fixed line, holds the rope against her waist, and walks sideways across the river. If something goes wrong, all she has to do is somersault over or swim under the rope to break free. Since there is always a possibility that the crosser could snag a lifejacket buckle or carabiner on the rope, the line shouldn't be anchored on both banks. Instead, use belay points on both banks or just tie off one anchor point and use a loose belay on the opposite bank.

Other Rope Rescues

STRONG-SWIMMER RESCUE

There may be times when a swimmer is caught against a midstream boulder and a throw-rope or boat-based res-

A fixed horizontal line supports the crosser but allows her to dive over or under the rope in an emergency. Don't anchor both ends of the line—you may have to let one end go if the crosser gets caught on the rope.

cue is simply impossible. If someone has to reach the swimmer to render assistance, one technique that might work is the strong-swimmer rescue.

The strong-swimmer rescue is a paradox in rescue procedures because it endangers the rescuer by placing her *inside* a rope loop while working in the current. Nevertheless, there may be times when other rescue techniques simply won't work and the increased risk is worth a victim's life.

The strong-swimmer rescue requires—at a minimum—a swimmer, a belayer, and a strong rope. A large, *very loose* loop is tied into one end of the rope and placed around the rescuer's chest. (The loop must be loose enough to push free if the rescuer runs into any trouble.) Once in the loop, the rescuer can be pendulumed to the victim from the far bank (in narrow streams only), or lowered downstream to the victim from an upstream boulder or island.

LOOSE HORIZONTAL LINE

A slightly safer alternative to the strong-swimmer rescue is an offshoot of the fixed horizontal line. In rescue situations, the fixed horizontal line can be rigged looser than usual so that the rescuer can make some *downstream* progress as she works her way out into the main channel. By slowly letting rope out from one of the belay anchors, the rescuer moves downstream while leaning her waist against the line. She can escape in an emergency by somersaulting away from the line

or having a belayer release one end of the rope.

THE TELFER LOWER

The Telfer Lower combines many of the rope tricks you've just learned but adds a raft as a rescue platform. The raft, in turn, is controlled by shore-based rescuers through the use of tag lines and fixed ropes. The Telfer Lower is so complex that it is rarely used—especially if a speedy rescue is necessary. However, it can provide one way to get to a wrapped raft or stranded swimmer when time isn't a critical factor.

The Telfer Lower requires, at a minimum: (1) an anchor line, (2) three carabiners, (3) two tag lines, and (4) a belay line. The anchor line is a fixed rope that

Strong-swimmer rescues: The rescuer can be pendulumed to the victim from the bank or lowered downstream from an island.

crosses the river 8 to 10 feet above the surface and 20 to 50 feet upstream of the rescue site. (If the anchor line is angled slightly downstream toward the rescue site the river will help push the raft toward the site with little help from shore.) From this anchor line, hang a chain of three interlinked carabiners. Next, attach two tag lines to the middle carabiner, with one line leading to each bank. Finally, add a belay line. This long, sturdy rope runs from the raft, up through the lowest carabiner in the chain, and back to the raft.

To operate the system, the shore belayers pull the tag lines until the raft is positioned upstream of the rescue site. Then the rescuers aboard the raft use the belay line to lower the raft to the rescue site.

There are many ways to set up a Telfer Lower—the belay rope can be run to shore and controlled by a shore belayer, two canoes can be used in place of a raft, and various types of friction brakes can be used to make the belay system more efficient—but each one takes a lot of planning and engineering skill. Accordingly, make learning a Telfer Lower one of your Sunday projects. Get a copy of *The Whitewater Rescue Manual* or *River Rescue* and try to set up the system on an easy river with some friends. Better yet, take a course in swiftwater rescue from Rescue 3 (see the Appendix), where you'll learn all the nuances of the system. Then, when the right calamity presents itself (hopefully, *never*), you'll be able to set up the Telfer Lower quickly and efficiently.

Wraps

You've probably seen it happen in photos or bloopers videos: A raft broadsides a big rock, pauses, then glues itself to the boulder like Canadian bacon on a hot

In this example of a Telfer Lower, the raft can be moved back and forth across the river by shorebound crewmembers pulling on the ropes tied to the center carabiner. At the same time the rescuer in the raft releases some slack in the rope looped through the bottom carabiner to move downstream.

tailpipe. If you've lived through the experience your-self, it was undoubtedly an ordeal you'll never forget.

Wraps provide rafters with an exciting opportunity to apply a grab bag of rescue skills and ingenuity—or leave them tapping their booties together and chanting, "There's no place like home, there's no place like home . . . " The goal, however, is to figure out the best way to overcome the tons of water holding the raft securely in place, and that takes muscle, sturdy equipment, and a bit of streamside engineering.

FIRST THINGS FIRST

Survey the Situation. Some river runners look at wraps as an outstanding chance to whip out all their rescue paraphernalia, blanket the landscape in nylon ropes and metal implements, and set up intricate raft-retrieval systems. Although some wraps require just that type of action, it is usually more efficient to select the most basic system for retrieving the raft quickly and without any complication.

Before setting up any ropes, survey the scene. Which bank is the raft facing? What obstacles wait downstream once the raft is freed? How much of the raft is left showing? How accessible are anchor points on the raft and along the banks? Will the raft be easier to remove in one direction than another?

Appoint a Director. Next, appoint someone to direct the rescue operation. The director should be a member of the shore crew, unless the only one who knows how to unwrap the raft is still sitting in the middle of the river. By putting one person in charge, rescuers can work together as a team under the guidance of a skillful coach. Keep in mind that the rescue process set out below is flexible and should be tailored to meet the needs of your situation.

Find an Anchor. Start the rescue operation by securely attaching one end of a strong rope to the raft. (Don't use your throw-bag rope on a severe wrap unless that's all you have available. It could easily snap under stress and injure a rescuer.) If the raft is left in a precarious position after all its passengers have washed free, reaching it could be very difficult. Proceed with great caution and choose the approach that is lowest in risk. That might mean that you'll have to set up a horizon-tal line, a strong-swimmer rescue, or even a Telfer Lower to reach the boat. Once at the raft you may be able to stand on the obstacle holding it in place or sit on the exposed tube. If an anchor point is submerged, try to have an assistant hold on to the rigger to keep him from getting pinned or swept beneath the surface.

Some raft rescue systems develop a tremendous amount of force—more force than most D-rings and handles can withstand. Since these attachments have a tendency to blow free during raft rescues, consider other anchoring options. In self-bailing rafts, try tying your rope around an exposed tube by threading it through the floor's drain holes; in standard-floor rafts, ropes can be tied to thwarts or multiple D-rings; on oarboats, ropes can always be tied to the frame.

BASIC ROPE SYSTEMS

The Tug-of-War. The first way to pull a raft loose is simply to join your fellow rafters in a riverside version of tug-of-war. The tug-of-war creates only a 1:1 mechanical advantage but it can pull lightly wrapped rafts free.

Vector Pull. A variation on this is the vector pull: Rather than pulling on the end of the rope, tie the end to an anchor point and attach a second rope to the center of the first rope at a 90-degree angle. Depending on the direction in which the second rope is pulled, a slightly greater amount of power can be transferred to the raft.

The 2:1 System. To double the power of your pulling system, anchor a pulley or a couple of cara-biners to the raft and run the rope through them. Then, with one end of the rope tied to an anchor point on shore, you can pull on the loose end of the rope and create a 2:1 mechanical.1 advantage.

The Rollover Line. A rollover line can also be used to help tug a raft free. The rollover line runs over the top of the exposed tube and down around the back of the raft, and attaches to the submerged D-ring or thwart. When pulled from upstream, this rope helps the raft dump water. Sometimes enough water can be dumped out of the raft with just one rollover line to pull the raft free. Other times, the rollover line can be used

You can often avoid setting up technical rescue systems with a strong rope and
a lot of muscle power.

"We might be here a while. Let's send out for pizza!" (P.S.: This is a wrap.)

with one of the other rope systems mentioned in this chapter to lessen the pressure on the system.

Z-DRAGS

The Z-drag is one of the most popular raft rescue systems in use today, and for good reason: The basic Z-drag system generates a 3:1 mechanical advantage and more complex Z-drags give even greater leverage.

It takes little more than some strong rope to build a rudimentary Z-drag system, but carabiners and pulleys cut down on rope friction wherever the rope makes a turn. (If you don't have carabiners or pulleys, use a figure eight or butterfly knot in their place. These knots are shown in the Appendix.)

The first step in setting up the Z-drag is to anchor the rope to the raft's thwarts, frame, or D-rings just as you would for tug-of-wars and vector pulls. At the same time, tie a sturdy tubular webbing sling or rope around a shore-based anchor and clip a carabiner and a pulley (if they're available) into the loop. Next, tie a figure eight or butterfly knot in the rope between the raft and the anchor loop. Since this knot will

move toward shore when you start pulling on the rope, it is important to tie it close enough to the raft so that it won't jam into the shore anchor. (If you're standing on the shore far from the raft, you might want to tie the figure eight or butterfly knot *before* you anchor the rope to the raft.) If you have another carabiner and pulley handy, clip them into this knot.

Now it's time to complete the system. Take the rope's loose end, thread it through the shore anchor carabiner or pulley, slip it back through the figure eight or butterfly knot, and run it back to shore. If you've done this correctly, the system will form a backward Z, just like the one shown in the accompanying diagram. To operate the system, just pull the free end of the rope.

Some rescuers add a *brake prussik* (shown in the Appendix) to the shore anchor loop. The brake prussik lets rescuers rerig the system if a knot approaches the anchor loop, and stops the rope from traveling backward through the system. Also, additional lines to the raft can be used to ease the burden on the Z-drag.

Z-drags can be rigged in many ways. By adding a 2:1 pull to the system, the mechanical advantage grows to

6:1, and by doubling the Z-drag, the mechanical advantage grows to 9:1. If nothing works—even one of the high-advantage Z-drag systems—it may be time to relieve the resistance caused by the floor. In self-bailing rafts with laced-in floors, cut the floor line and let the floor flap open. This may make the raft much easier to pull free. In standard-floor rafts, cut a hole at the point of greatest pressure, but beware the consequence of doing this: The whole floor might tear out. Although tubes could arguably be deflated to assist in the rescue, this lets water enter the tubes, which eventually damages the raft. The deflated tubes are also more likely to conform to the obstacle and make the wrap even worse.

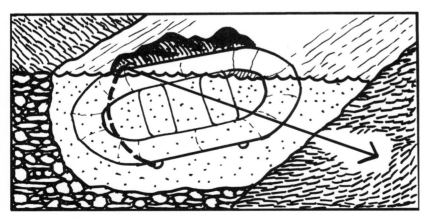

The three most basic ways to pull a raft free (from the weakest to the strongest) include the tug-of-war (A), the vector pull (B), and the 2:1 system (C). The tug-of-war generates no mechanical advantage. The vector pull can generate some mechanical advantage depending on the angle of pull. The 2:1 system, in which the rope runs from a shore anchor to the raft and back to shore, doubles your pulling power.

First Aid

As in any other form of outdoor recreation, rafters may be injured during a river trip. Fortunately, small cuts, bruises, and bouts with poison ivy are about the worst any first aid provider will see. In any event, it is important to be prepared for any type of first aid situation, from broken bones to near drownings.

Guides and private rafters alike should take the Red Cross basic first aid and CPR courses and should strive for higher levels of first aid certification. Rafters should know their physical limitations before embarking on a trip and should inform others of medical conditions that may affect patient care decisions. A first aid kit should accompany rafters on every trip. Especially on longer wilderness

The rollover line can be used alone or with other rescue systems to spill water from a pinned raft.

119

ventures, it is important not only to *have* all the items necessary to provide first aid, but to *know how to use* them effectively.

Hypothermia. The same water that provides a thrilling roller coaster ride for rafters can become a dangerous enemy for swimmers or underdressed passengers. Hypothermia—cooling of the body temperature—can happen whenever a swimmer is immersed in water for any length of time, or when cool air and spray drain the body's ability to stay warm. Hypothermia affects a rafter's judgment and can be life-threatening in its advanced stages, so it is important to take proper precautions and to know how to reverse the effects of hypothermia once it sets in.

Warm clothing, adequate food consumption, and constant activity provide the first line of defense against hypothermia, but one quick swim can drain even the hardiest rafter of internal warmth. If a rafter winds up in the river, get him out quickly. Water can drain body heat 20 to 30 times faster than air does, making even a short swim in very cold water dangerous.

It is important to know hypothermia's warning signs and how to treat victims once these signs are present. In the initial stages of hypothermia, victims may shiver vigorously, act cold, and appear pale. Treatment is easiest and most effective at this stage. Get the victim away from the river, into dry clothes, and near a source

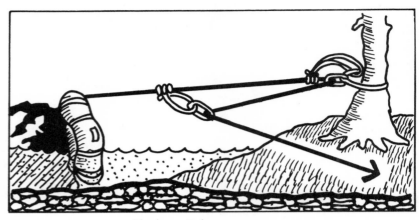

The basic Z-drag system.

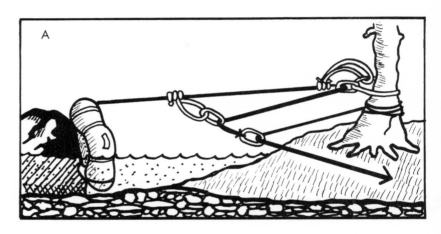

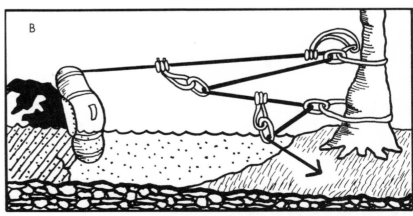

You can increase the mechanical advantage of a Z-drag to 6:1 by adding a second line (A) or to 9:1 by building in a second Z-drag (B).

of heat, such as in a warm car or by a campfire. If nothing is available, walk the victim along the bank until he warms up and stops shivering. Left untreated, the victim will progress to the next stage of hypothermia.

As the body's core temperature drops to 90 to 95 degrees Fahrenheit the victim may become confused, clumsy, and sluggish, and shivering may slow down. His speech may become slurred and his eyes dull. By the time these symptoms appear, the body has lost its ability to rewarm itself, and the basic treatment regimen won't work—an external source of heat is necessary. In a fix it may be necessary for a couple of people to climb into a sleeping bag with the victim and establish full-body skin-to-skin contact, letting their body warmth gently warm the victim. If a strong fire is available, seat the victim close to the heat with a backdrop of blankets or sleeping bags for insulation. Whatever is done, it must be done *before* the victim loses any more heat.

As the victim's core temperature drops further, his muscles will become rigid, he will become unconscious, and he may suffer a cardiac arrest. Immediate evacuation and hospitalization is mandatory in this situation.

10
ADVANCED RAFTING
RAFTING ON THE CUTTING EDGE

The phrase *Class V rafting* evokes a wild world of steep slides and menacing holes, barely penetrable boulder gardens and precipitous falls. Success and failure are often measured in terms of survival, and seemingly effortless descents border on artistry.

If you're an adrenaline junkie, Class V rivers can provide the ultimate test of your skills and mettle. Even if a Class V *river* isn't your cup of tea, an occasional Class V *rapid* will spice up your existence and keep you raving for months.

In this chapter we'll look at the methods and

mind-set necessary to raft difficult rivers. You'll discover specialized techniques for running everything from waterfalls and narrow chutes to giant waves. To the novice and intermediate rafter, a lot of these concepts will sound insane. After all, who in their right mind would *intentionally* slide a raft over rocks, drop off waterfalls, or surf holes in the middle of endless rapids? But for the advanced rafter these techniques not only exist—*they work!* If you're willing to step beyond conventional wisdom and use every part of the river to its fullest potential, you'll walk away with a broadened perspective of your raft's capabilities . . . and possibly your own.

Preparation

Class IV and V rivers present challenges rarely found on gentler streams. Whether these challenges manifest themselves as endless boulder labyrinths or minefields of boat-swallowing holes, the consequences of human miscalculations or equipment failure can be catastrophic. Accordingly, Class V rivers mandate that guides, passengers, rafts, and all supporting equipment be up to the rigors the river will present.

SKILLS AND CONDITIONING

Without the benefit of a professional guide, any rafters preparing to run a Class V river should already have two things going for them . . . the skills and confidence born of many hours on the river. These are not just skills well suited to a particular river or set of rapids, but skills that will translate well to any river situation: the ability to read and run confusing currents; full knowledge of the Z-drag and other rescue systems; the ability to quickly reright a raft; experience in swimming rapids; and an understanding of emergency medical procedures.

A Class V rapid is *not* the place to learn about advanced rafting. Instead, practice flipping and reflipping rafts in Class III rapids with safe pools. Swim Class II rapids, trying to catch eddies by swimming back and forth across the current. In a controlled setting, do everything that *could* happen in a Class V rapid and get good at fast rescues long before your first Class V adventure.

There's a fine line between tackling Class V whitewater and getting tackled yourself. If you want to stay in the game you've got to be in good physical condition. Being in shape will help your body withstand the stresses of powerful rapids. You'll have the strength to power swamped rafts around in pushy hydraulics, the ability to hold your breath during long swims, and the dexterity to leap to the high side when your raft collides with holes and boulders.

CHOICE OF RAFT

All sorts of high-quality rafts have been used on Class V rivers, but some rafts are better suited to extreme conditions than others. Self-bailing rafts and catarafts increase your level of safety during difficult descents by shedding water quickly and staying light and nimble in long rapids. Catarafts tend to stall less often in big holes, but they require much more hardware (frames) to operate. Self-bailing rafts can be paddled and can hold a lot of gear, but they aren't as agile as some catarafts. Rather than sweat over your options, choose the craft you are most comfortable operating and make sure it's ready for the river. When things get out of hand, this added confidence will give you just the edge you need.

There is also the question of whether to paddle or row. A lightly loaded self-bailing raft can easily be

Expert rafters can paddle some incredible rivers!
(Photo by Mike Doyle, courtesy of Beyond Limits Adventures)

123

portaged by a small team of strong paddlers and can even be deflated and carried through narrow ravines or tree-lined trails. When a frame is added to that same raft, portaging and lining become much more difficult. The frame will not only add weight during portages; it can snag rocks and branches and it will be more difficult to fit through narrow passages. Frames also add one more piece of equipment that can fail even if all else goes well. If you are catarafting, the frame is essential—but catarafts are usually lighter and less bulky than rafts to begin with.

Again, don't let my opinions shape your own! Only *you* know the rivers you'll be attempting, and only *you* know your own skills and preferences. Listen to your inner voice and you'll be much better off.

ACCESSORIES

Advanced rafters should surround themselves with top-quality equipment. Modern oars, paddles, helmets, lifejackets, throw bags, and rescue gear are designed to stand up to the rigors of the most demanding rapids and provide an enormous safety margin for intrepid river travelers. Still, rafters should check and recheck their gear for flaws. Carry spare equipment whenever possible in order to replace whatever breaks down, and bring enough rescue and first aid gear to meet or exceed the needs of any emergency situation.

STOWING GEAR

The combination of extra gear and raft-flipping rapids can be lethal. Catching a foot in a loose rope during a wrap might be all it takes to turn an adventure into a disaster. Pack gear as lightly and compactly as possible, remembering to leave safety gear readily accessible. Lash everything tightly to the raft where it won't interfere with the positioning or movement of rafters. (Remember that techniques like highsiding, beaching, and cross-bow draws require extra floor space.) Try to avoid carrying solid items—like ammo cans—in the passenger compartment. Soft-sided dry bags may work just as well and won't rearrange valuable body parts in the event of a collision.

THE CLASS V ATTITUDE

The definition of Class V rapids begins, "Extremely long, obstructed, or very violent rapids which expose a paddler to above average endangerment." Scary, huh? You bet! Try rowing a long Class V rapid—even after scouting it thoroughly—and you're likely to be on the edge of your seat until you're resting safely in a pool below.

Class V rapids take both a different mind-set and a different approach. First, don't focus on one or two objects in the river, such as a big rock or a wave. You'll end up getting tunnel vision and lose sight of everything going on around you. Open up your peripheral vision and expand your senses. Relax and take a couple of deep breaths above the rapid, and try to breathe normally once you're in whitewater. You'll have a much better feel for the rapid and you'll be able to react better if things go wrong.

Next, don't just sit on your butt and ride the raft

FEAR AND EXCITEMENT

There's a fine line between fear and excitement. Your perception of danger often depends on the crowd you're hanging with. Class III boaters with a few years of rafting behind them will have a much tougher time mustering up the courage to run a long Class IV boulder garden than Class V rafters accustomed to hairy situations. While one group is telling you about Billy Bob's butt-bruising swim back in '64, the other group will hustle you back in the raft to go run the rapid.

One of the best ways to pump your confidence level up a class or two is to join an outfitter on a Class V river trip. A skilled guide can get you through rapids you may have shied away from before, will practice the safety measures you'll need to know, and will show you what a raft can really do.

like a golf cart. Ski the rapids. Put more pressure on your legs and feet, and flex with the raft. If you're rowing, keep your butt barely on the seat so you'll be ready to highside in a flash. Do the same in a paddle raft so you can lunge into cross-bow draws or switch quickly from easy forward strokes to radical farback strokes.

It is important never to give up trying to navigate your raft upright through a rapid until it flips or wraps. If you're suddenly confronted by a big boulder or the largest hole of the day, it is often better to complete your maneuver than to look for a handhold. Your last-ditch effort might provide just enough momentum to bust through the hole or slip through the tight spot unscathed.

Finally, don't just run a Class V rapid in one mad dash—dissect it into bite-size portions. Rather than blasting downstream, use a zigzag approach. Jump from eddy to eddy, concentrating on each approaching eddy as you head downstream, then regrouping and reassessing your plan once you reach it. Use powerful ferries in the main channel to counteract the current and avoid turning broadside. This piecemeal approach to rapids will give you more control, more time to react, and more time to adapt your strategies to the demands of the river.

Rafting in the Third Dimension

HELPFUL HYDRAULICS

How many times have you stood above a rapid, shoulder to shoulder with fellow rafters, and said something like, "I'm going left of that hole, then right of the big boulder, then back to the center of those waves"? With minor variations, I've heard myself talk like that hundreds of times. The thought process of scouting rapids was always two-dimensional, locked into directions like upstream and downstream, left bank and right bank.

It was actually through kayaking that I discovered the missing link in my knowledge of rafting techniques . . . whitewater's *third dimension.*

Whitewater's third dimension is the river's vertical world, a world of steep waves, sharp holes, exposed rocks, and swelling boils. Up to now you have thought of many surface features as *obstacles*—things to be avoided or overcome—but now you can begin to think of them as natural *tools.* River features are tools that provide an extra link with gravity, friction, and hydraulic forces; they enhance your ability to outmaneuver a tough rapid and can make seemingly impossible rapids runnable.

WAVES

The same gravitational force that pulls a river downhill allows rafters to *surf* in place on a standard wave. When you pull your raft against the current on the upstream face of a wave—or in the trough between two waves—the raft will stall out dramatically. This is not only fun but a great way to buy some extra time to execute maneuvers.

The first time you use a wave to slow down, keep your raft parallel with the current. This will give you an extra second to make your next move. Once you get used to the feel of stalling on a wave, try turning your raft slightly to set a ferry angle, and then back-ferry. The wave will magnify the intensity and trajec-

It is much easier to turn on the crest of a wave than in the trough between waves.

tory of your ferry—in fact, by using medium-size waves (not those large enough to flip your raft) you can achieve some seemingly impossible ferries.

Waves can also act as *turntables,* making turns much easier. As your raft approaches the crest of a wave, the bow and stern become unweighted and for a split second the raft will spin more easily than it does in wave troughs. Start your turn high on the wave to save a lot of unnecessary effort—a turn started in the trough between two steep waves often produces nothing until the raft reaches a balancing point on the tip of the wave.

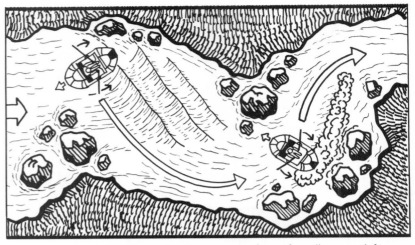

By surfing the upstream face of small waves (left) you can slow down or turn your raft and make some dynamic ferries. You can even surf small diagonal holes (right) to get where you want to go. Be prepared to highside at any moment, and don't surf big holes!

Once you get comfortable with wave moves, it will be easy to use them on other vertical features: large pillows, surging boils, and small breaking waves. Gravity acts as a maneuver turbocharger in all these situations. As long as you keep most of your crew's weight toward the downstream tube to avoid flipping broadside, you'll appreciate the usefulness of these hydraulics.

HOLES

Turn your angle of trajectory downward. Rather than slowing your ascent up the face of waves, control your rate of descent through holes and reversals. Since small holes rarely meet the textbook definition of a keeper (most provide an easy escape route at one end or the other) they can be surfed in place or cross-river just like waves. In fact, small holes sometimes present the only stopping point in the midst of a long rapid.

The concepts you just learned for wave surfing apply equally well—with some minor modifications—to hole surfing. As you approach a hole, look for the direction of its *kick*—the direction it will toss your raft as you plow into its backwash. If the hole angles downstream at one end, that's the direction it's going to kick you. Sometimes the hole will simply kick you toward the main outflow (the place where the most water exits the backwash). You can hit the hole and surf it toward the outflow, highsiding just enough to keep your boat upright. If highsiding won't be enough to keep you from swimming, *don't run the hole!*

V-HOLES

Take two holes or breaking waves and lay them midriver like a giant downstream

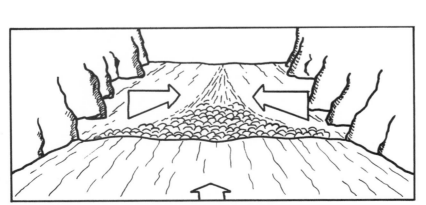

The hole's kick will help determine which way your raft is going to move. Enter this hole left and you'll move to the right. Drop in on the right and you'll move to the left.

V. Either side of the V can flush you toward a churning maelstrom known as a *maw*. Some maws are big enough to bite down on, chew up, and spit out rafts in varying states of disarray. Others are small enough for you to punch with momentum.

One way to survive the big, boat-eating maws—aside from walking around them—is to cut through the maelstrom to either side of the maw. Check out the accompanying diagram and see which route the raft takes. If you can make the diagonal move across the front of the maw and burst through the diagonal waves, go for it. Otherwise, get up a full head of steam and hit the maw as fast and hard as you

A big, powerful maw can form wherever two diagonal breaking waves meet. After scouting the rapid, decide whether it's best to hit the heart of the maw with lots of momentum or to angle to one side of it.

can. If the river gods aren't paying attention, you may sneak through unscathed.

EDDIES

You have already acquired the basic skills needed to enter and exit eddies. You have also learned that eddies house a variety of useful currents, some flowing upstream, some swirling downstream faster than the main current, and some sucking downward. Now you can expand your knowledge of eddies and tap into these currents for your own benefit.

It is possible to make some pretty dramatic stops and turns using eddies. Try entering an eddy high and deep with a lot of momentum. As you cross the eddy line, keep the downstream tube broadside to the eddy's upstream current and lean on it, staying

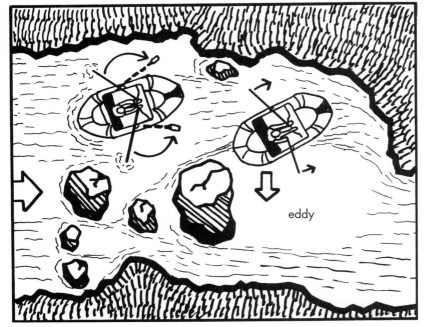

When it is impossible to set the proper angle to enter an eddy, try slowing your raft down ahead of time. If you are moving slow enough by the time you're next to the eddy, you can quickly pull across the eddy line.

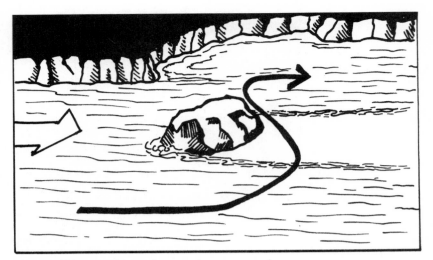

S-turns: Eddies can be used to accelerate your raft when you are ferrying across the river. Approach the eddy at a ferry angle and keep ferrying through the eddy. You will exit the far side with more upstream momentum than when you entered. (By linking eddies, you can actually use S-turns to climb upstream!)

greatly magnified by conveniently placed eddies. As the raft crosses the eddy, the eddy's upstream current will hurl the raft upstream against the main current faster than when it entered the eddy. The turbocharged effect of the transition from one side of the eddy to the other and back into the main current is very exciting, and can make some big, powerful moves possible. Try practicing it in a familiar rapid until you can get the raft to make S-turns back and forth across the river.

Boulders and Slots

BOULDERS

Early in my rafting career I treated solid obstacles as enemies—the nemeses of ill-fated rafters. I respected and avoided rocks and boulders, and portaged rapids I considered too boulder-choked to run. It took a bona fide Class V rafting adventure to change my perspective of these notorious river features.

In some instances shallow rocks and boulders provide midriver brakes when there are no eddies to be found. By running the raft onto partially submerged boulders (pay attention to your high side and don't pivot sideways), you can drag the raft to a halt, then spin off the boulder to continue downstream. Even if you don't want to stop completely, you can use the boulder to help make quick turns. This can be a real boon in the middle of a long Class V rapid. Also, shallow, wet boulders might provide the only feasible route through an otherwise impossible rapid. If the main channel is hopelessly boulder-choked, it would be senseless to try to raft it. On the other hand, wet boulders can be *boofed* with some momentum. In boofing, stiff, slick-bottomed rafts are paddled or rowed full speed across the tops of wet boulders and into the safety of the eddies below.

low in the raft so you don't fall out as the downstream tube dives downward. The raft will come to a gut-wrenching halt. If you're peeling out of an eddy, try leaning over the downstream tube—the raft will snap around faster as it crosses the eddy line.

In well-protected eddies, slamming across the eddy line into the upstream current might be impossible. An example of an elusive eddy is one that has many nearby boulders that prevent rafters from turning the raft at a ferry angle. If the raft can't be turned 45 or 90 degrees to the current, a fast and powerful entry technique is required.

An oar boat can frequently muster the energy to enter these types of eddies by backrowing early, then pulling into the eddy at the last possible second. A paddle raft, on the other hand, has to coordinate many paddlers to overcome its inertia. They too can start slowing the raft down ahead of time with forward or back ferries, then ferry the slowed raft into the eddy at the last moment.

Eddies can also be used to slingshot rafts cross river, or to spin the raft 180 degrees. A raft that begins ferrying in the main current will find its lateral momentum

This paddle team is negotiating a difficult rapid. To make it through the first narrow slot, the team has to lean to one side of the raft (lowside). Next, the team boofs over a shallow ledge.

LOWSIDING

Lowsiding is just the opposite of highsiding. While highsiding throws your body weight against an obstacle to keep a raft from wrapping, lowsiding throws your weight away from an obstacle to get you through tight squeezes. In the accompanying diagram, the raft is too wide to fit through a narrow chute. However, when the crew is seated on one side of the raft, the other tube rides up out of the water and slides over the obstacle.

On some rivers the only way to run narrow chutes may be to let some air out of the thwarts. Without the rigidity of fully inflated thwarts to keep the tubes their normal distance apart, the raft can flex inward and run narrower slots than would otherwise be possible. Of course, the tradeoff for this technique is a more flexible raft that might be harder to control.

Waterfalls and Steep Drops

Though I've hammered rafts over scores of waterfalls, I've yet to figure out a way to suppress the butterflies I get when I gaze out over a thundering, foam-spewing horizon line. In fact, often the only thing that has stood between me and predrop hysteria was the right choice of runnable waterfall and the techniques described here. My past choices haven't stopped me

from being munched by a couple of big drops, but they have increased my confidence in my raft and gotten me through a couple of close calls.

IRREGULAR LEDGES

Let's start the vertical ballgame easy. It's crazy to plunge over 15-foot waterfalls before you've got a handle on more manageable ledges. Ledges contain the same currents as their taller brethren and they provide a perfect place to learn how your raft handles when the river drops out from under it.

L-Shaped Ledges. L-shaped ledges often contain currents that overlap one another. Rafters call these *folded flows*. The indented seam that forms between the currents can inhale rafts and stuff them into some unfriendly hydraulics. Usually, the best way to avoid a wild ride is to stay on the top flow and to let the hole kick you to safety (see the diagram on page 130). If you have to stay on the bottom flow, steer clear of the top flow as best you can and paddle hard when you hit the hole!

V-Drops. Ledges can also take on a V shape (hence the name *V-drop*) such that part of the falls juts downstream like a big liquid gangplank. If the currents aren't too confused, and the gangplank is wide enough to hold your raft, you can get up a head of steam and ski jump right off the tip of the V. If the V points back into the ledge—forming an *upstream V*—some nasty

Irregular ledges contain some tricky pitfalls for unwary rafters. Here's the recommended route for running an L-shaped ledge (top), a downstream V-drop (center), and an upstream V-drop (bottom).

hydraulics can stack up in the notch, just like they do in L-shaped ledges. Avoid them by jumping the ledges to either side of the V.

Twisting Drops. Twisting drops can challenge your ability to stay upright if they're big, steep, and fast. Frequently, swollen pillows, funky reaction waves, and plunging currents will stack up against the outside walls of the drop. If you highside into them you may be able to stay upright. Sit on the low side of the raft and you'll be in next season's bloopers videos.

WATERFALLS

If you have managed to survive your ledge drops with all limbs—and sense of humor—intact, you're ready for the next step upward. You're ready for waterfalls.

Scouting. The first key to running waterfalls successfully is knowing which falls *not* to run. Check out the face of the falls. How far does it drop? Does the falls pour freely off a ledge or slide downward at an angle? Are there rocks in the falls that are going to throw the raft off course before it even hits bottom? A tall free-falling waterfall might flip your raft end over end, while a slanted falls might just feel like a high-intensity carnival ride.

Next, check out the hole at the base of the falls. Is it free of boulders and debris? Will the raft have enough momentum to break through the backwash, or

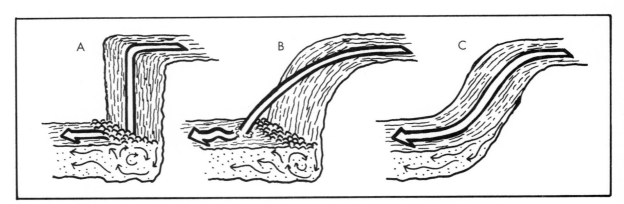

Three types of waterfalls: Waterfall A drops steeply over a ledge. If the falls is tall enough, the raft will flip. Waterfall B forms a rounded dome. Unless the falls is tall, the raft will kick outward and away from the waterfall instead of penciling straight down into the hole. Waterfall C is a slide. If there isn't a keeper hole at its base or sharp rocks in the face of the falls the slide may be runnable. (Note: Rafts usually flip in big falls.)

Doc Loomis and David Sacquety prepare to take a 30-foot plunge—one of the tallest vertical drops ever rafted! (Note: This shot is for entertainment purposes only!)
(photo by Joe Wilkins)

SCOUTING CLASS V RAPIDS

There's a lot more to scouting long, difficult Class V rapids than just linking together the best routes. Yeah, you need to look for clean, safe lines. But you also need to ask yourself: (1) Where's the most likely spot for a flip? (2) Can I swim this rapid? and (3) Which direction am I going to swim to save myself? If you answer "I don't know" or "No" to any of these questions, *portage!*

will the river be too powerful? What if you're swimming? Can you break free of the hole or will it be a keeper? Judge all these features carefully before you decide to run any waterfall, and always have a rescue team set up in case anything goes wrong.

Planning. Descending a waterfall is easy—sometimes you just hunker down and hold on. Knowing where to enter the drop can be the real challenge.

Ask yourself how you're going to know where to enter the falls. After all, you're going to see nothing but a big horizon line from your raft. Pick distinctive landmarks along the bank that will help point out your line ("I'll enter 10 feet left of that big boulder"). Other useful signposts are obvious hydraulic features ("We'll nick the right of that hole with our left tube, then drop over the falls") and tall downstream landmarks ("Paddle straight toward the tree").

No matter what you use to point your way, make sure you can see it from upstream or it won't do you any good! Walk upstream and look back down at the falls from a distance. Is your landmark still visible? If not, pick another one.

If you're about to run a large waterfall, figure out when the best time is to switch from maneuvering to holding on. Keep in mind that the strongest of grips won't do you any good if you quit paddling 20 yards above the lip of a waterfall, plop over it sideways, and flip in the hole. Figure out the last place

you can take a power stroke and, if you can, keep adjusting your raft's direction right up to the lip of the falls. If you're the paddle captain, get your crew down inside the raft a second or so before you reach the lip and steer the raft until the last possible moment. Also, make sure your handhold is easily accessible—it'll be much harder to find with your heart in your throat!

If you have a heavy crew, consider leaving some paddlers ashore. Smaller crews can unload passengers or gear from the bow compartment to help the bow snap up and away from the falls quickly.

Taking the Plunge. After you've tightly lashed down any loose gear and set out on the main current, begin visualizing the falls. Build up as much speed as possible to launch the raft out over the lip of the falls (this is called *ski jumping* or *airplane jumping*) and line the raft up so it drops down the falls towards the safest

Paddle as fast as you can over waterfalls so that the bow blasts through the hole. This is called ski jumping.

landing. This might require a straight descent in some falls, a diagonal descent in others.

Oar Rafts. Oar rafts are particularly dangerous in large waterfalls. Rafts flex and torque as they dive over the lip of a sharp drop, and they stop violently at the base. All this energy is transferred into the only mobile objects in the raft—passengers and oars. In response to this, rowers have developed two techniques. The first is to let go of the oars and hold onto the frame like a frightened barnacle. It

Rowing waterfalls: (1) Lean back and hold onto the oars; (2) balance on the seat and prepare for a jolt! It takes experience to avoid falling out of your seat! (By the way, always wear a helmet!)

Paddling waterfalls is tricky business—only run those that you know are safe. One way to run falls is to sit low in the raft (in self-bailers only), press your shins against a tube or thwart, and hold your paddles outside the passenger compartment. Hang on!
(Photo by John Hall/AAA Rafting)

works for keeping you on the raft, but subjects you and your passengers to the whims of wildly swinging oars—hence the development of technique number two.

In the second technique, the rower plants both feet firmly on the frame's footbar and leans as far back as possible. The oars are shipped with their handles facing the stern, and the rower's ability to anticipate the raft's gyrations gives him the balance to stay aboard. If there is a chance of getting tossed forward or losing an oar, try grasping the handles and frame together in each hand and hold on! Overall, the key to success is keeping your butt just off the seat so that it doesn't snap upward and catapult you overboard.

Paddle Rafts. Paddlers have the same concerns that rowers have—flying bodies and equipment—except that in paddle rafts, flying paddles replace flying oars. To minimize these hazards, paddlers should sit low in the raft, hold their paddles outside the raft, and grip handholds or grabloops with their inside hands. In self-bailing rafts, paddlers can sit right on the floor with their shins pressed against the thwarts to prevent them from sliding under the thwarts. Paddlers in standard-floor rafts have to sit higher off the floor or risk injury to their lower backs.

Dealing with Irregular Falls. Mother Nature, in her infinite wisdom, rarely makes two falls alike. The picture-perfect waterfall is seldom found beyond the cement walls of oversized city fountains. Accordingly, rafters have to learn how to deal with every waterfall configuration imaginable.

Waterfalls often take on the same L and V shapes as smaller ledges; you can look for runnable routes just as you've learned to do with ledges. However, waterfalls can also cascade over giant staircases, creating new hazards and concerns. A *staircase falls* bounces like a souped-up slinky down irregular ledges containing holes, pillows, boils, and weird cross-currents. If each ledge is small enough, you may be able to career right down the middle of the falls. But if the ledges are more widely spaced, you may be dealing with one potential keeper after another. As with any falls, scout it long and hard before you decide to run it.

Low- and High-Water Techniques

LOW-WATER TRIPS

Low-water trips demand a special style of river running—one that won't leave you high and dry on a gravel bar trying to bribe fishermen to help you out of the canyon. Rivers change at low water—the river moves more slowly and has less push, there are more obstacles to avoid, and there may be many shallow channels to select from. Slow currents decrease the possibility of a wrap but the constant maneuvering they require might drive you crazy.

There are many ways to make low-water rafting enjoyable. Start by picking a river that actually has enough water to float your raft, not one that is bone dry. Even if you are forced to line or portage a few rapids, pool-drop rivers are more fun at low water than rivers with continuous gradients because the pools between drops hold water. Low-water trips are also easier when you use small, sturdy rafts that will fit through tight slots and are easy to pull over shallow

bars. Finally, think about your feet. Sooner or later you'll ground out and have to pull your raft free. A solid pair of tennis shoes or hiking boots worn over neoprene socks will save your feet from the inevitable bashing of slippery rocks and hidden potholes.

When running rivers at low water your primary goal is to spot and stay in the deepest channels. Here are a few hints that will make your task easier:

1. Look for slick surfaces or long, even waves among smaller, choppier waves. These features reveal deeper channels.
2. Use the deep eddies behind big boulders to make cross-river maneuvers around shallow shoals. When a shallow bar is impossible to avoid, build up some momentum to help you slide over it into deeper water.
3. Lowside to lessen the amount of floor actually touching the water. The unweighting of one tube might be just enough to get the raft through a narrow slot.
4. Don't be afraid to spin or pivot your raft to and fro. Since the raft will inevitably snag rocks and shallow obstacles, pivots might get your raft off the rock before you have to jump out and pull it free.

HIGH-WATER TRIPS

When rivers bloat and swell after heavy rains or big snowmelts, they can become downright cantankerous. Currents speed up and eddies disappear. Holes become deeper and waves surge higher. It takes a dedicated crew with level heads (figuratively speaking, of course—my friends have round heads just like yours!) and strong river skills to match wits against big, powerful currents.

High-water runs demand some additional safety precautions. You need to plan for *every* contingency, but here are a few points to consider:

1. Every passenger should be a good swimmer and experienced in self-rescue, and there should always be rafts close by to help out in rescue situations.
2. It is safer to run rivers with nearby roads and easy evacuation routes in case the river turns out to be too dangerous.
3. Rafts should be big enough to survive the river's

hydraulics—the same raft that works late in the summer might feel like a helpless cork during the peak of spring runoff.

4. Rig fliplines onto the D-rings and install handholds inside the passenger compartment. Additional fliplines can be run under the raft and cinched tightly to the D-rings.

5. Consider using longer, more powerful oars on oar boats, and be sure you have enough paddlers to power a paddle raft.

6. Run the river more conservatively than you would under normal conditions.

When hitting big diagonal waves, get your mind off the main current for a second and drive straight through the wave. Here the left route drives perpendicularly through the wave and works out fine. The right route stays with the main current and results in a flip.

On the river, the techniques used during high water are the same as those used for any river trip, only more exact. Keep paddles and oars moving to keep your senses well tuned to the river's moods; keep the bow pointed squarely at waves and holes, not necessarily square with the current; keep standard-floor rafts bailed; and portegee or paddle hard through waves and holes to avoid stalling out in their troughs. If you find yourself on a collision course with a mighty hydraulic, maintain your momentum and hit it straight on. Also, don't try to pull off dramatic ferries in front of big haystacks or holes—you're likely to drift broadside into the hydraulics and flip.

High-water rafters need to know when to quit paddling, jump for the far tube, and highside like mad. You are much more likely to spend time highsiding

Big water excitement!

in gaping holes during high-water runs than you are during ordinary trips, so your ability to recognize the need for body-weight shifts will really help out.

Another difference between high- and low-water rivers involves scouting. During high water, rocks and shoreline landmarks might be invisible or moving too fast to be of much help. However, individual features like holes and waves become more significant and can provide signposts that are as effective as riverside landmarks.

No matter what you do, *avoid rivers at flood stage!* Flooded rivers are unpredictable and dangerous. Powerful downcurrents can hold you under for dangerous periods of time, and tree-lined banks can pose a serious threat to swimmers attempting to escape the river's grasp. If the river has water in it now, it will have water in it another day. But if you run it now, you might not be around to run it another day!

It's good to know what's over the next horizon line!

A Quick Course in Steep Creeking

READING THE HORIZON

When I first started rafting I scouted *everything!* I didn't care whether it was Class II or Class IV, I wanted to see exactly what I was getting myself into, and which way I was going to go once I was in it. Later on, as my river-reading skills developed, I spent less time on the bank and more time in my raft. Piloting a raft through Class II and III rapids became as familiar as piloting my feet along rocky forest trails. But Class IV and V drops still kept me ferrying toward the bank.

While shoreline scouting is the best way to go in *any* rapid, it isn't always possible. In fact, on some really high-gradient, steep-walled rivers, bank scouting

might be plum out of the question. In that case a whole new set of river-reading skills has to come into play—skills that will let you read blind drops without actually seeing what's going on up close.

One of the best examples of reading a blind drop is the perfect horizon line. There is nothing above the drop to hint of a safe passage route, but downstream of the drop there is a clear line of standing waves. As you learned in the Chapter 5, these waves usually show up wherever the current flows clear and unobstructed. If you had to place a bet on where to run the drop, the best bet would be to head straight for that part of the drop that leads into the waves. Check out the accompanying diagram and try to match it with a drop you've seen before. Still scout whenever possible, but keep these ideas in mind for the time they're really needed.

SLOWING YOUR DESCENT

In some parts of the world, rafters are descending creeks with gradients exceeding 300 feet per mile. That can add up to back-to-back waterfalls, long, tumbling ledge drops, and tough-to-catch eddies. If you're not paying attention, you can fly down a drop

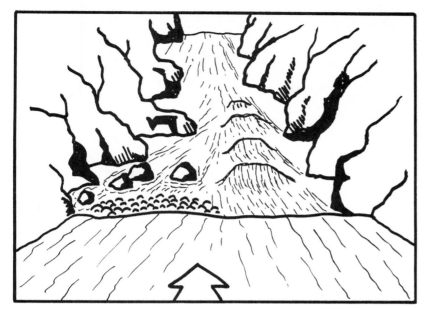

There may be times when you are forced to run a rapid that you can't scout. Look for clues—like the clean set of standing waves on the right side of the river—to mark the best point to approach the horizon line, and be prepared to alter your course quickly.

or two and disappear over an unrunnable falls before you know what's happening. That's where some specialized techniques come into play.

There's no set way to run ledges and falls. You don't *always* have to airplane jump straight downstream or paddle full speed ahead. Kayakers long ago discovered that you can paddle diagonally off a ledge, fly across the top of a hole, and land in the safety of an eddy. Although rafters have a tougher time making this maneuver work, there are times when it will keep you from slipping downstream farther than you want to go.

Another trick pulled from the kayaker's repertoire is using the hole's kick to propel you toward an eddy. If you control your rate of descent off a steep ledge with some well-timed backstrokes, you can let the hole stall and toss your raft in the direction of a safe eddy. The key to this stunt is picking holes that won't flip you.

If a straight descent down a big drop requires you to hunker down and hold on, you can at least have your paddle ready to throw in backstrokes the second the raft hits the hole. It's usually the impact with the hole

that throws you out of the boat; paddling is what can save you.

Again, there's no set formula for running every rapid. You've got to tailor your techniques to the river you're running.

R-2ing

Rafting with just two paddlers in a small raft—known as paddling R-2 *style* or *R-2ing*—is an exciting and challenging way to run rivers. The technique excels in small, steep creeks, but works well anywhere when used by skilled paddlers. When R-2ing, both paddlers must act together to accomplish moves. This can take a sixth sense, a keen knowledge of your partner's paddling traits, or just strong communication. On bigger, more powerful runs, a well-honed sense of balance also helps.

Technically, there are three ways to paddle R-2 style: side by side in the central compartment; end to end in the bow and stern; or diagonally in the bow and stern. However, with the advent of small rafts specially suited to the demands of R-2 paddlers, the diagonal formation (sitting as you would in a tandem canoe) is becoming the most popular seating configuration.

In the first R-2 formation, paddlers sit side by side in the central passenger compartment. This puts the pivot point in the center of the raft and makes both turning and power strokes easier.

The second R-2 technique—developed by rafters to meet the special demands of narrow, technical rivers—is sometimes called *sweep boating*. In sweep boating, the paddlers sit in the bow and stern and paddle over the ends of the raft. Specially mounted footcups—mounted sideways in tandem in the bow and stern compartments—keep the paddlers aboard. The sweep boat formation narrows the raft's profile considerably and distributes the paddlers' weight more evenly along the raft's long axis. This lets the raft slip

HAVE YOU DRIVEN AN R-2 LATELY?

It's almost inevitable. In our whitewater schools, we'll introduce rafters to every kind of inflatable river boat imaginable: big oar rafts, paddle boats, catarafts . . . the works. But in the end the odds-on favorite to win our students' hearts is the R-2. And for good reason: This sporty little raft is as irresistible as a sleek MG or a Jeep with the top down.

The explanation for the R-2's appeal is more than its high performance. True, the R-2's speed and agility are real crowd-pleasers. It can turn faster, catch tighter eddies, slide through narrower slots, handle lower flows, and even run smaller rivers that its heavier cousins.

But just as important, the R-2's logistics make life a whole lot easier. Small R-2s are lightweight, they inflate quickly, and they don't require a frame. This makes putting in and taking out easier than ever. Plus, you only have to find one other person to paddle an R-2. Basically, you get a taste of the simplicity that kayakers and canoers have long enjoyed.

Another key to the R-2's immense popularity is its low price. Pint-size R-2s require less material and hardware, which can put the price range barely above top-of-the-line canoes and kayaks.

Given the R-2's high performance, easy logistics, and low price, it is hard to beat for steep creeking, running small rivers, and making low-volume descents. These boats are just plain fun to drive!

—Bill Cross, coauthor, *Western Whitewater;* owner, Running Wild Whitewater School

over wet rocks and slink down incredibly steep and narrow rivers.

To maneuver the R-2 from the sweep position, the bow paddler lines the bow up into narrow slots and the stern paddler keeps the boat straight. Once in a steep drop, the stern paddler may discover a drawback of sitting in the stern—it is a veritable catapult. To avoid getting launched forward in steep drops, the stern paddler has to get low or the paddlers have to switch to the side-by-side formation.

In the final R-2 configuration, the paddlers sit in the bow and stern but paddle over the side tubes the same way two canoers would paddle a tandem canoe. This method regains the forward and back paddling power found in the side-by-side configuration and gives paddlers a more stable seating position.

An R-2 (two-person raft) can negotiate tight channels with ease.

11

SINGLE-DAY TO MULTIDAY TRIPS
CARRYING YOUR TOYS

Rafts provide the ultimate form of wilderness travel for those wishing to explore the outdoors without sacrificing their dependence on luxuries. Despite rafting's *float-and-bloat* reputation, it maintains its dignity; even the most brazen river explorers need rafts to carry passengers and gear down the world's great rivers.

Knowing how to load and safely take advantage of a raft's cargo-carrying capabilities is a skill that must be learned. In some ways, loading a raft with gear—whether for a one-day jaunt or a three-week expedition—is truly an art form. On multiday trips there may be sleeping bags, tents, kitchen equipment, portable potties, food, water, first aid boxes, and a plethora of other equipment crammed into one boat. Keeping all this gear dry and damage free takes some preliminary planning and some technical know-how.

Planning Ahead

Long before you start your raft trip, consider what you'll need to bring. Will you be on the river one day or five days? Will a few pairs of shorts and T-shirts constitute your entire wardrobe or will you need lots of clothing to stay warm? Do you plan to take small, easily prepared freeze-dried meals, or do you prefer to cook exotic riverside feasts? No matter how long a trip you plan, or what type of conditions you expect to encounter, the mere fact that you'll be *rafting* will change the type of food and equipment you'll have to carry.

Let's start with two simple assumptions. They may not always be correct, but working around them will make your river life much happier:

1. No matter how well you pack, the river is going to work its way into your gear cache, and even the best-packed gear is going to get jostled and bounced repeatedly.
2. The more gear you carry with you, the heavier and less maneuverable your raft will become.

Waterproof Containers

OK. *I lied.* Even though improperly packed gear is destined for a soaking, a number of modern technological wonders have made rafting drier and more enjoyable than ever. You really *can* keep your gear dry on the river.

In days gone by, rafters tried to keep the river out of their gear by packing it into sealed tins or by stuffing everything from riverwear to bagels into plastic trash bags, tying the bags closed, and avoiding waves. Nowadays rafters can choose from a long list of items specially designed to keep their gear dry and safe.

DRY BAGS

Dry bags are durable, specially designed waterproof sacks. When properly sealed—usually with foldover or zip-lock closures— dry bags usually keep their contents totally dry. Items that must stay absolutely dry can

be sealed in small plastic trash bags *before* they are inserted into dry bags. Smaller items can be separated into sandwich- and freezer-size Zip-lock bags before they go into dry bags. Not only will this help keep small things dry, but it will also make finding them in camp much easier.

AMMO CANS AND DRY BOXES

Some items—such as loaves of bread, patch kits, and camera gear—need to be stored in hard-sided dry boxes so they won't get smashed or tear their way through the soft sides of dry bags. Inexpensive army-surplus ammunition, or ammo, cans perform this function quite well. Durable O-ring seals render them totally waterproof, and they are available in a variety of sizes. Their only drawback is their sharp, square corners, which can easily injure passengers in the event of a collision. To avoid injuries, glue neoprene or foam to the outside of ammo cans or invest in high-quality plastic waterproof boxes such as Pelican Boxes. Dry boxes are frequently lighter than ammo cans, are available in a broader range of sizes and shapes, and often have precut foam inserts that can be customized to protect your valuables. The tradeoff for all of this is, of course, the added cost.

Dry bags are used to carry clothes, sleeping bags, personal items—anything that needs to stay dry. When properly sealed, they are waterproof.

Stowing Gear Safely

Veteran rafters take great pride in their ability to pack a raft. They can take piles of oddly shaped items and fit them neatly inside the raft like so many pieces of a puzzle. Some of you might be wondering why you can't just throw gear aboard and run a mile of rope around it. The answer is: Some day you're gonna flip. That's right! Sooner or later all the gear standing high *above* the tubes will be hanging far *below* the tubes as your upside-down raft floats downriver. And the longer it hangs there, the more likely you are to lose it. So rig that raft as if it's actually going to flip, and keep in mind some standard principles:

1. Keep the raft's center of gravity low: Lash all gear down with a low profile, and keep heavier items lower in the raft.
2. Keep the raft balanced: Store heavier gear toward the center of the raft and lighter items toward the ends.
3. Leave open spaces: Allow room for passengers' legs and room to bail. If you are rowing, make sure you have room to ship your oars and to lean backward during your strokes.
4. Protect your gear and your raft: Rather than laying gear directly on the floor—which can result in broken and torn equipment—use a suspended cargo platform to support everything. Also, keep hard-sided and sharp-cornered items away from the flight paths of bouncing passengers, tubes, and floors. These can do a lot of damage when the raft is ricocheting through wild rapids! (If you are packing light gear into a self-bailer, you may be able to load some gear directly onto the floor.)
5. Organize your gear for efficiency: Put commonly used items toward the top of the pile and rarely used items toward the bottom.

Fragile gear and food, such as cameras and bread, can be stored in waterproof ammo cans and dry boxes. O-ring seals around the inside of the lid keep water out when the box is clamped shut.

Label dry bags and containers with duct tape and waterproof magic markers to remind you where everything is.

6. Lash everything down tight: Make sure every item is securely fastened to the raft, whether encased in cargo nets or tarps, or merely tied down with ropes or straps. Buckled webbing works great for this purpose since it is available in many lengths and can be cinched tight without special knots. Use the best anchor points available. On a self-bailing raft, gear can be strapped to D-rings, floor drain holes, and even foot cups; on standard-floor rafts the D-rings and thwarts provide the main anchor points. On any oarboat, the rowing frame provides a great anchor for lashing down gear.
7. Don't overload your raft! If you don't really need an item, consider leaving it at home.

Rafts can carry everything but the kitchen sink. Although this raft is carrying a ton of gear, it is evenly loaded and remains maneuverable.

12
RIVER CAMPING AND COOKERY
LIFE AT THE RIVERSIDE INN

Camping and rafting make great travel companions. In fact, some of my less-adventurous friends have gone so far as to say that the river is little more than a hassle between campsites—a liquid highway to be traveled before the next park. Although few rafters see river running as a hassle, many would agree that camping is a ton of fun.

Riverside camping has a special air about it. There are no RVs parked in the next space, no pop machines or laundromats nearby, and, if you're lucky, no humans for miles around. Everything in camp was put there by Mother Nature or floated there in your raft. But that doesn't mean river camping demands a Spartan existence.

Rafts can carry hundreds, sometimes thousands, of pounds of new gear. If you want to be comfortable, pile on lounge chairs, lanterns, thick ground pads, spacious tents, and the rest of your toys. Sure, river camping can be as simple an experience as dropping your sleeping bag out under the stars, but it can also be as luxurious as playing guitars and drinking exotic concoctions whipped up in a battery-powered blender. The choice is yours.

Clothing and Camping Equipment

In Chapter 3 you learned a lot about river-wear: dry-suits, wetsuits, paddling jackets, booties. While that stuff works wonders on the river, there is nothing so delightful as slipping into warm, dry clothes at the end of the day.

On overnight camping trips, keeping items like clothing, tents, and sleeping bags totally dry can be a challenge; water-absorbent items like cotton shirts, canvas tents, and down sleeping bags invite long, damp nights in camp. Polyester and nylon fleece clothing works as well in camp as it does under your drysuit—it dries quickly and will keep you warm even when wet. A synthetic sleeping bag—filled with Hollofill, Quallofill, Polar-gaurd, or another space-age insulator—also works well even when damp.

Whatever you decide to take on your trip, keep in mind that you'll need to pack clothes and sleeping bags into dry bags. Don't carry personal items too large to stuff into a dry bag, and don't show up at the put-in with so much gear that you'll have to compromise your comfort by leaving some at home.

Campsite Selection

Some canyons offer a wide variety of terrain and campsites, while others contain few if any hospitable camping niches. It is best to find out about campsites before undertaking a raft trip. Peruse the local guidebooks for camping opportunities, or ask some friends who have run the river what to expect. If the river is unexplored, check topographic maps for broad valleys that may offer level, comfortable sites. There may even be a government agency that preassigns designated campsites to river travelers. If you are able to find out about campsites ahead of time, try to preselect sites that fit your travel plans. If the trip is two days long, pick a site midway so that both river days are enjoyable.

Whether or not you've learned about campsites before leaving the put-in, make sure that you're looking for a feasible site in daylight. There is nothing more petrifying, disheartening, or dangerous than traveling downriver after dusk! If the riverbank offers many ideal settings, you're in luck. You can choose campsites that will be sunny early in the morning or late in the day; campsites that slope gently into the water or involve a short hike away from the river; and campsites that offer shade or unobstructed vistas.

WIND AND WATER

One thing you certainly don't want is a riverside campsite that might disappear if the river comes up! If there is any chance that the river will rise—whether from heavy runoff or dam releases—pick a site high above the waterline that offers easy escape even in the dark of night. Unload small rafts in the evening and carry the gear and rafts up onto the shore. Tie the rafts off securely to solid anchors such as large trees or boulders and leave some slack in the line just in case the river gets too high. If you've prepared for a rising river, you'll only need to check your raft and gear occasionally as the river rises through the night. And even if the water comes up a few feet, you can spend the remainder of the night resting peacefully as the river roars many yards away.

There's one other thing to think about when you make camp for the evening: wind. If you've spread your paddle jackets, drysuits, T-shirts, and hats all over the rocks to dry out, they might not be where you left them come morning. Canyons have a way of focusing and amplifying local air currents, especially late in the afternoon. Make sure you secure all your belongings each time you *make* camp so that you'll still have them each time you *break* camp.

THE RIPARIAN ENVIRONMENT

Conscientious rafters strive to minimize their impact on the riparian environment. Thick, grassy banks or beaches lined with delicate shrubs are especially susceptible to human harm. On the other hand, broad sandy beaches and pebble-strewn bars can camouflage and erase your presence soon after your group leaves. Pick a site that has been used many times before or one that won't record your presence, and treat it with respect.

One trick to preserving the habitat is to use nothing but freestanding gear. Utilize tents that don't have to be staked out and kitchen tables that can be set up without the use of rocks or logs.

Campfires

One of the great joys of camping is sitting around the campfire. Campfires are soothing, enchanting, hypnotic. They also provide a valuable source of heat on cold trips and can be used for cooking if necessary. Still, campfires can leave unsightly scars on the landscape. In today's world it is probably best to save the campfire for designated campgrounds, to use gas-powered stoves for cooking, and to savor the warmth of friendship and the great outdoors rather than relying on a fire for that warmth.

FIREPANS

If you must have a fire, you can minimize its effect on the surrounding ground by using a fire pan. The fire pan is a large metal pan with high sides specially designed to accommodate small logs or charcoal briquettes. Place the pan on the shoreline below the high-water mark so that burn marks from stray coals will disappear with the next freshet. Fill the bottom of the fire pan with a thin layer of dirt or sand before adding firewood to avoid burning through the pan, and set it on rocks to avoid scorching the ground. You are now ready to enjoy a great fire.

Check the pan in the morning to make sure that the coals have totally cooled, then sprinkle the coals with water and shovel them into an ammo can so you can pack them out. The ashes can be used at the next camp to line the bottom of the pan and they will shrink each time they are reburned. Eventually the ashes will be little more than light dust, making it easier to pack them out.

Some camping gear can lessen your impact on the environment. Shown here are a roll-up table, portable chairs, a firepan (to free you from building a fire on the ground), briquette starter, and Dutch ovens. Many rafters use only gas-powered stoves since any kind of campfire can break free or scar the background.

CAMPFIRE CLEANUP

Fires built without pans are more difficult to clean up, and it takes a little more forethought to hide their marks. First, place the fire as you would one in a fire pan—below the high-water mark. Next, use rocks that will be easy to toss into the river channel the next morning. Don't build the fire near immovable boulders or trees that will bear blackened scars for many years to come. Finally, build the smallest fire practicable so that you won't have half-burnt logs lying around camp the next day. When the morning comes, douse the ashes with water and dismantle the site. Spend some extra time restoring the ground to its original condition . . . or better.

RIVER SAUNAS

If I haven't talked you out of building a *great* fire, I might as well talk you into building a river sauna. A river sauna is just as it sounds . . . a sauna built along the river. If that doesn't conjure any mental images, think of it as a sweat lodge, a steamy tepee. These ingenious contraptions spell instant relief for weary rafters and make a memorable impression on anyone who has ever tried one.

The river sauna starts with a big waterproof tarp and some imagination. Pick a site near the river and use paddles, tables, or whatever is available to build a small, tentlike structure with the tarp. The structure should be fully enclosed, with a sealable flap entrance, and barely big enough to fit you and your friends inside. Since you are going to be trapping steam and warmth inside this makeshift hut, the tighter and smaller it is, the better it will work.

Now, how do you add steam to the sauna? Well, that brings you back to the fire. Put a dozen or so clean, round, brick-size rocks in the fire when you first start building it. As the fire burns, these rocks will heat up and begin glowing. Once they're red hot, take them out of the fire with a shovel or some sturdy sticks and carry them over to the sauna. Put the rocks in a sandy hole, a big steel pot, or a steel can in the middle of the sauna, and keep a pot of cool water nearby. To get the steam going, just dab water on the rocks. In seconds your claustrophobic hut will transform into a dreamy chamber of soothing vapors.

To get the most out of your sauna experience bear a few things in mind. Keep the tarp sealed shut unless you're entering or exiting the sauna, getting short of breath, or feeling too hot. Each time you open the tarp, the steam escapes and you have to start over again. Pick a sauna site with a clear path to the river. (The river gives overheated steambathers a chance to cool down.) Choose your rocks carefully: Round igneous rocks without cracks give off a lot of heat and aren't prone to cracking but moist, misshapen rocks can explode violently. If you can't tell your igneous from your sedimentary, the best bet is to pick round rocks many feet above the high-water mark. Also, try mixing up the size of the rocks. Smaller rocks give off more heat, but big rocks stay warm longer. Finally, keep the rocks clean. There's nothing worse than mixing noxious smoke with steam when your lungs are wide open.

Human Waste

Sooner or later you're going to have to answer the call of nature. So what are you going to do? I've admittedly dashed behind a thousand trees in my day, but I don't profess it to be the best way to do things. With ever-increasing numbers of river runners flocking into the world's great canyons, your business might make things a little unpleasant for somebody else.

In earlier days, environmentally conscious rafters carried an 18-inch ammo can (known as a *rocket box*) for bathroom purposes. The can was lined with a new plastic bag each night and provided a convenient—though not exactly comfortable—place to deposit human waste. In fact, one of the rocket box's discomforting propensities was to leave a pair of reddened dents in your cheeks by the time you were done, well, you know. It was for this reason that these primitive toilets were dubbed *groovers*.

Today, federal law prohibits landfills from accepting human waste in plastic bags. You should still use a portable latrine in order to carry all human waste out of the canyon, so it will take a little forethought to

HUMAN WASTE

Here are some tips from the National Forest Service to make human waste management a bit easier:

1. Separate daily sewage into several smaller containers to make it more manageable rather than using a single sealed container.
2. Sand and paint the inside of ammo cans to simplify emptying and washing.
3. Use washable liners in ammo cans or buckets.
4. Use nonformaldehyde deodorizers like Pine-Sol, dry Clorox, or kitty litter to reduce odors.

bring your wilderness practices into compliance with the law. Fortunately, there are a few alternatives from which rafters can choose.

One option is to continue to use your ammo can, sans the plastic bag. Some federally controlled rivers now have *scat* machines (high-tech ammo can washers) that are specially designed to do your dirty work. For those of you who still insist on plastic bags, there are reusable plastic bags that can be taken to RV dumps when the trip is through. (Fittings for RV hoses make cleaning these bags easy.) Finally, rafters can use chemical holding tanks, also designed to be emptied at RV dumps, which are the easiest system to use but also the bulkiest and most costly.

To find out what is permissible on the river you're going to raft, contact the nearest federal agency. If one of the described latrines is required, check out the Appendix and contact one of the listed portable-toilet manufacturers.

Now, getting back to our primeval heritage...if neither a latrine nor a legal dump station is available, dig a single hole for your group 6 to 8 inches deep and at least 100 feet from the river and dispose of all human waste there.

River Cookery

Rafting—like any other form of outdoor recreation—burns calories. And if you're anything like me, much of your time will be spent figuring out how to restore those calories while keeping your taste buds amused. After a long day on the river, a tasty meal provides a soothing transition into the lazy hours after dusk, and bountiful lunch spreads will give you all the energy you need to get you down the river.

Riverside meals can be simple or elaborate, depending on your budget, available kitchen paraphernalia, carrying space, and gastronomic preferences. They can be simple one-pot meals, cheese and salami, or extravagant banquets. Riverside dining is limited only by your culinary creativity.

MENU PLANNING

Menu planning begins long before you make your first lunch stop or reach your first night's camp. In fact, it starts before you get to the local supermarket. Planning your river menu is only slightly different from planning your meals at home; of course, you are restricted by considerations of carrying space, refrigeration, and cooking utensils. Plan a menu that will make everyone happy, and get everyone involved in selecting meals either by listing items they do and don't like or by rotating menu responsibilities for each day on the river.

Try to plan meals around the length of the trip, your level of patience, and the amount of cookware available. On lengthy trips, select foods that are durable and won't spoil quickly. Most perishables are bulky and only last a few days in a cooler, but dehydrated food saves weight and lasts the longest.

If you are a patient cook and you have lots of kitchen gear, you can make some pretty fancy entrees. But if you'd rather relax and keep things simple, consider easier meals like one-pot stews, pasta dishes, and Mexican dinners. Also consider the season and weather. Do you *really* want to stand outside slow-simmering that special stew in the middle of a rainstorm?

PACKING FOOD

Food storage is dependent on the length of your trip, the number of people, and the amount of food you're carrying. On a one-day jaunt, with no more than a handful of rafters, you may be able to get by with string cheese, apples, and high-energy bars packed into a small dry bag. Heartier eaters may bring along a cooler—stored in either a rowing frame or a cooler frame—to carry cold beverages, fresh meats, and so on. On multiday journeys, even the chilly compartment of a cooler might not be enough to keep food fresh and edible. In this case, some creative menu planning and packing become necessary.

River runners tend to be an inventive and resourceful lot when it comes to packing food. The tricks of the trade are many. Since eggs break easily, they are better off broken ahead of time and stored in plastic bottles, ready for use in your morning omelette. Durable fruits and vegetables—such as potatoes, apples, watermelon, and cucumbers—are easier to keep fresh and undamaged than other types of produce and can be stored in tough bags. Canned meats, powdered milk, and freeze-dried items can be used to replace fresh goods—they'll last longer and they come in their own protective containers.

COOLERS

The ice chest is the most valuable tool for rafters in need of portable refrigeration. Filled generously with ice, a sealed cooler can keep perishables fresh for days.

Use your cooler wisely to maximize its efficiency. Since an open cooler warms quickly, make sure the lid is shut when it's not being used. By separating your meals ahead of time and designating certain coolers for use early or late in the trip, you can avoid opening and closing them at every food stop. (With duct tape and a waterproof pen, label the lid of each cooler to list its contents or specify which day it is to be used.)

Prefreeze your meats and use block ice if it is available; drain the meltoff daily to avoid a big pool in the bottom of the cooler. Another idea is to freeze plastic milk jugs full of water ahead of time—as the water melts inside the jugs it provides a source of fresh drinking water instead of just another mess. On really long journeys, consider packing the cooler with dry ice. Dry ice is much colder than regular ice, and if you pack every spare inch of the cooler with newspaper and keep it tightly sealed, the ice will last for days. One trick for keeping your cooler cool is to cover it with wet rags or other gear to shield it from the sun's warming rays.

It is a common misconception that coolers are waterproof. Evenly tightly strapped coolers can let water in if the raft flips or gets stuck in big hydraulics. Consider tying the cooler shut with bicycle inner tubes or strong bungee cords, and seal the food inside the cooler in individual plastic bags.

Coolers are great for carrying perishables and they can carry nonperishables as well if there is space, but sometimes food has to be divvied out among other containers—dry bags, ammo cans, and waterproof boxes. Some items, such as canned beverages, don't even need to be stored in containers but can simply be packed neatly away just like everything else in the raft.

SORTING FOOD

On trips longer than a couple of days, labeling and sorting meals becomes more important, especially if there is more food than can be packed into the avail-

able cooler space and you need to use additional containers. Rather than guess where your food is before every meal, or flip open every lid in search of one or two items, carefully divide food supplies between containers and label them ahead of time. One handy trick is to put all the ingredients of one meal—or one type of food, such as cereals, rice, and pasta—into one big plastic container and label it with a waterproof pen.

THE KITCHEN

Just about any manually powered tool you have in your home kitchen will work in your riverside kitchen. In fact, the kitchen list included in the Appendix is little different from what you'd expect to see in your own cupboards and drawers. Camp stoves, however, are different from those used at home. There are many excellent camping stoves on the market today, with those powered by white gas, propane, and butane leading the market. Though all of these fuel-burning stoves work fine, some rivers restrict the type of fuel rafters can use in camp. It might be helpful to find out about local regulations well in advance. To make camp cooking even easier there are roll-up kitchen tables and aluminum kitchen boxes designed especially for rafters.

Once in camp, set up the kitchen away from the gear pile. That way, people won't constantly pester the cook and make off with important ingredients before they hit the pan.

DUTCH OVENS

One remarkable cooking tool is the *Dutch* oven, or D.O. This cast-iron or aluminum pot and lid was first invented by Paul Revere and manufactured in the United States. Its widespread use by fur traders from Holland in bartering with Indians gave this American invention its *Dutch* name.

Dutch ovens are designed to absorb and spread heat evenly. (Because of this, some purists shun the aluminum ovens because they heat and cool faster and don't disperse heat as well. Nonpurists don't worry about this. They applaud aluminum's lighter weight and they prevent heat fluctuations by shielding the oven from the wind.) A typical 10-inch-diameter oven holds about 4.5 quarts and a 12-inch oven holds 7 quarts. Almost all have short legs to raise them above

The fully equipped river kitchen. *(Photo by Doc Loomis)*

the ground and a raised lip around the lid to hold coals. Charcoal briquettes or coals from the fire are placed evenly along the top of the lid and below the pot to create a hot cooking environment inside.

Before you use an iron D.O. you must season it by melting a tablespoon of shortening inside the pot. (Aluminum D.O.s don't require seasoning.) Remove the oven from the heat after the shortening liquefies and rub the oil into the pot and lid until it disappears, leaving a shiny, slick surface. Repeat this until the surface will take no more oil and then wipe it clean. Another method is to wipe the inner surfaces with cooking oil and bake the D.O. in your home oven for 20 minutes. (If you ever have to reseason the D.O., just scrape off any rust with steel wool and repeat the seasoning process. Clean it with mild soap and water only.)

Once you're ready to cook with your Dutch oven, place the food inside and close the lid. (You can cook anything, from stews to brownies, pan pizzas to pound cake.) Set the D.O. over a firepan to avoid scarring the ground. Lay coals along the edge of the lid and under the pot, about an inch from its sides.

The number of coals you use depends on what you're cooking. A 10- or 12-inch oven can heat to 375 degrees with about 25 briquettes. If you're making a stew, divide those briquettes evenly between the top and bottom of the oven; for baking, put about three-fourths of the briquettes on the top and one-fourth on the bottom. It's always better to underestimate the number of coals needed beneath the pot because the lower coals can quickly overheat the oven.

Once you start cooking, periodically turn the lid a quarter-turn, but avoid lifting it. Opening the oven will let out the heat and make cooking much more difficult. Even without lifting the lid, experienced Dutch-oven chefs can tell when their meals are done by smell alone.

DISHWASHING

Rancid dishes—much like those sitting in my kitchen sink right now—are a sure invitation for a host of gastric maladies. It's far better to clean your dishes daily than to risk losing your appetite from a stomach bug.

One time-tested way to clean dishes is what I call the *three-bucket technique*. Pour preboiled water into three buckets or large pots. (Boiling the water ahead of time decreases the risk of contamination.) Put some biodegradable soap in bucket 1, leave only pure water in bucket 2, and add two teaspoons of chlorine bleach to bucket 3. Scrub your dishes in the first bucket, rinse them off in the second, and disinfect them by dousing them in the third. (Some folks add one more bucket of pure water for rinsing off the dishes before washing them.) To keep your hands happy and soft you may want to wear some rubber gloves. Also, replace heavily soiled water with fresh water. When you're all done, strain the solid waste from the buckets and pack it out of camp in an ammo can. The residual water should be dumped in a small hole, deep enough so that animals won't try to dig it up, and far away from the river.

DRINKING WATER

It is disheartening to think that almost every raftable river poses a potential risk to humans if used for drinking water. Even the clearest streams can carry industrial pollutants and dangerous bacteria, including a nasty little bugger called *Giardia lamblia*. Nonetheless, it is important to maintain your level of hydration by drinking enough water every day. Fresh, safe drinking water demands some special attention, especially on long rafting trips.

The most obvious way to guarantee fresh drinking water is to carry your own supply. A few 2- to 5-gallon jugs strapped onto your raft might carry enough water to last a couple of days if used sparingly. If you're going to be on the river longer than that, or if there will be many people on the trip, you will have to produce your own safe, potable water.

There are three common ways to treat water for most living organisms. The first method is to boil the water for 10 to 20 minutes. (For every 1,000 feet you gain above sea level, add 1 minute of boiling time.)

The next method is to use a chemical purifier such as halizone, iodine or bleach. Halizone and iodine tablets come with instructions for proper dosages. However, if you're using tincture of iodine (2 percent), use 5 drops per quart of water and let it sit 30 minutes. (Double the time if the water is cold, and double the dosage if the water is cloudy.) Bleach is generally added to water at the rate of 8 drops per gallon and takes about 30 minutes to kill living organisms. None of these chemical treatments is foolproof, and each requires some patience and caution. Remember that it takes a little bit of time to kill the organisms, and that just one drop of untreated water can spoil the whole batch.

The third water treatment method—filtration—is the only one that can remove pesticides, solvents, and other artificial contaminants as well as living organisms. Portable filtration units (water filters) actually strain water through microscopic pores in the unit's filter element, and eject potable water out the tail end of the system. Rafters should carry large enough water filters to supply adequate water for everyone on the trip and bring replacement filter elements in case one clogs or breaks.

GARBAGE

Low-impact camping means carrying everything out of camp that wasn't there when you arrived. *Everything!* Garbage can be carried out in plastic buckets with airtight lids, in large ammo cans, in onion or potato sacks, or in plastic bags stuffed into dry bags. Even empty coolers can be used to haul garbage. Don't just strap trash bags to the raft: They're likely to burst open on the river and negate all your best environmental intentions.

13
ONE STEP FURTHER
RAFTING ALTERNATIVES

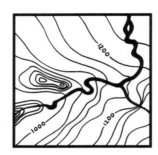

Adventurous rafters can expand their whitewater horizons far beyond the limits of everyday river running. For those willing to accept new challenges there await new rewards. In this chapter you will learn three new ways to look at rivers. First you will learn the basics of planning and carrying out exploratory trips and first descents. Next you will discover the growing sport of raft racing. Finally, we will explore playboating—an exciting endeavor that pits your skills and wit against the river's most exciting hydraulics. Even if you never intend to try these pursuits, this chapter will expand your rafting knowledge.

River Exploration

Exploring an unnavigated river can be an extraordinary experience. Some rafters feel an irresistible draw to this kind of trip, much the same as some travelers prefer forgotten backroads over popular highways. In many ways, exploratory descents mark the apex of all whitewater endeavors: They present you with so many unknowns that they inevitably test the full extent of your skills, judgment, and river prowess. First descents can combine the reverence of traversing untouched wilderness with the personal challenge of negotiating unnavigated canyons.

THE RESEARCH PHASE

Few exploratory descents—successful ones at least—take place without an enormous amount of preparation. In fact, pretrip planning can take longer than the trip itself, beginning weeks, months, or even years ahead of time. Learning everything there is to know about the river and the surrounding terrain ahead of time will minimize many of the risks inherent in wilderness exploration and running untested rapids.

Any exploratory descent should begin with a survey of all available information resources. Start with a copy of the region's best guidebooks, review paddling magazines and newsletters, and call around to local whitewater clubs. It is quite possible that your exploratory trip is really a second, third, or twentieth descent! Next, check out topographic maps. For North American paddlers, the United States and Canadian Geological Surveys maintain detailed topographic maps covering any river you can find, and these maps are a rafter's single most valuable resource.

When purchasing topographic maps, select the smallest scale possible. Large-area maps (with a scale of 1:100,000 or 1:250,000) usually offer too little detail to help much at all. However, smaller-scaled maps—particularly the 1:24,000 or 7.5-inch maps—are quite useful. Many of these have contour intervals of 20 to 40 feet, which can at least forewarn of the presence of large waterfalls.

Begin reading the map by looking at the width of the blue line denoting the river. Is it a *thick* blue line, indicative of a large-volume river, or is it a *narrow* line, indicating a small stream? Next, note the contour intervals (change in altitude between lines) and the mileage scale. Look at the section of river you wish to explore and break it down into ½-mile or 1-mile sections. Now, by counting the number of times the contour lines cross the river in a 1-mile section, and then multiplying by the contour interval, you can get the average gradient in feet per mile. (See the accompanying diagram.)

Knowing how to interpret gradient is important. Many popular streams drop 10 to 100 feet per mile.

More extreme whitewater rivers drop 100 to 200 feet per mile. On rare occasions rafters can descend rivers with gradients exceeding 200 feet per mile. Always keep in mind that even low-gradient rivers might descend very gradually, then drop many feet all at once over unrunnable falls!

One way to figure out whether your venture is worth the risk is to compare the river's gradient to the canyon's surrounding terrain. If the land adjacent to the river shows closely spaced contour lines, the river is in a canyon. This can be a genuine hazard if there are waterfalls, severe whitewater, or unrunnable rapids. A narrow canyon with a steep gradient is not the place to be unless you've scouted out everything by air or land ahead of time! However, put that same steep river on a map showing widely spaced contour lines traversing the adjacent land and it may be possible to portage anything.

While reading your map, look for obvious escape routes in the form of broad contour lines departing the river's edge. Note prominent landmarks such as giant peaks, cliffs, or major tributaries that will be visible from the river and will let you monitor your progress. Also figure out the total mileage between put-ins and take-outs to get a rough estimate of your expected river time.

Topographic maps are your guidebook during exploratory descents, so take good care of them. Keep them securely fastened and stored in waterproof containers when not in use, and keep a duplicate set of maps on another raft in case one set gets lost or destroyed.

Now that you have an imaginary picture of the river, it's time to gather more information. If you can, go to the river and scout as much of it as you can see. Many first descents started with long, arduous hikes along canyon rims to scout the rapids below, or with airplane and helicopter flights over the river to view hidden corridors. Talk to the locals—fishermen, hunters, and hikers—and glean as much information as they're willing to share with you. Also check with local paddling clubs to see if someone else has done some of your homework for you.

The final research stage is to obtain information on water levels. While the mental picture imparted by that thick blue line might be accurate, a gauge will tell you a lot more. Check with the local Geological Survey office, weather services, or water districts to see if the river has a gauge, then monitor the river level periodically. The Geological Survey can also provide historical watershed and drainage area information and flow data. When combined with information on local weather patterns, and a Water Supply Outlook (available from the U.S.G.S.), this information gives a strong indication of the river's reaction to factors like rain and snowmelt.

SELECTING THE CREW

In North America almost anything that *could* be rafted *has* been rafted. Accordingly, it is usually the most difficult and challenging rivers that remain unexplored. To meet that challenge you need a team of rafters who are compatible in both temperament and tenacity.

It takes much more than a positive mental attitude to confront and survive unknown hazards. Each team member should be comfortable with treacherous whitewater and should bring to the team a solid set of wilderness skills and useful technical abilities. By including rafters with medical expertise, rock–climbing skills, and intimate knowledge of the adjacent terrain, the team will have a broad range of useful skills and will be better prepared to handle difficult situations.

EQUIPMENT AND SUPPLIES

Since you'll be traversing unknown canyons, portaging with greater frequency, and relying on your equipment much more than ever before, it is imperative that your equipment be of top quality and in excellent shape. Take some time before the trip to double-check your raft. Pump it up tight and check for leaks. Repair any loose seams and seal any noticeable abrasions. Examine oars, frames, paddles, and other gear for flaws. If an irreparable defect shows up, don't risk bringing the item along!

The most important part of assembling your equipment for the trip is trimming weight. It is far easier to portage a light raft than one fully loaded with expendable luxuries. That *doesn't* mean that you shouldn't bring all the gear that is—or may be—*necessary!* You will be relying more on your gear now than ever

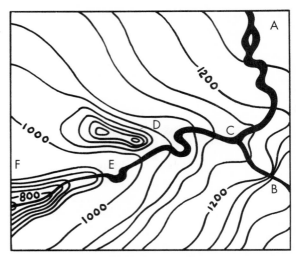

Topographic maps can provide a lot of valuable information. Here, the river winds through a broad valley while gradually descending through braided channels (A). A tributary descends over a big waterfall (B) before joining the main river (C). A big hill (D) might be seen from the river. If you did your homework, you'd know that the big eddy (E) is a clue that the river will soon steepen and enter a narrow canyon (F).

before, so bring everything that is essential to the success of your trip and leave the unnecessary frills at home. Try trimming your wardrobe by using layers of polypropylene clothing and waterproof outer shells. Instead of carrying several tents, bring a large tarp and ground pads. And when planning the menu, think like a backpacker: Bring freeze-dried food, one-burner stoves, and single pots rather than fresh foods and elaborate cookware.

SAFETY

One place you don't want to shave weight is in your safety gear selection. Bring extra safety equipment (climbing ropes, carabiners, throw bags, etc.) in case an emergency arises. Also carry a fully equipped expedition first aid kit along with a detailed medical handbook. The more remote and dangerous the trip, the more you should consider carrying a two-way radio and learning how to use it. Notify rangers, family, and friends of your itinerary before you leave, including your expected time of return. That way, if something does go wrong, a search party can be sent to find and help you.

GETTING TO THE RIVER

Many first descents and exploratory trips have been overlooked simply because of the difficulty of access to put-ins or take-outs. If you're willing to carry your gear long distances over adverse terrain, you may just find a whitewater paradise waiting at the end of the trail.

There are many ways to carry rafts to the river. For a self-bailing raft with a laced-in floor, remove the floor and divide the load between two or three team members. One strong person can carry a floor or a set of tubes draped over his shoulders for many miles. Another way to carry the raft is to use the *burrito roll* (see illustration). Start the burrito roll by laying on oar (or four or more long paddles) lengthwise down the center of the raft. Roll the raft around the oar lengthwise as tightly as possible and strap the roll closed. This will leave a long, thin bundle that can be carried on the shoulders of two or three rafters.

Keep in mind that additional gear—sleeping bags, riverwear, safety gear, and food—has to be carried to the river. If the hike down to the put-in is only a mile or two long, consider spending one day hiking back and forth to transport everything to the river. On the other hand, if you only have time to make one hike, load your gear into backpack-style dry bags. They hold a heavy load and won't interfere with carrying the raft on your shoulders.

Finally, for those of you who have too much gear or a little extra money, your hike to the river can be made easier by loading rafts on wheeled deer carts, pack animals, or even helicopters.

RUNNING THE RIVER

Whenever you're in a new canyon or on an unknown section of river, run more conservatively than you would otherwise. Make sure your gear is loaded down with bombproof straps or knots. Take a moment to ask yourself "What if . . . ?" before running blindly around a bend or over a horizon line. On remote rivers, a mistake could be costly and a serious injury could go untreated for days. Don't let paranoia overcome you, but do take a step back from your normal river bravado. By the time you reach civilization, the descent will take on heroic proportions anyway.

Racing

Raft racing is a dynamic and exciting sport for competitors and spectators alike. From downriver to slalom races, from rescue competitions to river orienteering events, the thrill of running rivers is magnified when every move becomes critical. In their effort to go fast and minimize errors, racers become totally focused. All the skills learned before—from raft control to route finding—come to a head. Sound skills shine and deficiencies become glaringly apparent.

It is in this process that another aspect of raft racing appears: Good racers make good river runners! The same precision that goes into running gates carries over to running rapids, and despite philosophical differences as to what river running is all

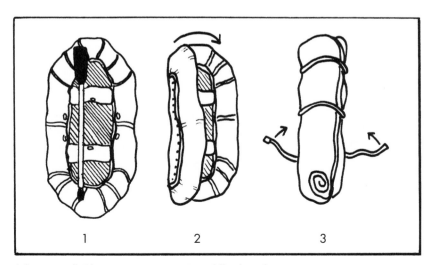

A burrito roll: Place an oar or some paddles lengthwise in the deflated raft; roll the raft tightly around the oar; keep the bundle tightly rolled with three or four straps. The burrito roll can be carried on rafters' shoulders.

about, racing and recreational rafting accent each other magnificently.

TYPES OF RACES

Raft races have varied over the years as much as the rivers that have hosted them. Today, most races involve one or more of these events: *slalom, giant slalom,* and *downriver* races. Some international rafting competitions add rescue, running, and orienteering events, but these rarely show up in North American races.

Slalom Races. Slalom competitions are the most dynamic and fascinating of the rafting events. Based on standardized canoeing and kayaking events, raft slaloms entail maneuvering rafts through a series of gates while racing against the clock. Slalom racers must balance speed with perfect technique because each tapped pole or missed gate adds significantly to the rafters' final time.

In regular slalom competitions, there may be as many as 21 gates set up over a short section of river. Once the rafts are in the gates, the action is fast and furious. Rather than progressing downstream at tremendous speed, rafts have to maneuver back and forth from gate to gate, sometimes turning into eddies to drive through upstream gates. Giant slaloms—especially those held during the same competition as the regular slalom events—have fewer gates and slightly longer runs. The giant slalom demands fewer drastic moves than the regular slalom; while precision maneuvering remains critical in the giant slalom, raw speed is a bigger factor of the final outcome.

Downriver Races. Downriver races—also known as *wildwater races*—are the purest form of raft racing. They are the sprints and marathons of the whitewater world, with no poles, gate judges, or penalties. They are simply races against the clock, in which the fastest overall time wins. It takes both physical conditioning and solid river-reading skills to compete effectively in the downriver race. The idea is to maintain fast, powerful strokes throughout the race while sticking to the fastest currents.

Rescue Events. Rescue competitions are the most exciting events; they can pump gallons of adrenaline through the veins of participants and spectators alike. In a typical rescue event there are four gates, four raft paddlers, and one designated swimmer. The paddlers sit in the raft at the starting line while the designated swimmer stands on the opposite bank. At the sound of "Go!" the raft team paddles across the river and through gate 1. The swimmer then dives into the river and climbs aboard the raft before it enters gate 2. Before negotiating gate 3, the paddlers must exit and flip the raft, then negotiate gate 3 upside down. Between gates 3 and 4 the team rights the raft, climbs aboard, and paddles through gate 4. The clock finally stops when all paddlers have reached a designated point along the bank.

PRERACE TIPS

A whole book could be written on raft racing, including chapters on technique, physical preparation, and equipment. But in many ways racing merely builds upon the techniques, fitness, and equipment experienced rafters already possess. The way to improve your racing results is to hone your skills, build your muscles and wind, and choose the fastest rafts available.

Before any race begins, spend enough time to learn all the rules and study the course. If you're on a paddle team, discuss and analyze the course together so that the moves can be executed without waiting for a paddle command. Scout the river to find the strongest currents, currents that will assist you with turns, and the fastest route from gate to gate. Finally, form an indelible mental image of the course so you can plan every stroke ahead of time.

DURING THE RACE

Since the racer's goal is to make the run as fast and penalty-free as possible, it can be difficult to relax at the starting line. Before the starter says "Go," set your oar or paddle in the catch position so you can make the first stroke immediately. Keep your grip relaxed so as not to waste energy, and keep a vision of the course in your head.

Paddling and rowing during a race is no different from any other time. However, paddlers should concentrate on executing short, fast, and powerful strokes, and should keep their heads up to widen their field of vision. Since the tail end of the forward stroke delivers little energy to the raft, chop it off and begin each

Whitewater racing combines skill and endurance!

stroke's recovery phase sooner than usual. Rowers should strive for fast stroke rates and smooth oar motions. To save energy, use the large, strong muscles of the back and legs; don't lift the oars too high out of the water after each stroke; and let only the blade dip beneath the surface during the stroke.

In slalom events, the fastest way to run the course is to keep the raft running *smoothly* from gate to gate. This means avoiding momentum-draining corrective strokes and choppy turns, and running minimally offset gates with subtle draw or sweep strokes to shift the raft's position. When making turns, turn *above* or *in* the gate so you don't have to struggle to change the raft's direction after the gate. Also, as you enter each gate, figure out which pole you should run closer to; watch the poles and your raft's tubes to make sure there are no touches; and always concentrate on the next gate downstream.

WILDWATER TIPS

Prepare for wildwater races just as for slalom races: Review the rules, scout the river, and discuss the course with your team. Find the fastest currents and the cleanest route through rapids—the route that makes the straightest line and requires the fewest maneuvers. An ideal route will require no backpaddling and few, if any, turning strokes.

When running the river, avoid eddies, holes, and pockets of shallow, slower-moving water. Although wave trains generally signify fast water, run the shoulders of waves rather than their peaks. (The peaks will increase your vertical motion, slap your raft around, and make it tougher to paddle, all of which will slow you down.) If you're doing really well, you may even catch up to the raft in front of you. Plan to overtake the front raft carefully. Don't waste energy trying to pass the raft in slower water. Pick a broad, fast channel with even currents, announce your intentions, and only pass when it's legal.

Playboating

Rafting has long been a way to get from point A to point B. Even advanced river running does little more than connect clean routes and eddies in an effort to reach the take-out in one piece. But playboating can change all that.

Other whitewater boaters—kayakers and canoers—have long known that waves and holes can provide an endless source of amusement and challenge. Whether gently gliding their craft down the face of a wave or doing 360s on the shoulders of a hole, playboaters develop and hone their boating skills while connecting with some of the river's most exciting hydraulics. Now that rafters have self-bailing rafts and catarafts, they too can join in the fun.

EQUIPMENT

A self-bailing raft or cataraft is a must for playboating. With a standard-floor raft, the river will flood the passenger compartment and become difficult to maneu-

FAST WATER

The key to winning wildwater races is finding—and staying on—the fastest currents. Even though that sounds easy, it can be a bit tricky at times. So here are some tips:

1. It's faster to run the shoulders of waves than to hit the crests.
2. Lines of foam or bubbles leading downstream across slow-moving pools usually signify the fastest current.
3. The current along the outside of a bend—barring any obstacles—is usually faster than the inside.
4. On windy days, it may be easier to paddle closer to the bank than usual.

ver. Bare paddle rafts make better playboats because they have no dangerous frames or oarstands to injure you if the raft flips. However, frames work fine on paddle cats since they are harder to flip.

Before jumping onto a wave or into a hole, double-check all of your gear. Make sure that there are no loose items or ropes and that each person is fully outfitted with helmets, insulating outerwear (you *will* swim sooner or later!), and lifejackets.

SKILLS

Before you think about playing around on waves and holes, learn to distinguish forgiving hydraulics from perilous keepers. If you know what the river is likely to do to your raft ahead of time, you'll be able to anticipate the river's actions and adjust accordingly. Since flips are common in playboating, you must be comfortable rerighting a flipped raft and swimming out of holes. Finally, you should be adept at maneuvering your raft in powerful hydraulics.

PLAYING ON WAVES

Surfing a river wave with a raft relies on the same gravitational force that pulls a surfer down the face of an ocean wave. But while the surfer is light and streamlined, the raft is heavy and it creates a lot of surface drag. To surf a wave, the rafter must overcome the friction created by the raft.

Start off by picking a medium-size wave (about 2 to 4 feet high) just downstream of an eddy. Try to leave the eddy with an upstream ferry, slide over to the middle of the wave, and line your raft up parallel with the current. As you hit the trough of the wave, slow your raft down by pulling it upstream. As you do this, you should feel the raft stall. Work hard to keep your raft straight, since any change in its angle relative to the current will throw the raft off the wave.

To keep the raft stalled in the wave's trough, rudder with paddles or oars and stroke upstream just enough to keep the raft from slipping free. Don't overpower your strokes or the raft will bury in the trough and get pushed off the wave.

To further improve your chances of staying on a wave, center the raft's weight over the trough. For paddle rafts this might mean unloading the bow compartment. Also, use your most powerful stroke. For oar rafts this means that backsurfing will be easier since it relies on the more powerful backstroke, while paddle rafts will have an easier time forward paddling against the current.

PLAYING IN HOLES

Small holes make perfect play spots since their backwash creates natural raft catchers and eliminates the need to keep perfect angles like you would on waves. In holes, all you have to do is stabilize your raft, then focus your attention on spinning maneuvers, bronco riding, and eventually busting free of the hole.

Getting In There. The techniques used for entering holes are similar to those used on waves, with some minor changes. To reach the hole, start parallel to or just upstream of the hole and ferry across to it with a steep upstream angle. As you reach the hole, drive the raft upstream over the backwash and into the trough.

What you do at this point depends on the size of the hole. In large holes it can be dangerous to turn the raft broadside because this gives the river a better shot at flipping you, so strive to keep the bow pointed upstream. Hole size will also tell you whether to shift your body weight to the high side (the downstream tube) or the low side (the upstream tube). In very small holes, the only way to stay in the hole is to lean upstream into the trough, but in medium to large holes the upstream lean is a sure invitation for a flip. Lean downstream (highside) in stronger holes.

Once you're in the hole, wait a moment until things feel stable and then think of what you want to do. The longer you sit sideways in the middle of the hole, the more likely you are to take on water, stall out, or flip, so move toward the shoulder of the hole and try to spin. Let the bow snag the downstream current passing the shoulder of the hole and turn. At the same time, try to rotate the stern back into the middle of the hole. Voilá! Your first *180!* Next time, try to spin the raft *360 degrees* by turning the bow and stern all the way around. If the river is deep and safe and has a big pool below in which to reclaim your gear, you can even paddle right into the falls, lean forward, and shoot the raft straight up in the air. This maneuver—called a

THE SECOND SEASON

Long before you started flipping through this book, I'd already spent countless hours convincing my friends I wasn't nuts. While they were home in bed, or shoveling snow off their driveways, or sitting in front of the fireplace, I was donning my drysuit and heading down my favorite rivers. While they were adjusting their thermostats, I was adjusting my attitude. My addiction to whitewater was insatiable, pausing for neither the changing of the seasons nor for a drop in the mercury level.

For the well-prepared rafter, winter is a magical time of year to float rivers. Transient storm-fed streams burst to life with winter rains, and familiar summer runs take on a whole new appearance. Still, good judgment and some extra preparation are required on winter outings, so here are some tips to make your next trip safe, fun, and comfortable:

1. Select shorter trips so you don't get caught on the river after dark.
2. Only run rivers that you know intimately and that are well within your skill level.
3. Avoid iced-over rivers.
4. Pick rivers with short, easy shuttles and leave warm, dry clothes at the take-out.
5. Dress extra warm with dry suits or dry tops, helmet liners, gloves, and thick booties.
6. Stay active on the river and eat well. Carry Power Bars or granola to provide a burst of energy if you feel tired or cold.
7. Learn how to recognize and treat hypothermia.

pop up or *endo*—is fun once in a while, but can slam unsuspecting paddlers into the boulder or ledge. Use it sparingly!

Getting Out of There. When you finally get weary of surfing a hole, exit by backpaddling downstream over the backwash or by slipping sideways over the shoulder of the hole. If all else fails, have someone on shore toss you a throw bag and pull your raft free.

Playboating teaches rafters many skills that can't be learned by simply floating downriver. Here, the rafters paddled into the trough of a breaking wave and pulled off a kayaker's trick known as a pop-up or endo.

14
STAY IN SHAPE
GEAR MAINTENANCE AND REPAIR

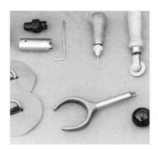

Rafting equipment is built to withstand abuse—collisions with rocks, chafing from poorly loaded gear, the damaging effect of ultraviolet rays. But owner abuse—poor maintenance, careless storage, or improper use of gear—will greatly shorten the life expectancy of almost every item in your rafting arsenal.

It takes only a little bit of care and common sense to keep rafting equipment healthy and kicking long after the warranties expire. In this chapter you'll learn the simple techniques gear owners use to maintain rafts and rafting accessories as well as ways to repair gear once it breaks down.

Raft Care

I've got to admit that I love a shiny new raft. It looks great on the water, and the extra boost it gives my psyche actually makes me feel like I'm rafting better. But whether it's new or old, I expect my raft to support gear, bounce off rocks, and surround my crew with a buoyant, resilient, and reliable cushion of immovable air on every trip. Although that sounds like an awful lot to demand of one boat, it really isn't; you can demand a lot if you're willing to give some care in return.

There is a multitude of ways to damage or destroy a raft, but most raft damage results from overinflation, tearing, abrasion, ultraviolet decay, and water damage. Here are some simple guidelines for avoiding these common problems:

1. Don't let oar frames rub against tubes. Wrap the frame with foam tubing or apply a rubbing strake to the tops of the tubes. Check metal frames for burrs and file them off.
2. Rinse sand and dirt from shoes and gear when boarding a raft so they don't grind their way into the fabric or valves.
3. Don't step on a deflated raft. There may be rocks or sharp objects on the ground that could puncture the material.
4. Carry—don't drag—a raft while putting in, taking out, or portaging.
5. When pulling ashore, pull your raft to a point where it won't rock or rub against the bank.
6. Don't overload a raft or load gear directly on the floor (light gear can be loaded on a self-bailing floor).
7. Don't overinflate a raft; check periodically for correct air pressure, especially on hot or sunny days.
8. When transporting a raft, make sure it isn't rubbing against the sides of the trailer or the interior of the trunk or truck bed.

TAKEDOWN, ROLLING, AND STORAGE

A surprising amount of damage can occur after the raft trip is over—damage that won't show up until the raft is blown up again before the next outing. To avoid this type of damage, take a few extra minutes after each trip to prepare the raft for storage.

At the take-out, unload your gear and rinse the raft thoroughly with clean water. Let the raft air dry by leaning it on its edge against some paddles or a wall. (If it's raining, this will have to wait until later.) When it is dry, gently wipe off any residual dirt and lay the

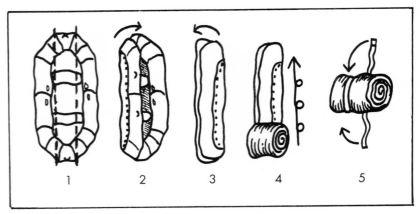

There are five steps to follow when rolling up your raft: (1) Mentally divide the raft into three long sections; (2) fold the left over the middle; (3) fold the right section over the middle; (4) roll the raft up from the end; and (5) run a strap around the roll to hold it in place.

raft back on the ground. If there are wet ropes still tied to the raft, remove them so that the water doesn't damage the boat when it is in storage. Deflate the tubes just as you inflated them: Let air out of each chamber evenly and slowly.

Before you roll up your raft, press or pump all remaining air out of the chambers. As we discussed in Chapter 13, look down at the fully deflated raft and divide it mentally into three long sections: (1) the left tube and the left part of the floor, (2) the center part of the floor, and (3) the right tube and the right part of the floor. To begin the roll, take the left third and fold it across the center, then fold the right third over the left. Now the raft is folded lengthwise like a loose burrito, one-third its original width. To complete the roll, begin at one end of the raft and roll it toward the other end as you would a sleeping bag. Use a strong strap to hold the roll tightly closed, being careful to avoid chafing.

Raft manufacturers recommend that you store your raft completely dry and semi-inflated. A raft containing just enough air to maintain its shape is less likely to suffer fabric stress and delamination when it is rolled up. But if you are anything like me, you don't own a trailer, garage space is a precious commodity, and storing a raft semi-inflated is out of the question. Simply make a tight roll at the river as described, then relax the roll before putting the raft into a safe storage place away from direct heat, sunlight, chemicals, and sharp objects. The loose roll lets air circulate freely around the tubes and floor.

Raft Repair

I'd like to tell you that you'll never have to use the following information, but I'd probably be wrong. Just by looking at the number of sharp rocks in a typical river and applying the law of averages, you'll see that sooner or later your raft is going to get a hole.

Lucky rafters get small holes in their tubes just before they reach the take-out. They manage to limp the raft to shore and then apply a clean, permanent patch at home under controlled conditions. Truly unfortunate rafters get holes in their boats far from the nearest take-out and have to make repairs on the river. These types of repairs are usually nothing more than sophisticated Band-Aids designed to get the raft downstream. On-river repairs are the same as those made at home—they just take a little patience and imagination to work out as well as home repairs.

The first step in repairing a raft is to figure out where the hole is. Though big tears are easy to find, pinhole leaks can be deceptive. In fact, sometimes they go unnoticed for years! The best way to find a pinhole leak is first to listen for the telltale whistle of escaping air, then to rub the suspected tube with soapy water. The water will bubble where it hits the leak.

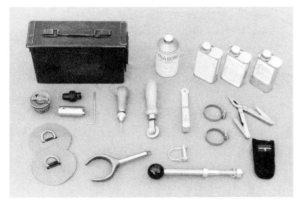

Always carry a repair kit with you.

Once you spot the leak it'll be easier to figure out what type of patch you need.

An easy way to think about the patching process is to divide it into three stages: (1) selecting the materials that will be needed, (2) preparing the workplace, and (3) applying the patch.

MATERIALS

Patching materials include glues, solvents, and fabrics that work with your raft's fabric. There are a number of one- and two-part glues available. One-part glues require no catalyst but can soften and lose their grip in temperatures as low as 150 degrees Fahrenheit (which can happen on a hot day). Two-part glues require the addition of a catalyst, but they cure faster and remain stable at higher temperatures. Unfortunately, the working time of many two-part glues is frustratingly short, so you must be prepared to apply your patch as soon after mixing the glue as possible.

Ask your raft dealer what type of glue your raft will need. Also, buy your glue from the dealer—it'll probably be better suited to rafts and of higher quality than those you'll find in a hardware store. Purchase small cans of glue and replace them at least once a season. If a can has been opened it may last as little as 30 days, so always have a fresh batch handy.

Solvents are used for thinning glues, cleaning the raft, and breaking down the raft's surfaces in preparation for receiving a patch. Typical solvents include toluol, which is used on Hypalon and neoprene rafts, and MEK (methyl ethyl ketone), which is used on PVC and urethane rafts. Note that all solvents—and glues, for that matter—are extremely toxic. Use them only in well-ventilated areas while wearing gloves and safety goggles. If you're around raft solvents a lot, consider wearing a breathing mask with an activated-charcoal filter.

The fabric used for the patch will be the same as the fabric of the raft. Cut loose pieces of fabric into patches large enough to overlap the edges of the hole by 1 to 2 inches. Round and bevel the edges and corners of the patch so they won't pull up later. Since really large tears *are* a possibility, it is a good idea to carry along as large a swath of fabric as your repair kit will hold. For additional items to use in making repairs, see checklist in the Appendix.

THE RAM PATCH

In an ideal world rafts would never tear, or they'd magically mend themselves without any human assistance. In the real world we've got to make do with current technology. The Ram Patch is the closest thing to magic for making on-river repairs.

This amazing little tool seals small tears by squeezing the raft's fabric between two rubber-faced disks—one for the inside of the tube and one for the outside. The Ram Patch kit includes a specially designed key for tightening the patch in place, as well as a miniature razor blade for making small holes large enough to accept the disks.

Carry a Ram Patch in your repair kit. If all goes well you'll never use it, but if you ever do need it you'll be glad you have it.

A Ram Patch provides a quick and convenient way to repair small holes.

THE WORKPLACE

The ideal workplace is clean and windless, with low humidity and an ambient temperature between 50 and 80 degrees Fahrenheit. Set up the workplace by laying out all your tools (listed in the Appendix) and preparing the glues, raft surfaces, and patches for use. Lay the loose patch over the hole and trace it with a pen so that you will know where to apply the glue. If the raft is constructed from Hypalon or neoprene, sand the area around the hole and one side of the patch. This will roughen the fabric surface and greatly increase the strength of the bond. Clean off excess grit with a clean cloth (cheesecloth works best) soaked in toluol. PVC and urethane don't require sanding (though some urethane is so tough that sanding is necessary). Instead, just rub them vigorously with MEK to soften the coating. Finally, prepare the glue following the manufacturer's directions. If the glue is not prethinned, thin it by adding about 20 to 30 percent of the solvent you'll be using.

APPLYING THE PATCH

There are seven steps in applying patches:

1. Arrange and mark the patches so you'll know where each one goes.

2. Wipe clean the patch and raft surfaces with a clean cloth soaked in solvent.

3. Apply a very thin first coat of glue, overlapping the patch outline by ¼ inch, and let it dry completely. (Use long, quick strokes when applying glue to keep it from balling up, and don't touch glued surfaces—body oils will affect the bond!)

4. Apply a second thin coat of glue and let that coat dry completely.

5. Reactivate the glue by wiping it quickly with a cloth wet with solvent. Wait about 15 to 30 seconds.

6. Carefully match up the patch and the outline, press the patch against the tube, and firmly press it down with a roller, being sure to force all air bubbles out from under the patch.

7. Clean up excess glue with solvent or a hard eraser, and let the patch dry completely (24 hours).

PATCHING TIPS

Moving beyond the basics, there are some simple tips that make the patching process much easier. Try presanding patch surfaces and prethinning glues at home so they'll be ready for on-river repairs. To avoid glue splatter, outline the mark you drew on the raft with masking tape before you start painting on any glue.

Really big rips can be particularly tough to repair. In times past, many rafters used an awl and heavy-duty thread to sew the tear with a baseball stitch before patching it. Though this method is still used occasionally, the thread causes an irregularity in the patch, making it tougher to mend the surfaces flat. If you need to repair a big rip, start by thoroughly drying out the torn chamber. Use bias tape or radiator-hose repair tape inside the tube to bring the torn edges back together. Working on a flat surface, carefully insert the tape into the tube through the tear with the sticky side up and press the rip down against the tape. This will make it much easier to apply the outside patch. An inside patch can be used in place of the tape and applied in the same way as an outside patch.

MAJOR REPAIRS

Major repairs include tears near seams and blown baffles. Although it is usually best to leave these repairs to the pros, experienced amateurs can make both types of repair.

Repairing seams or adjacent materials differs little from other patch jobs except that the seam may have to be peeled away from the raft to repair adjacent materials. To save some big headaches, start by giving your raft's manufacturer a call. Chances are you'll get sound advice and some technical guidance. Next, buy a hot-air gun; this is used to heat the seams and to loosen the glue. To begin the repair, hold the hot-air gun 4 to 6 inches from the seam and warm the seam very gradually, taking care not to melt the fabric coating. Check the seam every couple of minutes to see if it can be pulled away from the remaining material. When the seam is pliable, peel it back with a pair of pliers and proceed with the repair as you would with any other patch.

WELDING

As rafting technology evolves, the need for glues and solvents will begin to wane. There are already some handheld fabric-welding units that can be used to make bombproof raft repairs at home. Because welding actually melts the patch right into the raft's fabric, the patch becomes part of the raft rather than just adhering to it. If you have a choice, have your major tears welded to ensure that the repairs will last the life of the raft.

D-RINGS

Hot-air guns are also needed to heat and loosen torn or blown D-rings. Again, heat the D-ring gradually to avoid melting the surrounding material and try pulling it free with a pair of pliers every couple of minutes. Once it has pulled loose, replace it with a similar D-ring using the same gluing methods as you would to patch your raft.

VALVES

Depending on the type of valve used in your raft, valve repair can be a quick and easy task or a real nightmare. However, most of the newer valves are designed for easy replacement with nothing more than a few tools and some basic know-how.

Many military-style and AD-1 valves fit into a recessed circular boot on the raft and are fixed in place with screws. To replace these, just undo the screws, remove the damaged valve, and screw a new valve in place.

Halkey-Roberts valves consist of two pieces and are held in place by a male face and female backing screwed together. To replace a Halkey-Roberts valve you will need a specially designed valve tool. This tool

PATCHING SECRETS

On cold, rainy days, it can be frustrating—if not impossible—to apply a good patch to your raft. To make things easier, carry chemical heat packs in your repair kit. Lay the heat packs over the patch to hasten the glue's cure time and counteract the effects of uncooperative weather.

—Les Bechdel, author, *River Rescue*

fits inside the male face and is used to unscrew the outer half of the valve while you hold the inner half in place. When the two halves separate, the male face will pop free. Hold the female backing in place by pinching the tube around it with your free hand, then use the valve tool to screw in a new male face.

If both halves of a Halkey-Roberts fail, or if valve replacement makes you nervous, let a professional handle the job.

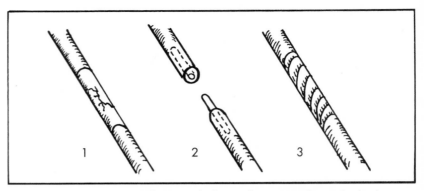

Broken oar shafts can be repaired. Cut the broken section away and drill ½-inch-wide holes 4 inches deep into the open ends. Insert an 8-inch-long by ½-inch-wide steel pin into the holes, using epoxy to hold it in place. Finally, wrap the shaft with fiberglass.

Oar Maintenance and Repair

You learned in Chapter 3 that wooden oars—unlike aluminum and fiberglass oars—need to be treated and sealed before they're ready for the river. Since water wear, chipping, and abrasion from oar locks or clips will slowly damage oar surfaces, wooden oars need to be retreated periodically in the same way. If a wooden oar breaks or cracks, there is still a chance that it can be repaired. Breaks that go straight across the shaft are usually oar killers—throw the oar away or use it for firewood. If you are hopelessly attached to that particular oar, trim the splintered ends square and drill a hole 4 inches deep and ½ inch wide into each end. Insert an 8-inch-by-½-inch steel pin into the holes and hold it in place with epoxy glue. If you wrap the break with overlapping layers of fiberglass, the oar will make a serviceable spare on future outings. Use only epoxy resins to seal fiberglass because polyester resins may damage the wood.

Diagonal cracks in wooden oar shafts can be repaired much more easily. Bend the shaft so that the crack opens up and work some epoxy glue into the crack. When the glue has set the oar will be as good as new.

Even large cracks or splits in oar blades can be repaired with epoxy. Cut away a rectangular piece of blade ¼ inch larger than the crack on all sides. Carefully whittle and sand down a piece of hardwood until it is identical in size to the open rectangle and cement it into place with epoxy. To make the repair more bombproof, wrap the blade with fiberglass tape using epoxy resins.

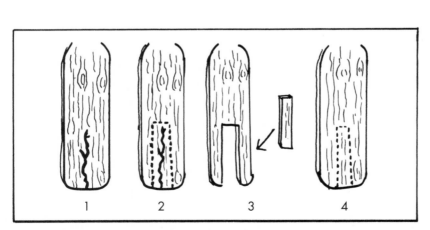

Oar blade repairs: (1) Locate the crack or split; (2) cut out a block around the crack; (3) use the block to trace and cut a new block from a fresh piece of wood; (4) epoxy the new block in place and wrap the blade tip with fiberglass.

When storing oars and paddles, don't lay them on the floor or lean them at an angle in the corner of your garage. Prop them up as vertically as possible in an out-of-the-way place to keep them from warping or being damaged.

Riverwear

Drysuits, wetsuits, paddle jackets, and booties take an enormous amount of abuse on river trips. Twigs and snags can rip the fabrics, body oils start to stink up your neoprene items, and ultraviolet rays slowly wear away the lifespan of nylon.

NEOPRENE CLOTHING

Wetsuits and booties start seeing abuse the moment you go to put them on. Neoprene can tear if stretched or pulled too hard, so use care when you're putting it on and taking it off. If a rip does develop, repair it before it spreads. The easiest way to repair a damaged suit is to use an iron-on neoprene patch (available at dive shops), but neoprene cement and Aquaseal (a special glue for use in water) work better and don't leave a raised section of material. Both Aquaseal and neoprene cement come in small cans with simple directions for gluing the torn edges back together.

To keep a wetsuit clean and strong (as opposed to strong *smelling*), wash it periodically. Use a special wetsuit detergent instead of harsh laundry soap, and clean it by hand or on the rinse cycle in a washing machine. Once the suit is dry, sprinkle it with talcum powder and store it in a dry place.

DRYSUITS

Drysuits are more delicate and expensive than many wetsuits, so be sure to take good care of them. Never try to zip a rear-entry drysuit by yourself—have someone do it for you. (The zippers are very expensive and can be damaged easily if tugged or bent the wrong way.) Take good care of your suit's neck, wrist, and ankle seals and cuffs, which are particularly vulnerable to drying, splitting, and tearing. Swab the seals with generous amounts of Seal Saver (a food-grade silicone) or 303 Protectant before or after each trip. Don't use

anything on the seals that contains petroleum, and avoid spilling solvents on them.

If a seal or cuff ever tears, it can be replaced by the factory or by some whitewater shops. If you want to do it yourself, here's how:

1. Tear off the old cuff, being sure to get rid of all the excess latex and glue.
2. Find a container large enough to fully expand the opening where the cuff will be mounted and insert it into that opening.
3. Apply a thick coat of Aquaseal to the outside of the drysuit opening where the new cuff will go, being sure to spread the Aquaseal an extra ¼ inch past the cuff line.
4. Stretch the new gasket with your hands and lay it over the glue-coated opening of the suit.
5. Hold the seal in place with tape and let it dry for 24 hours.

Repair tears to drysuits with Vinyl Bond—a general-purpose glue—and a small patch made of the same material as your drysuit. Simply use a dab of Aquaseal to repair small holes or tears.

Other Equipment

LIFEJACKETS

Lifejackets are tough survivors if properly maintained. The key to lifejacket longevity is to keep from using them as seats, cushions, or rags. Don't stuff them into small spaces, and strive to keep them clean and safe from ultraviolet rays and heat.

PUMPS

Manual pumps have moving parts that work better and last longer when lubricated. Keep the cylinders of hand pumps clean and lubricate them in accordance with the manufacturer's specifications (waterproof grease often works well). Electric pumps will last a long time if they're used only to pump rafts up to shape; they'll die fast if they're used to top rafts off.

15

THE REST OF THE STORY
BECOMING A PROFESSIONAL GUIDE

Becoming a Professional Guide

OPENING DOORS

Every guide has heard the questions before: "How deep's the river?" "What do you do in the winter?" "How many times have you done this river?" "How'd you become a guide?"

The last question has always made me smile. There's a mystique surrounding river guides. To an outsider it probably seems as if guides are the lucky few who can play in paradise and still pull in a paycheck. But any guide who's been around a while will tell you that it's quite easy to become a professional. All you have to know is what to do and where to go.

GETTING YOUR TICKET TO RIDE

There are a few basic steps that any prospective guide has to take. Start by picking up all the accreditations you'll need to land a job. In some regions, all you'll need is a valid CPR and First Aid card from the Red Cross; elsewhere you'll need a guiding license as well.

That may mean enrolling in a preseason course offered by whitewater instructors and passing a series of standardized tests to show you have the necessary skills to become a guide.

GUIDE-TRAINING SCHOOLS

Once your accreditations are in place, it's time to honestly evaluate your skills. You may already have a few years' experience as a private rafter—enough experience to start right up as a professional guide. Even if you lack experience, a guide's license will show that you have at least enough expertise to guide gentler rivers although you may need more training. An outfitter's guide-training program will give you additional hands-on experience, an inside look at the operation of a commercial rafting company, and an introduction to a potential employer. The trick is to find a company that both trains and hires guides. But that can be easy too. Read on.

There are lots of ways to find reputable outfitters that offer guide-training programs. You can find their ads in the back of outdoor and paddling magazines and on the brochure racks at your local outdoor store. The National Forest Service, the Bureau of Land Management, and departments of tourism for individual states often maintain lists of outfitters. (Also check the Outfitters Organizations section of the Appendix.) Gather phone numbers and call around to see what's available. Ask for brochures, schedules, and price sheets. At the same time, introduce yourself and ask whether they'll be hiring any guides for the next season. The bigger companies (often the ones with the slick, full-color brochures) will usually have the greatest seasonal turnover of guides and thus the most job openings.

When researching guide schools, don't be afraid to ask questions. Check out the school's reputation and safety record. Will it offer both classroom and hands-on instruction? What is the student-to-teacher ratio? Will you get to run different rivers and use different equipment, or will you use just one raft on one river? If you really do want to become a guide, will they hire you or recommend you to other outfitters? What are the instructors' qualifications? The answers to these questions may vary widely, but lucky for us rafters, guide schools abound. Pick the one that sounds the best, and *have fun!*

THE INSIDE TRACK

The insider's trick to finding guiding jobs is to pick a popular river and then target the outfitters that offer trips there. Rivers like the South Fork of the American (California), the Youghiogheny (Pennsylvania), the Nantahala (North Carolina), the Arkansas (Colorado), and the Ottawa (Ontario) host tens of thousands of rafters each year and have become meccas for first-year guides. If you have the necessary skills and a warm, outgoing personality, and you don't mind traveling to see the outfitters before the season gets rolling, chances are you'll find a job.

Keep in mind that every outfitter on every river needs guides. Some of the best jobs are with small

EIGHT QUESTIONS FOR RESEARCHING GUIDE SCHOOLS
1. Does the company have a solid reputation and safety record?
2. Will you get plenty of hands-on experience?
3. What are the instructors' qualifications?
4. What is the student-to-teacher ratio?
5. Will you get to try out different types of rivers and equipment?
6. Will you learn how to row and paddle?
7. If you want to become a professional guide, will the company help you land a job?
8. Do you get good vibes from the people you talk to?

companies on obscure rivers. Heck, I've only paddled a couple of the rivers I just listed, and I've had a lot of success as a guide. So keep your ears open, talk to plenty of outfitters, and go with the companies that give you the best vibes.

LANDING THE PREMIER JOBS

Once you've mastered the basics of guiding, you may be chomping at the bit to try more demanding rivers. Most outfitters will want you to prove yourself before they'll let

A guide takes a big group of passengers down Alberta's majestic Bow River.

THE GUIDING REPERTOIRE

Riding the bus alongside one of our favorite commercial rivers toward the put-in, Bill started in with his time-worn colloquy.

"Hey, Jeff, look at the river. One-in-Ten is really cranking today!"

"Wow! That's about as gnarly as I've ever seen that rapid!"

"Are you gonna to run it?"

"Umm . . . I don't know. Do you think we can make it?"

The bus was silent. The passengers were about to embark on their first rafting trip and didn't know quite what to expect. Worse yet, they had no idea they were being teased.

"Why do you call it 'One-in-Ten?'" inquired one of the bolder members of the group.

"Because one in ten paddlers ends up swimming it. By the way, how many of you are there today?"

The passenger paused and tentatively muttered, "Ten."

Bill and I burst into laughter. "Gotcha! Hey, did I ever tell you about the time . . ."

Seasoned guides are more than paddle captains, repairmen, and cooks: They're entertainers. Wry, warped, or witty, the best guides put on the best show and display an innate ability to turn river *trips* into river *adventures*. They can pull a seamless stream of tall tales and informative lectures from their bag of tricks and make every moment into something special. They can catch an eddy in the middle of a Class V rapid, give a quick chat on geology, explain how to finish the rapid, and guide the team to safety. Masters of river psychology, they know exactly what to say to keep fears in check or to turn Class III rapids into epic adventures.

To keep your interest piqued (and your tips rolling in), you should constantly strive to expand your guiding repertoire. Let your mind drift beyond the confines of rafts and rapids. Take a little time to learn about the area's flora and fauna, bone up on the region's history, and store up a supply of animated campfire tales. The more you know, the more you have to share with your customers.

you advance to more difficult whitewater. That usually means you've got to have the necessary skills to run a safe trip and a flair for keeping the passengers happy.

To land a premier job you should do whatever it takes to become a real pro. You'll need certain skills to guide multiday trips in the Grand Canyon and other skills to guide paddle teams down high-gradient creeks. You'll also need to become a recognized member of the river-running scene. Run Class IV and V rivers in your spare time, take up kayaking or canoeing, and perfect your rescue skills. Swiftwater rescue courses—whether offered by Rescue 3 (listed in the Appendix) or by your outfitter—will teach you rescue techniques you may never have used before and will make you a more well-rounded employee. Watch whitewater videos and read river magazines to keep the latest lingo and hottest rivers on the tip of your tongue. As your experience and credentials improve, so will your chances of landing that perfect job.

Whitewater Photography

There's nothing like whitewater rafting for in-your-face excitement. But long after the trip's over and the last drops of water have dried from your river gear, the best way to relive your adventures is through photographs and videos. Once you master the basics of whitewater photography, you can freeze moments in time and capture emotions that would otherwise fade away. In this section we'll take a look at the equipment and techniques that whitewater photographers use to produce dazzling images.

EQUIPMENT

There is a vast spectrum of photography equipment available to today's photographers, from inexpensive point-and-shoot cameras to high-tech 35mm SLR (single-lens reflex) systems.

If you're on a budget, you may want to try a waterproof compact model with a zoom or telephoto lens option. Many compact cameras come with a permanently installed 35mm wide-angle lens. That's OK for some shots, but a short lens can flatten out the image and shrink your subject. Zoom and telephoto lenses

extend your shooting range from wide-angle shots to greatly magnified images. With just a flick of a button you can capture a broad swath of canyon or home in on nearby wildlife.

Folks with a few extra bucks may want to use one of the more versatile and higher-quality 35mm SLR systems available today. The 35mm system starts with a camera body that accepts a variety of lenses. With a twist of your wrist you can install an ultra-wide-angle 24mm lens to grab a panoramic view of your riparian world or a long 300mm telephoto lens to compress the scene so tight that the entire river becomes one steep falls.

Video cameras add to this zoom option the tantalizing element of motion. There are several water-resistant video cameras that are perfect for whitewater videography.

PROTECTING YOUR GEAR

Unless you own a waterproof still or video camera, the most important thing you can do for your gear is to keep it dry. Put your camera in a hard-sided Pelican box or a padded ammo can and keep it there until you're sure you're not going to get splashed. Always make sure that camera cases are sealed before you head downriver and that they're strapped tightly to a thwart or to the floor. At the end of each trip, check out the O-ring seals inside the case openings to make sure they're intact, and replace them if they're damaged.

If you don't want to limit your photography time to those moments when your raft is still and dry, you may want to purchase an EWA Marine or comparable underwater housing. This will let you hold onto your camera even while getting pounced upon by waves.

FILM

The first choice you have to make when choosing film is whether you want slides or prints. Slides can be shown on the wall, made into prints, or sold to magazines. Prints, on the other hand, can be stuffed into an album and carried along anytime you want to show them off. Slides may take longer to get back from the developer and they require a deeper understanding of photography to get premium results. Prints may only take an hour or so to get back from a developer but they may not capture a scene as truly as a slide will.

Your next choice is film speed—commonly known as ASA or ISO. Film speeds of 25, 50, or 64 produce amazingly detailed images, but they're often too slow to use for shooting whitewater. Film speeds of 200 or 400 let you freeze whitewater scenes with fast shutter speeds, but they may produce grainier shots. Many whitewater photographers choose 100 ASA film or they shoot with 50 ASA film and *push* it. By setting the camera at 100 ASA but shooting 50 ASA film, and then telling the developer to push the film one stop, you can get tight grains *and* fast shutter speeds.

LIGHTING AND EXPOSURE

Whitewater photography provides some of the greatest challenges a photographer will ever face. You usually have to shoot with fast shutter speeds (½₅₀ to ⅟₁₀₀₀ second) to freeze the action, while dealing with shadows, fickle lighting, and extreme contrasts.

Very sunny days can produce stark differences between bright whitewater and dark shadows, and the reflected light can throw off your exposure meter, resulting in dark, muddy images. Fortunately, you can often override your light meter by choosing an exposure compensation setting of +1 or +1.5 (this is the same as selecting an f-stop one stop larger or a shutter speed one stop slower than the meter chose for you).

You can also control the color and detail in your photos and minimize flares and shadows by positioning yourself with the sun partially or completely behind you. On cloudy days, light is more evenly disbursed, which reduces contrast and harsh shadows. This diffusion will still provide good color saturation if there is sufficient light.

Experiment with back-lighting by placing the subject between the sun and the camera. If you do it just right, you can turn an exploding wave into a veil of shimmering liquid pearls enshrouding a raft.

SHOOTING ANGLES

Your choice of shooting angle will make a dramatic difference in your photographs. If you want to eliminate some annoying background scenery and accentuate the on-river action, climb a few yards up a nearby bank and shoot down at the river. Conversely, you can hunker down in your raft or on the bank and shoot from below eye level to incorporate scenic backdrops into your photos.

THE LEARNING CURVE

After you get back a batch of slides or prints, take some time to see how well you did. Are you pleased with the results? Could you have framed a particular scene better? Do any of your photographs give you new ideas for your next trip? Constantly analyze your photography skills and pore over the photographs in your favorite paddling magazines. Soon you'll be well on your way to capturing photographs that inspire passion and pride.

Rafting for the Physically Challenged

As I reflect upon my many years as a river guide, some of my warmest memories are of river trips with physically challenged rafters. After a few trips with these remarkable folks I realized that the term *handicap* referred to a flaw in my *expectation* of physically challenged people's abilities, not to a *limitation* on those abilities.

Over a period of 10 years I have had the good fortune to guide passengers with a variety of disabilities—blindness, deafness, paraplegia, even quadriplegia. By the end of each of these outings, both passengers and guides had learned a little bit more about themselves. Some of that knowledge had to do with the special preparations and considerations that are involved in handicapped raft trips.

When rafting with physically challenged passengers, you should adapt your equipment and techniques to the special needs of your crew. Sometimes these accommodations are relatively minor. For example, I have had great success with guiding deaf paddle teams when I seated an interpreter in the bow to relay my commands to the crew with sign language. With blind paddlers I have learned to give short, vivid descriptions of things like oncoming waves and rocks to help the crew lean and balance through rapids.

On one particularly memorable trip, I met a paraplegic gentleman at the put-in and thought I was going to be taking him on a casual ride in the bow of my raft. Much to my delight, he had brought his own specially modified rafting equipment and was going to be rowing his own boat that day! It took only minor modifications to the raft's seat (the addition of a seat belt) and a little assistance from the shore before he could row the river as well as anyone else on the trip.

At the far end of the spectrum, raft trips can be shared with quadriplegics and other individuals with severe physical disorders. However, the utmost consideration must be given to their comfort and care. Extra padding is required to provide a safe, comfortable seat, and plenty of warm, dry layers of insulation are necessary to preserve their body heat. Since a flip or a swim is always a possibility—even on Class II rivers—each disabled passenger should have two assistants (one on either side of the passenger) ready to help out in an emergency.

Before undertaking any raft trip with disabled passengers, consult one of the books for physically challenged rafters listed in the Appendix, and contact the American Canoe Association (also in the Appendix) for additional assistance. Finally, choose a river that poses minimal hazards should a mishap occur, and have fun. It may be one of your most memorable outings ever!

Rafting with Children

Kids are popping up all over the outdoors these days, and raft trips are no exception. Pint-size lifejackets, helmets, and paddling garb has turned whitewater rafting into a safe pursuit for tykes of all ages.

In this section we'll take a look at rafting with children aged 5 to 11. There's plenty of room for debating suitable ages and maturity levels for rafting trips, but I've seen 13-year-olds tackle Class V rapids that made me shiver! So size up your children and read on; you may be entering a whole new realm of family adventure.

START ON THE RIGHT FOOT

The first key to convincing kids that rafting is fun is to whet their appetite on a short, warm, gentle river. Pick a run you're familiar with, and share your confidence with your kids or they get antsy before the trip even begins. Next, pick the psychological ploy that

works best with your young ones. The river can be a roller coaster ride, a trip down an endless water slide, or a wilderness exploration . . . whatever fires your children's imagination. No matter what you do, the first trip will be the litmus test. If you're able to get your kids down the river once—smiling—chances are they'll become instant river addicts and share in your joy of whitewater rafting.

RAFT SAFELY

Watching out for your children's safety starts with a trip to your local whitewater shop. Pick lifejackets, helmets, wetsuits, and paddle jackets that are sized to your children. Remember that they don't have the same experience and sensibility you have and that they're less likely to know how to help themselves if they go for a swim. Dressing them in warm, buoyant gear will take the shock out of a trip overboard.

Make more conservative decisions while floating the river. Why roll the dice on making it through a Class IV or V rapid when you can just as easily portage? When bouncing through Class II or III rapids, have your kids hold on and stay low in the raft. Also, make sure there's another boat along just in case you get into trouble.

KEEP THEM ENTERTAINED

To keep your children entertained and enthusiastic, let them set the pace; if you force them to keep to your schedule, you're asking for trouble. (If you picked a short river trip, this should be no problem.) Bring along plenty of snacks—it's amazing how happy taste buds will improve your children's attitude. Finally, make up games to liven up the flat stretches. Give points for spotting wildlife, birds, or yellow boats and reward them with something special at the end of the trip. Let them try rowing or paddling on gentle riffles, or let them swim in calm pools.

Remember, you control your children's whitewater destiny. Choose a path that will make them happy and appreciative of rivers.

Other Whitewater Craft

If you've made it this far into the book, I don't have to convince you that rafting provides enough thrills and spills to fill a lifetime of river journeys. However, if *wetter and wilder* is what you're looking for, you might want to jump ship and try out some new craft. If you're willing to shed the bloated confines of your trusty vessel and invest a little time in learning new skills, you can also run rivers in inflatable kayaks, hardshell kayaks, canoes . . . even riverboards. These craft heighten the level of intimacy between you and the river by putting you closer to the river's surface. The closer and more attuned you become to hydraulics and river features, the better you are able to manage them when you climb back into your raft.

Children love running rivers!

INFLATABLE KAYAKS

Inflatable kayaks have long been the favorite craft of rafters looking for new challenges. Part raft and part kayak, they combine the sporty feel of hardshell kayaks with the familiar buoyancy and portability of whitewater rafts. Their diminutive design lets them skitter across the river's surface and squeeze through tiny slots like no raft ever will. Their shallow draft allows them to slip over the shallowest streambeds when your favorite river gets too low to raft. And you don't even have to learn how to roll them before you start paddling whitewater. Skilled rafters have tackled forgiving Class III rapids on their first day of inflatable kayaking and emerged with nothing worse than a weary smile.

One key difference between inflatable kayaks and rafts is the way they're paddled. Most folks sit in the inflatable kayak's cockpit and paddle with a double-bladed paddle rather than the old familiar single-bladed raft paddle. This demands a whole new set of techniques, but they're easy to learn. Just grab a copy of *The Complete Inflatable Kayaker* (see the back page of this book), throw an inflatable kayak in the trunk, and head for the river. You're guaranteed to get hooked!

INFLATABLE CANOES

Inflatable canoes differ little from many inflatable kayaks; they can be paddled sitting down with a typical kayak paddle. However, inflatable canoes can also accommodate the kneeling position used by most canoers. While incorporating many of the same design characteristics found in inflatable kayaks, inflatable canoes often have slightly larger tubes and lash points for installing seats or saddles.

SIT-ON-TOPS

Sit-on-tops are the latest craze to hit the river-running market. Stiffer than inflatable kayaks, but more forgiving than hardshell kayaks, sit-on-tops combine the stiff plastic hulls of hardshell kayaks with the open cockpits of inflatable kayaks. In fact, anyone who has paddled an inflatable kayak will find a lot of familiar features on sit-on-tops, such as thigh straps and self-bailing floors. If you don't mind the extra space that a sit-on-top takes up, you'll surely appreciate the fact that its plastic hull will never pop or deflate.

KAYAKS

Hardshell kayaks are the sports cars of the whitewater world. Their rigid hulls and sleek profiles let paddlers

Inflatable kayaks (top two boats) provide a logical next step for rafters. Traditional kayaks (bottom) are the sports cars of the river world.

cut serpentine paths from eddy to eddy and drop to drop. Skilled kayakers can surf a wave, spin on the shoulder of a hole, and pop straight up out of the river. In fact, there are so many ways to go kayaking these days, there's probably a specialized kayak to feed just about any passion you have. From ultra-low-volume *squirt* boats (designed to execute all sorts of tricks by using submarine currents) to high-volume *creekin'* boats (designed to surface quickly after running steep drops), kayaks come in myriad shapes, sizes, and materials.

As with a sports car, it takes practice before you can harness the kayak's potential. Since you're wearing the kayak, you've got two choices when you flip upside down: roll up or bail out. It takes some time to learn the *Eskimo roll* (the technique used to reright yourself), bracing techniques, and the paddle strokes that make kayaks special, but once you've got them down, you're on the edge of a new realm of whitewater travel. You can kayak just about anything you can raft . . . and more.

CANOES

Canoeing is steeped in legend and lore. It has been passed down from generations of Indians and voyageurs.

Canoes have traveled the world's major rivers and have introduced thousands of contemporary paddlers to river travel.

Modern recreational canoes run the gamut from stable cruisers to highly rockered whitewater boats. They can carry hundreds of pounds of gear along a chain of lakes or run steep drops side-by-side with kayaks and rafts. If you're used to paddle rafting, chances are you've already learned some of the basic strokes you'll need to paddle a canoe.

RIVERBOARDS

Riverboards are—both literally and figuratively—the ultimate way to get *into* whitewater.

Riverboards are like overgrown boogie boards with added flotation, enhanced durability, and special design features like handles and body-hugging grooves. At first glance they look like the deranged creation of a fun-starved river runner, but that assumption disappears the first time you try one. They are so safe, in fact, that they are used by swiftwater rescue teams as part of their standard equipment!

Riverboarders attain a level of intimacy with the river environment that can only be surpassed by swimming a rapid with your lifejacket on. To use the board you simply lie on it chest down and use swimming and kicking strokes to maneuver across the surface of the river. You wear knee and shin pads, a helmet, and hand and foot fins to protect your limbs and enhance the performance of your strokes. To keep warm and comfortable you add a wetsuit and a thick lifejacket.

After a few sessions on the board you can run an amazing variety of rapids. You can catch body-sized eddies and surf behemoth holes. You can dive under keeper hydraulics and slip through channels too narrow for rafts. Today's most experienced riverboarders take them down runs considered extremely challenging by even the best rafters.

16
CONSERVATION
PRESERVING THE RIVER RESOURCE

It is worth remembering that, long after we are gone, these rivers will still run to distant seas, and that our daughters and sons will want to stand on the banks, as we have done, transfixed by the magic of a river's music and lulled by its flow. . . . They deserve their inheritance. Their children do, as well.

—Paul Vasey, *Rivers of America*

I have been fortunate, over these past two decades, to witness the joy, the thrill, and the challenge that only whitewater rivers can bestow. While sliding down a smooth tongue, gliding toward the heart of a rapid, I feel a return to the elements, to primal forces far more powerful than the human spirit. On the river I gain a deeper understanding of my own roots, and begin to understand humanity's reliance upon water for the sustenance of life itself. And when away from the river I feel a profound sense of displacement that affects every aspect of my daily life, as if a part of me were left at the last take-out.

This sense of interconnectedness has been shared by my predecessors and captured in timeless prose for boaters of all generations. John Muir, the grand architect of environmentalism, wrote, "The rivers flow not past, but through us, thrilling, tingling, vibrating every fiber and cell of the substance of our bodies, making them glide and sing." Henry David Thoreau wrote in his journal, "The river is my own highway, the only wild and unfenced part of the world hereabouts." And Chief Seattle's words have inspired many followers: "The rivers are our brothers, they quench our thirst. The rivers carry our canoes and feed our children . . . and you must give to the rivers the kindness you would give any brother."

While contemporary whitewater enthusiasts look upon flowing waters with reverence and respect, others eye rivers as exploitable resources, a raw product to be harvested, transformed, and sold. The latter group appears in many forms—regional irrigation districts, private utility companies, the Army Corps of Engineers. They come to the rivers not to float and enjoy the wonders of the wilderness but to dam and divert them, shackling eternal waters behind transient insults of concrete and steel.

I have struggled to articulate my own feelings on this kind of river use but have fallen quite short of my goal. Instead, I have deferred to the poetry of Margaret Hindes, whose beautiful verse I found in William O. Douglas's *My Wilderness*:

> Gone, desecrated for a dam—
> Pines, stream, and trails
> Burned and bare
> Down to dust.
> Now water fills the hollow,
> Water for power,
> But the bowl of wilderness
> Is broken, forever.

Rivers are the veins of the earth, the lifeblood of the planet. They nourish the land and rinse away the trivial monuments of human arrogance, mindless of humanity's misbegotten pride. Rivers are there for all

RAFTERS (NOT ALWAYS) WELCOME

Next to river conservation issues, few topics stir so much emotion as river access. As rafters, we are reliant on open corridors across lands adjacent to runnable rivers. Without these corridors, we would be unable to partake in our sport.

North American rivers traverse a wide variety of privately and publicly held lands. This has resulted in a complex collection of access regulations and permit systems.

Access to rivers—especially those in more populated regions—may be limited to specific locations. Access easements, public recreation corridors, or commercial access points might be the only way to reach the river without trespassing on private landholdings. If you aren't sure who owns the land or what your rights are, check out the area's leading guidebooks for put-ins and take-outs. Next, verify the guidebook's accuracy by talking to other boaters, landowners, or government officials.

If your river falls within national forest, national park, Bureau of Land Management, or other federally owned lands, contact the managing agency in advance of your trip to determine whether boating permits are required. Dozens of popular western rivers restrict rafting to those rafters who hold permits. These permits are usually granted many months in advance—either by lottery or by waiting list—so begin planning your trip anywhere from 3 to 12 months before your actual travel date.

A few state and provincial agencies have jumped on the federal bandwagon by restricting river use to permit holders. Though these agencies usually establish less stringent regulations, it can be equally frustrating—and costly—if you fail to pay the proper access fees or obtain the correct permits.

Rafters are a strong force in the river community. Nonetheless, river access is likely to become increasingly limited as the pressure on our natural resources grows. Accordingly, today's rafters must treat rivers and rafting privileges with respect and care in order to ensure open river corridors for the boaters of tomorrow.

to view, to float, and to enjoy. They carry our dreams, and the dreams of future generations.

Whether you raft rivers for inner peace, an adrenaline rush, or financial gain, it is you who can help preserve rivers for everyone. Take the first step by getting involved—join your local whitewater club or support national environmental groups. Then, let the river's own wealth of inspiration kindle your energies and foster your own desires to preserve free-flowing water for everyone to enjoy.

I leave you with these words, passed along by Tanaka Shozo: "The care of rivers is not a question of rivers, but of the human heart."

Put some heart into your rivers and they'll last forever.

A P P E N D I X

Safety Code of the American Whitewater Affiliation

(Reprinted with permission of the American Whitewater Affiliation)

This code has been prepared using the best available information and has been reviewed by a broad cross section of whitewater experts. The code, however, is only a collection of guidelines; attempts to minimize risks should be flexible; not constrained by a rigid set of rules. Varying conditions and group goals may combine with unpredictable circumstances to require alternate procedures.

I. PERSONAL PREPAREDNESS AND RESPONSIBILITY

1. Be a competent swimmer, with the ability to handle yourself underwater.

2. Wear a life jacket. A snugly fitting vest-type life preserver offers back and shoulder protection as well as the flotation needed to swim safely in whitewater.

3. Wear a solid, correctly fitted helmet when upsets are likely. This is essential . . . for . . . rafters running steep drops.

4. Do not boat out of control. Your skills should be sufficient to stop or reach shore before reaching danger. Do not enter a rapid unless you are reasonably sure that you can run it safely or swim it without injury.

5. Whitewater rivers contain many hazards which are not always easily recognized. The following are the most frequent killers:

a. High water. The river's speed and power increase tremendously as the flow increases, raising the difficulty of most rapids. Rescue becomes progressively harder as the water rises, adding to the danger. Floating debris and strainers make even an easy rapid quite hazardous. It is often misleading to judge the river level at the put-in, since a small rise in a wide, shallow place will be multiplied many times where the river narrows. Use reliable gauge information whenever possible, and be aware that sun or snowpack, hard rain, and upstream dam releases may greatly increase the flow.

b. Cold. Cold drains your strength, and robs you of the ability to make sound decisions on matters affecting your survival. Cold-water immersion, because of the initial shock and the rapid heat loss which follows, is especially dangerous. Dress appropriately for bad weather or sudden immersion in the water. When the water temperature is less than 50 degrees Fahrenheit, a wetsuit or drysuit is essential for protection if you swim. Next best is wool or pile clothing under a waterproof shell. In this case, you should also carry waterproof matches and a change of clothing in a waterproof bag. If, after prolonged exposure, a person experiences uncontrollable shaking, loss of coordination, or difficulty speaking, he or she is hypothermic and needs your assistance.

c. Strainers. Brush, fallen trees, bridge pilings, undercut rocks, or anything else which allows river current to sweep through can pin boats and boaters against the obstacle. Water pressure on anything trapped this way can be overwhelming. Rescue is often extremely difficult. Pinning may occur in fast current, with little or no whitewater to warn of the danger.

d. Dams, weirs, ledges, reversals, holes, and hydraulics. When water drops over an obstacle, it curls back on itself, forming a strong upstream current which may be capable of holding a boat or a swimmer. Some holes make for excellent sport; others are proven killers. Paddlers who cannot recognize the differences should avoid all but the smallest holes. Hydraulics around man-made dams must be treated with utmost respect regardless of their height or the level of the river. Despite their seemingly benign appearance, they can create an almost escape-proof trap. The swimmer's only exit from the "drowning machine" is to dive below the surface when the downstream current is flowing beneath the reversal.

e. Broaching. When a boat is pushed sideways against a rock by strong current, it may collapse and wrap. . . . Even without entrapment, releasing pinned boats can be extremely time-consuming and dangerous. To avoid pinning, throw your weight downstream towards the rock. This allows the current to slide harmlessly underneath the hull.

6. Boating alone is discouraged. The minimum party is three people or two craft.

7. Have a frank knowledge of your boating ability, and don't attempt rivers or rapids which are beyond that ability.

a. Develop the paddling skills and teamwork required to

match the river you plan to boat. Most good paddlers develop skills gradually, and attempts to advance too quickly will compromise your safety and enjoyment.

b. Be in good physical and mental condition, consistent with the difficulties which may be expected. Make adjustments for loss of skills due to age, health, fitness. Any health limitations must be explained to your fellow paddlers prior to starting the trip.

8. Be practiced in self-rescue, including escape from [beneath]an overturned craft. . . .

9. Be trained in rescue skills, CPR, and first aid with special emphasis on the recognizing and treating of hypothermia. It may save your friend's life.

10. Carry equipment needed for unexpected emergencies, including footwear which will protect your feet when walking out, a throw rope, knife, whistle, and waterproof matches. If you wear eyeglasses, tie them on and carry a spare pair on long trips. Bring cloth repair tape on short runs, and a full repair kit on isolated rivers. Do not wear bulky jackets, ponchos, heavy boots, or anything else which could reduce your ability to survive a swim.

11. Despite the mutually supportive group structure described in this code, individual paddlers are ultimately responsible for their own safety, and must assume sole responsibility for the following decisions.

a. The decision to participate on any trip. This includes an evaluation of the expected difficulty of the rapids under the conditions existing at the time of the put-in.

b. The selection of appropriate equipment, including a boat design suited to their skills and the appropriate rescue and survival gear.

c. The decision to scout any rapid, and to run or portage according to their best judgment. Other members of the group may offer advice, but paddlers should resist pressure from anyone to paddle beyond their skills. It is also their responsibility to decide whether to pass up any walk-out or take-out opportunity.

d. All trip participants should constantly evaluate their own and their group's safety, voicing their concerns when appropriate and following what they believe to be the best course of action. Paddlers are encouraged to speak with anyone whose actions on the water are dangerous, whether they are a part of your group or not.

II. BOAT AND EQUIPMENT PREPAREDNESS

1. Test new and different equipment under familiar conditions before relying on it for difficult runs. This is especially true when adopting a new boat design or outfitting system. Low-volume craft may present additional hazards to inexperienced or poorly conditioned paddlers.

2. Be sure your boat and gear are in good repair before starting a trip. The more isolated and difficult the run, the more rigorous this inspection should be.

3. Flotation. . . . Inflatable boats should have multiple air chambers and be test-inflated before launching.

4. Have strong, properly sized paddles or oars for controlling your craft. Carry sufficient spares for the length and difficulty of the trip.

5. Outfit your boat safely. The ability to exit your boat quickly is an essential component of safety in rapids. It is your responsibility to see that there is absolutely nothing to cause entrapment when coming free of an upset craft. This includes . . . loose ropes which cause entanglement. Beware of any length of loose line attached to a whitewater boat. All items must be tied tightly and excess line eliminated; painters, throw lines, and safety rope systems must be completely and effectively stored. Do not knot the end of a rope, as it can get caught in cracks between rocks.

6. Provide ropes which permit you to hold on to your craft so that it may be rescued. . . . Rafts and dories may have taut perimeter lines threaded through the loops provided. Footholds should be designed so that a paddler's feet cannot be forced through them, causing entrapment. Flip lines should be carefully and reliably stowed.

7. Know your craft's carrying capacity, and how added loads affect boat handling in whitewater. Most rafts have a minimum crew size which can be added to on day trips or in easy rapids. . . .

8. Car top racks must be strong and attach positively to the vehicle. Lash your boat to each crossbar, then tie the ends of the [ropes]directly to the bumpers for added security. This arrangement should survive all but the most violent vehicle accident.

III. GROUP PREPAREDNESS AND RESPONSIBILITY

1. Organization. A river trip should be regarded as a common adventure by all participants, except on instructional or commercially guided trips as defined below. Participants share the responsibility for the conduct of the trip, and each participant is individually responsible for judging his or her own capabilities and for his or her own safety as the trip progresses. Participants are encouraged (but are not obligated) to offer advice and guidance for the independent consideration and judgment of others.

2. River Conditions. The group should have a reasonable knowledge of the difficulty of the run. Participants should evaluate this information and adjust their plans accordingly. If the run is exploratory or no one is familiar with the river, maps and guidebooks, if available, should be examined. The group should secure accurate flow information; the more difficult the run, the more important this will be. Be aware of possible changes in river level and how this will affect the difficulty of the run. If the trip involves tidal stretches, secure appropriate information on tides.

3. Group equipment should be suited to the difficulty of the river. The group should always have a throw line available, and one line per boat is recommended on difficult runs. The list may include carabiners, prussik loops, first aid kit, flashlight, folding saw, fire starter, guidebooks, maps, food, extra clothing, and any other rescue or survival items suggested by conditions. Each item is not required on every run, · and this list is not meant to be a substitute for good judgment.

4. Keep the group compact, but maintain sufficient spacing to avoid collisions. If the group is large, consider dividing into smaller groups or using the "buddy system" as an additional safeguard. Space yourselves closely enough to permit good communication, but not so close as to interfere with one another in rapids.

a. The lead paddler sets the pace. When in front, do not get in over your head. Never run drops when you cannot see a clear route to the bottom or, for advanced paddlers, a sure route to the next eddy. When in doubt, stop and scout.

b. Keep track of all group members. Each boat keeps the one behind it in sight, stopping if necessary. Know how many people are in your group and take head counts regularly. No one should paddle ahead or walk out without first informing the group. Weak paddlers should stay at the center of a group, and not allow themselves to lag behind. If the group is large and contains a wide range of abilities, a designated "sweep boat" should bring up the rear.

c. Courtesy. On heavily used rivers, do not cut in front of a boater running a drop. Always look upstream before leaving eddies to run or play. Never enter a crowded drop or eddy when no room for you exists. Passing other groups in a rapid may be hazardous; it's often safer to wait upstream until the group ahead has passed.

5. Float plan. If the trip is into a wilderness area or for an extended period, plans should be filed with a responsible person who will contact the authorities if you are overdue. It may be wise to establish checkpoints along the way where civilization could be contacted if necessary. Knowing the location of possible help and preplanning escape routes can speed rescue.

6. Drugs. The use of alcohol or mind-altering drugs before or during river trips is not recommended. It dulls reflexes, reduces decision-making ability, and may interfere with important survival reflexes.

7. Instructional or Commercially Guided Trips. In contrast to the common adventure trip format, in these trip formats, a boating instructor or commercial guide assumes some of the responsibilities normally exercised by the group as a whole, as appropriate under the circumstances. These formats recognize that instructional or commercially guided trips may involve participants who lack significant experience in whitewater. However, as a participant acquires experience in whitewater, he or she takes on increasing responsibility for his or her own safety, in accordance with what he or she knows or should know as a result of that increased experience. Also, as in all trip formats, every participant must realize and assume the risks associated with the serious hazards of whitewater rivers. It is advisable for instructors and commercial guides to acquire trip or personal liability insurance.

a. An "instructional trip" is characterized by a clear teacher/pupil relationship, where the primary purpose of the trip is to teach boating skills, and which is conducted for a fee.

b. A "commercially guided trip" is characterized by a licensed, professional guide conducting trips for a fee.

IV. GUIDELINES FOR RIVER RESCUE

1. Recover from an upset [and get out of the way of the raft]. . . if there is imminent danger of being trapped against rocks, brush, or any other kind of strainer.

2. If you swim, hold on to your boat. It has much flotation and is easy for rescuers to spot. Get to the upstream end so that you cannot be crushed between a rock and your boat by the force of the current. Persons with good balance may be able to climb on top of a . . . flipped raft and paddle to shore.

3. Release your craft if it will improve your chances, especially if the water is cold or dangerous rapids lie ahead. Actively attempt self-rescue whenever possible by swimming for safety. Be prepared to assist others who may come to your aid.

a. When swimming in shallow or obstructed rapids, lie on your back with feet held high and pointed downstream. Do not attempt to stand in fast-moving water; if your foot wedges on the bottom, fast water will push you under and keep you there. Get to slow or very shallow water before attempting to stand or walk. Look ahead! Avoid possible pinning situations including undercut rocks, strainers, downed trees, holes, and other dangers by swimming away from them.

b. If the rapids are deep and powerful, roll over onto your stomach and swim aggressively for shore. Watch for eddies and slackwater and use them to get out of the current. Strong swimmers can effect a powerful upstream ferry and get to shore fast. If the shores are obstructed with strainers or undercut rocks, however, it is safer to "ride the rapid out" until a safer escape can be found.

4. If others spill and swim, go after the boaters first. Rescue boats and equipment only if this can be done safely. While participants are encouraged (but not obligated) to assist one another to the best of their ability, they should do so only if they can, in their judgment, do so safely. The first duty of a rescuer is not to compound the problem by becoming another victim.

5. The use of rescue lines requires training; uninformed use may cause injury. Never tie yourself into either end of a line without a reliable quick-release system. Have a knife handy to deal with unexpected entanglement. Learn to place set lines effectively, to throw accurately, to belay effectively, and to properly handle a rope thrown to you.

6. When reviving a drowning victim be aware that cold water may greatly extend survival time underwater. Victims of hypothermia may have depressed vital signs so they look and feel dead. Don't give up; continue CPR for as long as possible without compromising safety.

Water-Level Information

Bureau of Reclamation, Commissioner's Office, Department of the Interior, C Street, between 18th and 19th Streets, Washington, DC 20240; (202) 343-1100

Hydrological Information Unit, United States Geological Survey, 419 National Center, Reston, VA 22092; (703) 860-7531

National Weather Service, National Oceanic and Atmospheric Administration, Department of Commerce, 8060 13th Street, Silver Springs, MD, 20910; (301) 427-7622

United States Army Corp of Engineers, Public Affairs Office, 20 Massachusetts Avenue, N.W., Washington, DC 20314-1000; (202) 272-0010

NOTE: If you can't find a telephone number for water-level information in your area, call a local outfitter or paddle shop. They may be able to help you out.

United States Maps

BUREAU OF LAND MANAGEMENT

Office of Public Affairs, Bureau of Land Management, Department of the Interior, Washington, DC 20240; (202) 343-9435

Denver Service Center, Bureau of Land Management, Denver Federal Center, Building 50, P.O. Box 25047, Denver, CO 80225-0047; (303) 236-6452

NATIONAL CARTOGRAPHIC INFORMATION

National Cartographic Information Center, 507 National Center, 12201 Sunrise Valley Drive, Reston, VA 22092; (703) 860-6045

NATIONAL FOREST SERVICE

Region 1 (Northern ID, MT): Regional Forester, Northern Region, Forest Service, Federal Building, P.O. Box 7669, Missoula, MT 59807; (406) 329-3011

Region 2 (CO, NB, SD, WY): Regional Forester, Rocky Mountain Region, Forest Service, 11177 West 8th Avenue, Lakewood, CO 80225; (303) 234-4185

Region 3 (AZ, NM): Regional Forester, Southwestern Region, Forest Service, 517 Gold Avenue S.W., Albuquerque, NM 87102; (505) 766-2444

Region 4 (Southern ID, NV, UT, WY): Regional Forester, Intermountain Region, Forest Service, Federal Building, 324 25th Street, Ogden, UT 84401; (801) 625-5182

Region 5 (CA): Regional Forester, Pacific Southwest Region, Forest Service, 630 Sansome Street, San Francisco, CA 94111; (415) 556-0122

Region 6 (OR, WA): Regional Forester, Pacific Northwest Region, Forest Service, 319 S.W. Pine Street, Portland, OR 97208; (503) 221-2877

Region 8 (AL, AR, FL, GA, KY, LA, MS, NC, SC, TN, TX, VA): Forest Service Information Center, Southern Region, 1720 Peachtree Road N.W., Room 850S, Atlanta, GA 30309; (404) 347-2384

Region 9 (MD, PA, WV): Regional Forester, Eastern Region, 310 West Wisconsin Avenue, Room 500, Milwaukee, WI 53203; (414) 291-3693

NATIONAL PARK SERVICE

Pacific Northwest, 83 South King Street, Suite 212, Seattle, WA 98104; (206) 442-5366

Rocky Mountains, P.O. Box 25287, Denver, CO 80225; (303) 969-2000

Western, 450 Golden Gate Avenue, P.O. Box 36063, San Francisco, CA 94102; (415) 556-8313

Southwest, P.O. Box 728, Sante Fe, NM 87504-0728; (505) 988-6886

Midwest, 1709 Jackson St, Omaha, NE 68102; (402) 221-3482

Mid-Atlantic, 143 South Third Street, Philadelphia, PA 19106; (215) 597-7386

Southeast, 75 Spring Street SW, Atlanta, GA 30303; (404) 331-5838

U.S. GEOLOGICAL SURVEY

Mapping Distribution, U.S. Geological Survey, Box 25286 Federal Center, Building 41, Denver, CO 80225; (303) 236-7477

Canadian Maps

Map Distribution Office, 615 Booth Street, Ottawa, Ontario K1A 0E9

Canadian Heritage Rivers Board, c/o Canadian Parks Service, Environment Canada, Ottawa, Ontario K1A 0H3

Regional Guidebooks (United States)

Armstead, L. D. *Whitewater Rafting in Eastern America: A Guide to Rivers and Outfitters for Beginning and Advanced Whitewater Rafters.* Chester, CT: The Globe Pequot, 1974.

Armstead, L. D. *Whitewater Rafting in Western America: A Guide to Rivers and Professional Outfitters.* Chester, CT: The Globe Pequot, 1990.

Bennett, J. *Class Five Chronicles: Things Mother Never Told You 'Bout Whitewater.* Portland, OR: Swiftwater Publishing Company, 1992.

Cassady, J., B. Cross, and F. Calhoun. *Western Whitewater: From the Rockies to the Pacific.* Berkeley, CA: North Fork Press, 1994.

Hulick, K. and L. Wright. *Paddler's Atlas of U.S. Rivers West.* Harrisburg, PA: Stackpole Books, 1993.

Penny, R. *The Whitewater Sourcebook: A Directory of Information on American Whitewater Rivers.* Birmingham, AL: Menasha Ridge Press, 1989.

Shears, N. *Paddle America, A Guide to Trips and Outfitters in All 50 States.* Washington, DC: Starfish Press, 1992.

Wood, P. *Running the Rivers of North America: A Guide to Canoeing, Kayaking, and Rafting Down More Than 50 US and Canadian Rivers—From Lazy Streams to White Water.* Barre, MA: Barre Publishing, 1978.

Local Guidebooks (United States)

FAR WEST (CA AND NV)

Cassady, J. and F. Calhoun. *California Whitewater: A Guide to the Rivers.* Berkeley, CA: North Fork Press, 1990.

Cassady, J. and F. Calhoun. *River Maps: Forks of the Kern, Upper Kern, Lower Kern, Tuolumne and South Fork American.* Berkeley, CA: Cassady and Calhoun River Publications, misc. years.

Cassidy, J. *A Guide to Three Rivers: The Stanislaus, Tuolumne, and South Fork of the American.* Stanford, CA: Friends of the River Books, 1981.

Holbeck, L. and C. Stanley. *A Guide to the Best Whitewater in the State of California.* Stanford, CA: Friends of the River Books, 1984.

Margulis, R. K. *The Complete Guide to Whitewater Rafting Tours: California Edition 1986.* Palo Alto, CA: Aquatic Adventure Publications, 1986.

Quinn, J. M. and J. W. Quinn. *Handbook to the Klamath River Canyon.* Medford, OR: Educational Adventures Inc., 1983.

Robinson, K. and F. Lehman. *South Fork of the American River: From Chili Bar Dam to Salmon Forks Road.* Fremont, CA: Lore Unlimited, 1982.

Robinson, K. and F. Lehman. *Stanislaus River: From Camp Nine to Parrots Ferry.* Fremont, CA: Lore Unlimited, 1982.

Robinson, K. and F. Lehman. *Tuolumne River: From Lumsden Bridge to Ward's Ferry.* Fremont, CA: Lore Unlimited, 1982.

PACIFIC NORTHWEST (AK, OR, AND WA)

Bennett, J. *A Guide to the Whitewater Rivers of Washington: A Comprehensive Handbook to Over 150 Runs in the Cascades and Beyond.* Portland, OR: Swiftwater Publishing Company, 1991.

Campbell, A. *John Day River: Drift and Historical Guide.* Portland, OR: Frank Amato Publishers, 1980.

Embick, A. *Fast & Cold: A Guide to Alaska Whitewater.* Valdez, AK: Valdez Alpine Books, 1994.

Jettmar, K. *The Alaska River Guide: Canoeing, Kayaking, and Rafting in the Last Frontier.* Seattle, WA: Graphic Arts Center Publishing Center, 1993.

Furrer, W. *Water Trails of Washington.* Edmonds, WA: Signpost, 1979.

Garren, J. *Oregon River Tours.* Portland, OR: Garren Publishing, n.d.

Korb, G. *A Paddler's Guide to the Olympic Peninsula: A Comprehensive Guide to 69 River Runs on Washington's Beautiful Olympic Peninsula.* Self-published, 1992.

North, D. *Washington Whitewater.* Seattle, WA: Mountaineers, 1992.

Quinn, J. M. and J. W. Quinn. *Handbook to the Klamath River Canyon.* Medford, OR: Educational Adventures, Inc., 1983.

Quinn, J. M., J. W. Quinn, and J. G. King. *Handbook to the Illinois River Canyon.* Medford, OR: Educational Adventures, Inc., 1979.

Quinn, J. M., J. W. Quinn, and J. G. King. *Handbook to the Rogue.* Medford, OR: Educational Adventures, Inc., 1979.

Quinn, J. W., J. M. Quinn, and J. G. King. *Handbook to the Deschutes River Canyon.* Medford, OR: Educational Adventures, Inc., 1979.

Wilderness Public Rights Fund. *Whitewater Primer: Including Selway and Illinois Rivers.* Portland, OR: Wilderness Public Rights Fund.

Willamette Kayak and Canoe Club. *Soggy Sneakers Guide to Oregon.* 2d rev. ed. Corvallis, OR: Willamette Kayak and Canoe Club, 1986.

NORTHERN ROCKIES (ID, MT, AND WY)

Amaral, G. *Idaho: The Whitewater State.* Boise, ID: Watershed Books, 1990.

Conley, C. and J. Carrey. *The Middle Fork and Sheepeater War.* Cambridge, ID: Backeddy Books, 1977.

Conley, C. and J. Carrey. *River of No Return.* Cambridge, ID: Backeddy Books, 1978.

Conley, C. and J. Barton. *Snake River of Hell's Canyon.* Cambridge, ID: Backeddy Books, 1979.

Fischer, H. *The Floater's Guide to Montana.* 2d ed. Helena, MT: Falcon Press, 1986.

Garren, J. *Idaho River Tours.* Beaverton, OR: Touchstone Press, 1980.

Graeff, T. *River Runner's Guide to Idaho.* Boise, ID: Idaho Department of Parks and Recreation, 1986.

Huser, V. and Buzz Belknap. *Snake River Guide: Grand Teton National Park.* Boulder City, NV: Westwater, 1972.

Moore, G. and D. McClaren. *Idaho Whitewater: The Complete Guide for Canoeists, Rafters and Kayakers.*

McCall, ID: Class VI Whitewater, 1989.

Quinn, J. M. et al. *Handbook to the Middle Fork of the Salmon.* Medford, OR: Educational Adventures Inc., 1979.

Wilderness Public Rights Fund. *Whitewater Primer: Including Selway and Illinois Rivers.* Portland, OR: Wilderness Public Rights Fund.

Lewis, D. *Paddle and Portage: The Floater's Guide to Wyoming Rivers.* Casper, WY: The Wyoming Naturalist, 1991.

SOUTHWEST (UT, CO, AZ, NM, AND TX)

Aitchison, S. *A Naturalist's San Juan River Guide.* Boulder, CO: Pruett, 1983.

Anderson, F. and A. Hopkinson. *Rivers of the Southwest: A Boaters' Guide to the Rivers of Colorado, New Mexico, Utah and Arizona.* 2d ed. Boulder, CO: Pruett, 1987.

Baars, D. and G. Stevenson. *San Juan Canyons: A River Runner's Guide.* Boulder City, NV: Westwater, 1986.

Banks, G. and D. Eckardt. *Colorado Rivers and Creeks.* Boulder, CO: Moenkopi Digital Formations, 1995.

Belknap, Bill and Buzz Belknap. *Canyonlands River Guide.* Boulder City, NV: Westwater, 1974.

Belknap, Buzz. *Grand Canyon River Guide.* Boulder City, NV: Westwater, 1969.

Cassady, J. and F. Calhoun. *River Maps: Upper Arkansas, Lower Arkansas, and the Rio Grande.* Berkeley, CA: Cassady-Calhoun River Publications, misc. years.

Crumbo, K. *History of the Grand Canyon: A River Runners's Guide.* Boulder, CO: Johnson, 1981.

Evans, L. and Buzz Belknap. *Desolation River Guide.* Boulder City, NV: Westwater, 1969.

Evans, L. and Buzz Belknap. *Dinosaur River Guide.* Boulder City, NV: Westwater, 1969.

Hamblin, W. K. and J. K. Rigby. *Guidebook to the Colorado River, Part I: Lee's Ferry to Phantom Ranch in Grand Canyon National Park.* 2d ed. Salt Lake City, UT: Brigham Young University Press, 1969.

Hamblin, W. K. and J. K. Rigby. *Guidebook to the Colorado River, Part II: Phantom Ranch in Grand Canyon National Park to Lake Mead, Arizona-Nevada.* Salt Lake City, UT:

Brigham Young University Press, 1969.

Hayes, P. T. and G. C. Simmons. *River Runner's Guide to the Green and Colorado Rivers with Emphasis on Geologic Features.* Vol. I, *River Runner's Guide to Dinosaur National Monument and Vicinity, with Emphasis on Geologic Features.* Denver, CO: Powell Society, 1973.

Maurer, S. G. *A Guide to New Mexico's Popular Rivers and Lakes.* Albuquerque, NM: Heritage Associates Inc., 1983.

Humphrey, M. *Running the Rio Grande: A Floater's Guide to the Big Bend.* Austin, TX: AAR/Tantalus, 1981.

Kirkley, G. *A Guide to Texas Rivers and Streams.* Houston, TX: Lone Star Books, 1983.

Mutschler, F. E. *River Runner's Guide to the Green and Colorado Rivers with Emphasis on Geologic Features.* Vol. II, *Rivers Runner's Guide to Canyonlands National Park and Vicinity with Emphasis on Geologic Features.* Denver, CO: Powell Society, 1977.

Mutschler, F. E. *River Runner's Guide to the Green and Colorado Rivers with Emphasis on Geologic Features.* Vol. IV, *Rivers Runner's Guide to Desolation and Gray Canyons with Emphasis on Geologic Features.* Denver, CO: Powell Society, 1972.

New Mexico State Park Division. *New Mexico Whitewater: A Guide to River Trips.* Santa Fe, NM: New Mexico State Park Division, 1983.

Nichols, G. C. *River Runner's Guide to Utah and Adjacent Areas.* 2d ed. Salt Lake City, UT: Univ. of Utah Press, 1986.

Nolen, B. M. and R. E. Narramore. *Texas Rivers and Rapids.* Vol. VI. Bandera, TX: Ben Nolen Graphics, 1983.

Pearson, L. R. *River Guide to the Rio Grande: General Information.* Big Bend National Park, TX: Big Bend Natural History Assoc., 1982.

Pearson, J. R. *River Guide to the Rio Grande.* Vol. I, *Colorado and Santa Elena Canyons.* Big Bend National Park, TX: Big Bend Natural History Assoc., 1982.

Pearson, J. R. *River Guide to the Rio Grande.* Vol. II, *Mariscal and Boquillas Canyons.* Big Bend National Park, TX: Big Bend Natural History Assoc., 1982.

Pearson, J. R. *River Guide to the Rio Grande.* Vol. III, *The Lower Canyons.* Big Bend National Park, TX: Big Bend Natural History Assoc., 1982.

Rigby, J. K. et al. *Guidebook to the Colorado River, Part 3: Moab to Hite, Utah, Through Canyonlands National Park.* Salt Lake City, UT: Brigham Young Univ. Press, 1969.

Simmons, G. C. and D.L. Gaskill. *River Runner's Guide to the Green and Colorado Rivers with Emphasis on Geologic Features.* Vol. III, *River Runner's Guide: Marble Gorge and Grand Canyon.* Denver, CO: Powell Society, 1969.

Stevens, L. *The Colorado River in the Grand Canyon: A Comprehensive Guide to Its Natural History.* Flagstaff, AZ: Red Lake Books, 1986.

Stohlquist, J. R. *Colorado Whitewater.* Buena Vista, CO: Colorado Kayak Supply, 1982.

Wheat, D. *The Floater's Guide to Colorado.* Helena, MT: Falcon Press, 1983.

SOUTHERN APPALACHIANS (AL, GA, KY, NC, SC, AND TN)

Benner, F. *Carolina Whitewater: A Canoeist's Guide to the Western Carolinas.* 5th ed. Hillsborough, NC: Menasha Ridge Press, 1987.

Benner, F. and T. McCloud. *A Paddler's Guide to Eastern North Carolina.* Hillsborough, NC: Menasha Ridge Press, 1987.

Burmeister, W. F. *Appalachian Water IV: Southeastern U.S. Rivers.* Oakton, VA: Appalachian Books, 1974.

Burmeister, W. F. *Appalachian Waters V: The Upper Ohio and Its Tributaries.* Oakton, VA: Appalachian Books, 1974.

Foshee, J. *Alabama Canoe Rides and Float Trips.* Huntsville, AL: Strode Press, 1975.

Nealy, W. *Whitewater Home Companion.* Vol. I, *Southeastern Rivers.* Birmingham, AL: Menasha Ridge Press, 1981.

Nealy, W. *Whitewater Home Companion.* Vol. II, *Southeastern Rivers.* Birmingham, AL: Menasha Ridge Press, 1984.

Sehlinger, B. et al. *Appalachian Whitewater.* Vol. I, *The Southern Mountains.* Birmingham, AL: Menasha Ridge Press, 1986.

Sehlinger, B. *A Canoeing and Kayaking Guide to the*

Streams of Kentucky. Hillsborough, NC: Menasha Ridge Press, 1978.

Sehlinger, B. and B. Lantz. *A Canoeing and Kayaking Guide to the Streams of Tennessee.* Vol. I. Hillsborough, NC: Menasha Ridge Press, 1981.

Sehlinger, B. and B. Lantz. *A Canoeing and Kayaking Guide to the Streams of Tennessee.* Vol. II. Hillsborough, NC: Menasha Ridge Press, 1983.

Sehlinger, B. and D. Otey. *Northern Georgia Canoeing.* Hillsborough, NC: Menasha Ridge Press, 1980.

Sehlinger, B. and D. Otey. *Southern Georgia Canoeing.* Hillsborough, NC: Menasha Ridge Press, 1986.

Smith, M. *A Paddler's Guide to the Obed-Emory Watershed.* Hillsborough, NC: Menasha Ridge Press.

CENTRAL APPALACHIANS (MD, OH, PA, VA, AND WV)

Burmeister, W. F. *Appalachian Waters I: The Delaware River and Its Tributaries.* Oakton, VA: Appalachian Books, 1974.

Burmeister, W. F. *Appalachian Waters III: The Susquehanna River and Its Tributaries.* Oakton, VA: Appalachian Books, 1974.

Burmeister, W. F. *Appalachian Waters IV: Southeastern U.S. Rivers.* Oakton, VA: Appalachian Books, 1974.

Burmeister, W. F. *Appalachian Waters V: The Upper Ohio and Its Tributaries.* Oakton, VA: Appalachian Books, 1974.

Matacia, L. J. and D. Cecil. *Blue Ridge Voyages.* Vol IV, *The Shenandoah River.* Oakton, VA: Matacia, 1974.

Combs, R. and S. E. Gillen. *A Canoeing and Kayaking Guide to the Streams of Ohio.* Vol. I. Hillsborough, NC: Menasha Ridge Press, 1983.

Combs, R. and S. E. Gillen. *A Canoeing and Kayaking Guide to the Streams of Ohio.* Vol. II. Hillsborough, NC: Menasha Ridge Press, 1983.

Corbett, H. R. *Virginia Whitewater.* Springfield, VA: Seneca Press, 1977.

Davidson, P. and W. Eister, with D. Davidson. *Wildwater West Virginia.* Vol. I, *The Northern Streams.* 3rd ed. Hillsborough, NC: Menasha Ridge Press, 1985.

Davidson, P. and W. Eister, with D. Davidson. *Wildwater West Virginia.* Vol. II, *The Northern Streams.* 3rd ed. Hillsborough, NC: Menasha Ridge Press, 1985.

Falcomer, K. and R. Corbett. *The Delaware River.* Oakton, VA: Appalachian Books, 1981.

Grove, E. et al. *Appalachian Whitewater.* Vol. II, *The Central Mountains: The Premier Canoeing and Kayaking Streams of Pennsylvania, West Virginia, Maryland, Delaware, and Virginia.* Hillsborough, NC: Menasha Ridge Press, 1987.

Matacia, L. J. and O. S. Cicil III. *An Illustrated Canoe Log of the Shenandoah River and Its South Fork.* Oakton, VA: Matacia, 1974.

Matacia, L. J. and R. Corbett. *Blue Ridge Voyages.* Vol. III, *An Illustrated Guide to Ten Whitewater Canoe Trips.* Oakton, VA: Matacia, 1972.

Nealy, W. *Whitewater Home Companion.* Vol. I, *Southeastern Rivers.* Birmingham, AL: Menasha Ridge Press, 1981.

Nealy, W. *Whitewater Home Companion.* Vol. II, *Southeastern Rivers.* Birmingham, AL: Menasha Ridge Press, 1984.

NORTHERN APPALACHIANS (CT, MA, ME, NH, NY, AND VT)

Schweiker, R., ed. *River Guide.* Vol. I, *Maine.* Boston, MA: Appalachian Mountain Club Books, 1986.

Schweiker, R., ed. *River Guide.* Vol. II, *New Hampshire and Vermont.* Boston, MA: Appalachian Mountain Club Books, 1986.

Schweiker, R., ed. *River Guide.* Vol. III, *Massachusetts, Connecticut and Rhode Island.* Boston, MA: Appalachian Mountain Club Books, 1986.

Yates, K. and C. Phillips, eds. *River Guide, Maine.* New York, NY: Appalachian Mountain Club Books, 1991.

Tuckerman, S., ed. *River Guide, Massachusetts, Connecticut, and Rhode Island.* Boston, MA: Appalachian Mountain Club Books, 1990.

Burmeister, W. F. *Appalachian Waters I: The Delaware River and Its Tributaries.* Oakton, VA: Appalachian Books, 1974.

Burmeister, W. F. *Appalachian Waters II: The Hudson River and Its Tributaries.* Oakton, VA: Appalachian Books, 1974.

Burmeister, W. F. *Appalachian Waters III: The Susquehanna River and Its Tributaries.* Oakton, VA: Appalachian Books, 1974.

Burmeister, W. F. *Appalachian Waters V: The Upper Ohio and Its Tributaries.* Oakton, VA: Appalachian Books, 1974.

Connelly, J. and J. Porterfield. *Appalachian Whitewater.* Vol. III, *The Northern Mountains: The Premier Canoeing and Kayaking Streams of Connecticut, Massachusetts, Eastern New York State, Vermont, New Hampshire, and Maine.* Hillsborough, NC: Menasha Ridge Press, 1987.

Gabler, R. *New England Whitewater River Guide.* Boston, MA: Appalachian Mountain Club Books, 1981.

OZARKS (AS AND MO)

Kennon, T. *Ozark Whitewater: A Paddler's Guide to the Mountain Streams of Arkansas and Missouri.* Birmingham, AL: Menasha Ridge Press.

NORTHWOODS (MI, MN, AND WI)

Breining, G. and L. Watson. *A Gathering of Waters: A Guide to Minnesota's Rivers.* St. Paul, MN: Minnesota Dept. of Natural Resources, 1977.

Palzer, F. and J. Palzer. *Whitewater/Quietwater: A Guide to the Rivers of Wisconsin, Upper Michigan and NE Minnesota.* 5th ed. Two Rivers, WI: Evergreen Paddlers, 1983 (supplt. 1985).

Local Guidebooks (Canada)

Harrington, R. *River Rafting in Canada.* Alaska Northwest Publishing Company (WA), 1987.

Madsen, K. and G. Wilson. *Rivers of the Yukon: A Paddling Guide.* Whitehorse, Yukon: Primrose Publishing, 1989.

Northwest Brigade Canoe Club. *Canoe and Kayak Trip Guide for the Central Interior of British Columbia.* Prince George, BC: Northwest Brigade Canoe Club (updated yearly).

Pratt-Johnson, B. *Whitewater Trips and Hot Springs in the Kootenays of British Columbia: For Kayakers, Canoeists and Rafters.* Seattle, WA: Adventure Publishing, 1989.

Pratt-Johnson, B. *Whitewater Trips for Kayakers, Canoeists and Rafters in British Columbia: Greater Vancouver Through Whistler, Okanagan and Thompson River Regions.* Seattle, WA: Adventure Publishing, 1986.

Pratt-Johnson, B. *Whitewater Trips for Kayakers, Canoeists and Rafters on Vancouver Island.* Seattle, WA: Pacific Search Press, 1984.

Smith, S. *Canadian Rockies Whitewater.* Jasper, Alberta: Headwaters Press, Ltd., 1995.

VanDine, D. and B. Fandrich. *Rafting in British Columbia, Featuring the Lower Thompson River.* Sureey, BC: Hancock House, 1984.

International Guidebooks

Bangs, R. and C. Kallen. *Rivergods: Exploring the World's Wild Rivers.* San Francisco, CA: Sierra Club Books, 1985.

Bennett, J. *Class Five Chronicles: Things Mother Never Told You 'Bout Whitewater.* Portland, OR: Swiftwater Publishing Company, 1992.

Bennett, J. and J. Cassady. *World Whitewater: River Running Around the Globe.* (Work in progress!)

Dawson, S. *Corsica Whitewater.* Oxford, U.K.: T. Storry, n.d.

Flakstad, N. and L. Ongstad. *White Water Canoeing Guide To Southern Norway.* No publishing information.

Fox, A. *Run River Run: Canoeing Britain's Finest Rivers.* London: Diadem Books, 1990

Gallo, R. and M. Mayfield. *The Rivers of Costa Rica, A Canoeing, Kayaking and Rafting Guide.* Birmingham, AL: Menasha Ridge Press, 1988.

Haas, J. *Gems of Whitewater of the High Alps.* Germany: Rosgarten Verlag, 1990.

Holbek, L. *The Rivers of Chile.* Phoenicia, NY: American Whitewater Association, 1992.

Knowles, P. and D. Allardice. *Whitewater Nepal.* Birmingham, AL: Menasha Ridge Press and Rivers Publishing (U.K.), 1992.

McLaughlin, C. and Y. McLaughlin. *The Rivers and Lakes of Victoria.* Hampton, Australia: Macstyle Publishing, 1991.

McLaughlin, C. and Y. McLaughlin. *The Rivers and Lakes of New South Wales*. Hampton, Australia: Macstyle Publishing, 1990.

McLaughlin, C. and Y. McLaughlin, Y. *Canoeing the Rivers and Lakes of Queensland*. Hampton, Australia: Macstyle Publishing, 1988.

Robey, T. *A Gringo's Guide to Mexican Whitewater*. Heritage Associates (NM), 1992.

Wales, S. *Alpine Canoeing*. Lincoln, U.K.: Alpine Canoeing Holidays, 1990. (Covers Bavaria and Austria.)

Walker, W. *Paddling the Frontier, Guide to Pakistan's Whitewater*. No publishing information.

Books for Physically Challenged Rafters

Canoeing and Kayaking for Persons with Physical Disabilities. American Canoe Association, P.O. Box 1190, Newington, VA 22122; (703) 550-7495

A Guide to Canoeing with Disabled Persons. British Canoe Union, Mapperley Hall, Lucknow Avenue, Nottingham, NG3 5FA, England

International Directory of Recreational Oriented Assistive Devices. Life Boat Press, P.O. Box 11782, Marina Del Ray, CA 90295

Introduction to Kayaking for Persons with Disabilities. John Galland, Vinland National Center, 3675 Ihduhapi Road, Box 308, Loretto, MN 55357

Resource Manual on Canoeing for the Disabled. Canadian Recreational Canoeing Association, Box 500, Hyde Park, Ontario, N0M 1Z0, Canada

Additional Canada Information

Ministry of Tourism, Parliament Buildings, Victoria, B.C. V8V 1X4

Ministry of Environment and Parks, Conservation and Parks Division, 4000 Seymour Place, Victoria, B.C. V8V 1X5

Department of Lands, Forests and Resources, Parliament Buildings, Victoria, B.C. V8V 1X4

Department of Tourism, 7-155 Carlton Street, Winnipeg, Manitoba R3C 3H8

Department of Tourism Information Service, Box 12345, Fredericton, New Brunswick E3B 5C3

Parks Division, Department of Culture, Recreation and Youth, P.O. Box 4750, St. John's, Newfoundland A1C 5T7

TravelArctic, Government of the Northwest Territories, Yellowknife, NWT X1A 2L9

Director, Park Management Branch, Ministry of Natural Resources, Public Information Centre, Room 1640, 99 Wellesly Street West, Toronto, Ontario M7A 1W3

Parks and Recreation, Place de la Capitale, 150 East Street, Cyrille Boulevard, Quebec City, Quebec G1R 2B2

Saskatchewan Economic Development and Tourism, 1919 Saskatchewan Drive, Regina, Saskatchewan S4P 3V7

Tourism Yukon, Box 2703, Whitehorse, Yukon Y1A 2C6

Periodicals

American Whitewater (The Journal of the American Whitewater Affiliation), P.O. Box 85, Phoenicia, NY 12464.

Canoe & Kayak, 10526 NE 68th, Suite 3, Kirkland, WA 98033.

Currents, National Organization for River Sports, P.O. Box 6847, Colorado Springs, CO 80934.

Outside, P.O. Box 54729, Boulder, CO 80322-4729.

Paddler, P.O. Box 697, Fallbrook, CA 92028.

Rafting Equipment Catalogs

Alpenglow Marine and Sport, Inc., I-70 and Colfax, 885 Lupine Street #B, Golden, CO 80401; (800) 274-0133

B & A Distributing Co., 201 S.E. Oak Street, Portland, OR 97214; (503) 230-0482

Cascade Outfitters, P.O. Box 209, Springfield, OR 97477; (800) 223-RAFT (7238)

Clavey Equipment, P.O. Box 1149, Point Reyes Station, CA 94956; (415) 663-1921

Colorado Kayak Supply, P.O. Box 3059, Buena Vista, CO 81211; (800) 535-3565

Down River Equipment Company, 12100 W. 52nd Avenue, Wheat Ridge, CO 80033; (303) 467-9489

Downstream Products, Inc., 12112 N.E. 195th, Bothell, WA 98011; (206) 486-0220

Four Corners Rivers Sports, P.O. Box 379, Durango, CO 81302; (303) 259-0379

Long Beach Water Sports, 730 E. 4th Street, Long Beach, CA 90802; (310) 432-0187

Nantahala Outdoor Center, Outfitters Store, 41 Highway 19 West, Bryson City, NC 28713-9114; (800) 367-3521

North American River Runners, U.S. Route 60, P.O. Box 81, Hico, WV 25854; (800) 950-2585

Northwest River Supplies, 2009 S. Main, Moscow, ID 83843-8913; (800) 635-5202

Pacific River Supply, 3675 San Pablo Dam Road, El Sobrante, CA 94803; (415) 223-3675

Predator, 1652 Duranleau, Granville Island, Vancouver, B.C. V6H 3S4; (604) 688-1928

Recreational Equipment Incorporated (REI), Department N2045, Sumner, WA 98352; (800) 426-4840

Sierra South, P.O. Box Y, Kernville, CA 93238; (619) 376-3745

Water's Edge, Inc., P.O. Box 26823, Tucson, AZ 85726; (800) 999-RAFT

Wildwater Designs, 230 Penlynn Pike, Penlynn, PA 19422; (215) 646-5034

Wyoming River Raiders, 601 S.E. Wyoming Boulevard, Casper, WY 82609; (800) 247-6068

Raft Manufacturers

Achilles Inflatable Craft, 1407 80th Street S.W., Everett, WA 98203; (206) 353-7000

AIRE, Inc., P.O. Box 3412, Boise, ID 83703; (208) 344-7506

All River Equipment (distributor for Star Inflatables), 232 Banks Road, Traveller's Rest, SC 29690; (803) 836-2800

Avon Seagull Marine, 1851 McGaw Avenue, Irvine, CA 92714; (714) 250-0880

B & A Distributing Co. (Riken and Momentum Rafts), 201 S.E. Oak Street, Portland, OR 97214-1079; (503) 230-0482

Colorado Headwaters, Inc., 18800 E. Clarke Road, Parker, CO 80134; (303) 840-8776

Custom Inflatables, P.O. Box 80, Albright, WV 26519; (304) 329-2359

Demaree Inflatable Boats, P.O. Box 307, Friendsville, MD 21531; (301) 746-5815

ERC Manufacturing, Inc. (Wing rafts and catarafts), P.O. Box 279, Arcata, CA 95521; (707) 826-2887

Gemini Boats, P.O. Box 9326, Bend, OR 97708; (503) 383-0756

Hyside Inflatables, P.O. Box Z, Kernville, CA 93238; (619) 376-3723

Incept River Boats, 3347 Highway 8, East #7, Moscow, ID 83843; (208) 882-2844

Jack's Plastic Welding, 115 S. Main, Aztec, NM 87410; (505) 334-8748

Maravia Corporation, Box 404, Boise, ID 83701; (208) 322-4949

Northwest River Supplies, 2009 S. Main, Moscow, ID 83843; (800) 635-5202

Osprey Whitewater, 561 Merlin Road, Merlin, OR 97532; (503) 474-7656

Sevylor, 66511 E. 26th Street, Los Angeles, CA 90040; (213) 727-6013

Waterwolf, P.O. Box 3341, Telluride, CO 81435; (800) 358-3169

Whitewater Manufacturing, 1700 S.W. Nebraska Avenue, Grants Pass, OR 97527; (503) 476-1344

Zodiac of North America, Inc. (Metzler), P.O. Box 400, Stevensville, MD 21668; (410) 643-4141

Portable Toilets

Canyon R.E.O., P.O. Box 3493, Flagstaff, AZ 86003; (602) 526-4663

Four Corners Marine, P.O. Box 3173, Durango, CO 81302; (303) 259-5380

Jack's Plastic Welding, 115 S. Main, Aztec, NM 87410; (505) 334-8748

Northwest Dories, 1127B Airway, Lewiston, ID 83501; (208) 743-4201

Partner Steel Co., 3187 Poleline Road, Pocatello,

ID 83201; (208) 233-2371

Professional River Outfitters, 1802 W. Kaibab
Lane, Flagstaff, AZ 86001; (602) 779-1512

Thetford Corp., P.O. Box 1285, Ann Arbor, MI
48106; (313) 769-6000

Waterman Welding, Kanab, UT 84741;
(801) 644-5729

Outfitters Organizations (US)

America Outdoors, P.O. Box 1348, Knoxville, TN
37901; (615) 524-4814

National Organization of Canoe Liveries and
Outfitters; R.R. 2, Box 249, Butler, KY
41006-9674; (606) 472-2205

North American Paddlesports Association, 12455
North Wauwatosa Road, Mequon, WI 53092;
(414) 242-5228

Outfitters Organizations (CANADA)

Ministry of Tourism, Queen's Park, Toronto,
Ontario M7A 2R9

The Quebec Outfitters Association, 2900,
Boulevard Saint-Martin Quest, Laval,
Quebec H7L 2J2

TravelArctic, Yellowknife, N.W.T. X1A 2L9

Yukon Outfitters Association, Bag Service 2762,
Whitehorse, Yukon Y1A 5B9

Private Boaters Organizations

American Canoe Association (ACA), 7432 Alban
Station Boulevard, Suite B226, Springfield, VA
22150; (703) 451-0141

The American Whitewater Affiliation,
P.O. Box 85, Phoenicia, NY 12464

The National Organization for River Sports,
Box 6847, Colorado Springs, CO 80934

The North West Rafters Association,
P.O. Box 19008, Portland, OR 97219

Rafting Schools

Running Wild Whitewater School, P.O. Box 658,
Ashland, OR 97520; (503) 482-WAVE (courses
for both private boaters and professional guides)

Many outfitters offer top-notch guiding schools. To
locate outfitters offering professional guiding
schools contact one of the outfitters organizations.

Safety Instruction Organizations

Rescue 3 International, P.O. Box 519, Elk Grove,
CA 95759; (800) 45RESCU

Rescue 3 Northwest, 12112 N.E. 195th, Bothell,
WA 98011; (800) 234-4644

Rescue 3 Canada, 5075 Angus Drive, Vancouver,
B.C., Canada, V6M 3M6; (604) 263-3580

For additional safety instruction programs, contact
one of the outfitters or rafting schools in your area.

Conservation Groups

American Rivers, 800 Pennsylvania Avenue S.E.,
Suite 303, Washington DC 20003; (202) 547-6900

Environmental Defense Fund, 2728 Durant,
Berkeley, CA 94704

Friends of the Earth, 530 7th Street S.E.,
Washington DC 20003; (202)543-4312

Friends of the River, Fort Mason Center, Building C,
San Francisco, CA 94123; (415) 771-0400

National Audubon Society, 950 Third Avenue,
New York, NY 10022

The Nature Conservancy, 1800 North Kent Street,
Arlington, VA 22209; (703) 841-5300

The River Conservation Fund, 323 Pennsylvania
Avenue N.E., Washington DC 20003;
(202) 547-6900

River Watch (see American Rivers, above)

The Sierra Club, 730 Polk Street, San Francisco,
CA 94109

Wilderness Society, Suite S 176, 3900 Wisconsin
Avenue, N.W., Washington DC 20016

Checklists

CLOTHING
bathing suit
river sandals/shoes
polypropylene underwear
helmet
helmet liner
wetsuit/drysuit
paddle jacket/dry top
gloves
booties
other: _____

GEAR FOR DAY TRIPS
raft
frame
oarlocks/pins and clips
oars
paddles
pumps
bow and stern lines
bail buckets
straps
safety/rescue gear (separate list)
first aid kit (separate list)
repair kit (separate list)
waterproof containers
water and food

REPAIR KIT
Ram Patch
duct tape
patch materials (6" x 48")
glue and catalyst
solvent (MEK or toluol)
mixing cup
paintbrush
roller
rag (cheesecloth)
scuffing tool/sandpaper
pen
hard eraser
nitrile gloves
pliers
scissors
large needle & cord
bailing wire
wirecutters
screwdrivers
valve tools
spare parts
other: _____

SAFETY/RESCUE GEAR
carabiners
river knives
throwbags
flip lines
whistles
pulleys
web slings
static rope
prussik loops
Z-drag crib cards
anchor slings
paddle hooks
other: _____

CAMPING AND COOKING GEAR
dry bags/boxes
ammo cans
tent/tarp
sleeping bag
ground pad
lantern & fuel
pillow
clothing
toiletries
camera gear
firepan
presto log
portable commode
stove & fuel
matches/lighters
cooler
water containers
eating utensils
pots and pans
cups, plates, bowls
can opener
spatula
seasonings
scouring pads
biodegradable soap
trash bags
portable table
Dutch oven
washing buckets
food
ice
water filters/purifiers
other: _____

FIRST AID KIT
first aid book
Band-Aids
butterfly closures
adhesive tape
gauze (4" x 4")
roll gauze (2")
compresses
ace bandages
triangular bandages
sam splint
paramedic shears
10% proridine-iodine solution
19% hydrocortisone cream
Neosporin ointment
high-spf sunblock
small tweezers
knife
needles
safety pins
razor blades
CPR face shield
thermometer
disposable gloves
alcohol swabs
small package liquid soap
oral glucose/sugar/candy
powdered sports drink
penlight
large syringe/rubber bulb

moleskin
venom extraction kit
space blanket
Tylenol/ibuprofen
Lomotil
Ex-lax
Dramamine
Robitussin DM
eyedrops
antacids
prescription medications
waterproof carry case
other: _____
(NOTE: Consult a physician
before taking any prescription
medications or using any topical or
oral medications included in this
list. Many of the items included in
this list require some expertise to
use effectively. Obtain adequate
first aid and CPR training through
the Red Cross or other certified
medical training programs.)

TRIP PLANNER
assemble group of rafters
choose river from
    guidebooks/brochures
research guidebooks to check best
    seasons, access points, rapids, etc.
gain knowledge from local boaters
    and outfitters
call government agency to check
    permit requirements
acquire any necessary permits
check for additional governmental
    regulations (toilets, gear, etc.)
plan shuttles
plan menu
review equipment list
review safety/rescue gear list
review first aid kit list
review kitchen and camping gear
    list
obtain any missing gear
check water levels
check weather forecast

have fun!
other: _____
(This is primarily designed to be
used as a basic guideline for inexperienced rafters. There are many
more steps that go into a pretrip
agenda. As your river experience
grows, so will your ability to
quickly assemble groups of rafters
and plan river trips.)

CONVERSIONS
1 cubic foot per second = .0283
    cubic meters per second
1 cubic meter per second = 35.3
    cubic feet per second
1 mile = 1.6 kilometers
1 kilometer = .6214 miles
1 foot = 0.3 meters
1 meter = 3.28 feet

Knots

bowline

1   2   3

water knot (ring bend)

1   2

3   4

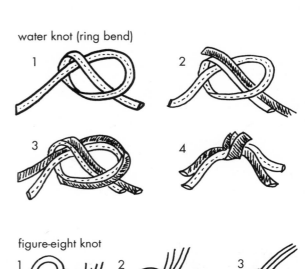

butterfly knot

1   2   3   4

figure-eight knot

1   2   3

double fisherman's knot

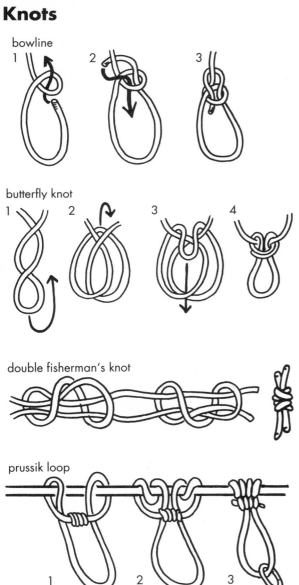

double half hitch

square knot

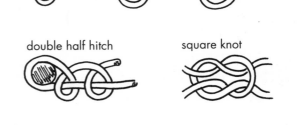

prussik loop

1   2   3

trucker's hitch

Knots

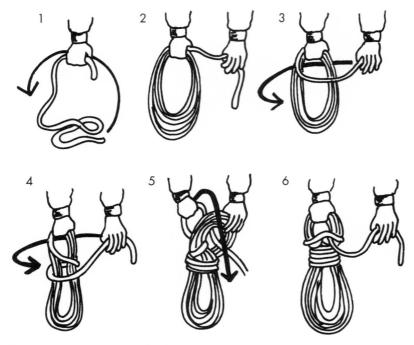

Suggested rope-storing method.

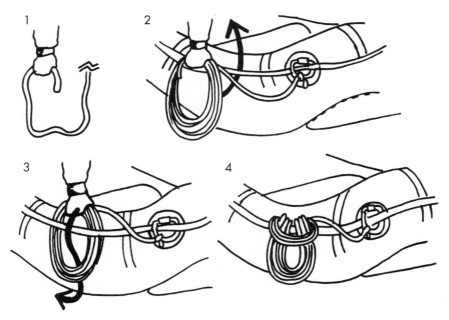

Rope-storing method using exterior handline.

GLOSSARY

Baffle: a diaphragm that divides the interior of tubes into separate compartments

Bank: the river's shore

Bar: a shallow part of the river channel made up of sand, gravel, or small rocks

Belay: a method of slowing or stopping a rope from sliding

Big water: rivers with large volume and powerful hydraulics

Blade: the wide, flat part of a paddle or oar

Boat: raft

Boater: rafter

Boils: ascending currents that rise above surface level unpredictably

Boulder garden: a rapid densely strewn with boulders

Bow: the front or nose of a raft

Bowline: the rope tied to the front or nose of a raft (also a type of knot)

Brace: to use the paddles to stay in the raft or to prevent the raft from flipping

Breaking wave: a standing wave that falls upstream

Bulkhead: see *baffle*

Cfs: cubic feet per second; measures the current's velocity past a fixed point in the river (35.3 cfs equals 1 cubic meter per second)

Cms: cubic meters per second

Carabiner: a metal clip used to attach lines to rafts, to secure gear, or to substitute for a pulley

Chamber: one interior compartment of a raft tube

Chute: a narrow, constricted portion of the river

Clean: free of obstructions; used to describe a route through a rapid

Classification: a system for rating the difficulty of whitewater rapids

Confluence: the point where two rivers or streams meet

Current: moving water

Cushion: see *pillow*

D-ring: a steel ring attached to the raft and used as a tie-down point

Diaphragm: see *baffle*

Downstream: in the direction of the river's flow (a.k.a. *downriver*)

Draw stroke: a stroke used to move the raft sideways by placing the paddle out to the side of the raft and pulling it toward to the raft

Drop: a steep, sudden change in the level of the river bottom (often called *waterfalls* when they are taller than 6 to 7 feet)

Dry bag: a waterproof bag designed to keep its contents dry

Drysuit: a waterproof suit that encloses a paddler in impermeable layers of fabric; designed to be worn over insulating layers of clothing

Eddy: a pocket of water downstream of an obstacle that flows upstream or back against the main current

Eddy line: the interface between the eddy current and the main current (a high eddy line is called an *eddy fence*)

Entrapment: a situation in which a raft or a rafter is pinned against an obstacle by the river's current

Falls: a drop where the river plummets steeply over boulders or broken river bottom (can refer to a waterfall or to the upstream side of a hole)

Feather: to turn a paddle or oar blade horizontal to the water

Ferry: a maneuver used to move a raft back and forth across the river

Flipline: a short rope used to pull a flipped raft upright

Footcup: a loop, cone, cup, or stirrup mounted to the raft's floor and used to brace the foot

Frame: a structure fixed to a raft's tubes to secure and provide a fulcrum for oars

Gradient: the measurement of a river's descent in feet per mile or meters per kilometer

Guide: the person in charge of a raft (see also *paddle captain*)

Handle: the handgrip of a paddle or oar

Haystack: a large, unstable standing wave

Helmet: rigid headgear designed to protect a rafter's head from impact

Highside: lean on the downstream side of the raft to prevent a flip or a wrap

Hole: a swirling vortex of water wherein the river pours over an obstacle and drops toward the river bottom, leaving a pocket behind the obstacle into which an upstream surface current flows

Hydraulics: a change in currents that causes surface features that can deflect, slow, or speed up a raft's descent (e.g., holes, waves, and eddies).

Hypothermia: a lowering of the body's core temperature

Keeper: a large hole or reversal that can keep and hold a raft or swimmer for a long period of time

Lifejacket: a personal flotation device designed to float a swimmer in water

Lining: a technique used to maneuver unmanned rafts around difficult rapids with the use of ropes

Lowsiding: unweighting one tube to help a raft slip through narrow slots.

Psi: pounds per square inch; a measurement of air pressure

Pillow: a cushion of water that forms on the upstream side of an obstacle

Pivot: to turn the raft in place

Pool: a flat section of river with no rapids

Pool-drop: a type of river consisting of intermittent rapids followed by long, easy sections of calm water

Portage: to carry a raft

Portegee: a push stroke with oars

Power face: the side of an oar or paddle blade that normally pulls against the current

Pry stroke: a stroke used to turn or sideslip a raft away from the paddle

Put-in: the place where a raft trip begins

Rapid: a place where the river leaves its two-dimensional state and enters a three-dimensional state complete with faster currents, rocks, and various types of liquid surface features

Reversal: see *hole*

Riffle: a shallow, gentle rapid caused by rocks or streambeds

River left: the left side of the river when you are looking downstream

River right: the right side of the river when you are looking downstream

Roller: a big curling wave that falls back upstream on itself

Rooster tail: a fountain of water that explodes in a fan pattern off a submerged obstacle

Scout: to walk along a bank to inspect the river

Section: a portion of river between two points

Shaft: the pole between the blade and the handle of a paddle or oar

Sneak route: the easiest route through a rapid (a.k.a. *cheat route*)

Standing wave: a stationary river wave

Stern: the back end of a raft

Steep creeking: running high-gradient, low-volume streams.

Stopper: a hole, reversal, or breaking wave capable of stopping, holding, or flipping a raft or a swimmer

Strainer: an obstacle, such as a tree, that lets water flow freely through it but catches swimmers, rafts, and debris (a.k.a. *sweeper, logjam, boulder sieve*)

Sweep stroke: a turning stroke wherein the blade is swept in an arc pattern fore or aft

Tail waves: standing waves that form at the base of a rapid

Take-out: the place where a raft trip ends

Technical: containing many obstacles and requiring constant maneuvering; used to describe rapids

Throw bag: a bag that holds a long coiled rope, used as a rescue device to be tossed to swimmers (a.k.a. *throw rope, rescue bag*)

Thwart: the cross-tube of a raft

Tongue: a smooth V of fast-moving water that frequently appears at the top of a rapid

Undercut: an overhanging rock or ledge under which water flows

Upstream: in the direction from which the river flows

Volume: the amount of water in a river

Waterfall: see *drop*

Wave: a hump in the river's flowing water

Wave train: a series of standing waves

Whitewater: rapids (a.k.a. *fun!*)

Wrap: a raft pinned flat against an obstacle by river currents

Z-drag: a pulley system used to rescue pinned or wrapped rafts

I N D E X